Early praise for *Practical Microservices*

Practical Microservices is, indeed, practical. It's also the clearest and most complete example of how and why to build an event-driven architecture that presents a unified example that isn't overly simplistic or overly complex. This would've changed my approach to microservices if it had been available five years ago.

➤ **David Bryant Copeland**
Co-author of *Agile Web Development with Rails 6*

This book sets straight the microservices phenomenon—decoupled evented microservices style is the only way to achieve antifragility and maintain simplicity at the same time.

➤ **Adrian Bilauca**
Director, R&D, TotalSoft S.A.

Practical Microservices

Build Event-Driven Architectures
with Event Sourcing and CQRS

Ethan Garofolo

The Pragmatic Bookshelf

Raleigh, North Carolina

Many of the designations used by manufacturers and sellers to distinguish their products are claimed as trademarks. Where those designations appear in this book, and The Pragmatic Programmers, LLC was aware of a trademark claim, the designations have been printed in initial capital letters or in all capitals. The Pragmatic Starter Kit, The Pragmatic Programmer, Pragmatic Programming, Pragmatic Bookshelf, PragProg and the linking *g* device are trademarks of The Pragmatic Programmers, LLC.

Every precaution was taken in the preparation of this book. However, the publisher assumes no responsibility for errors or omissions, or for damages that may result from the use of information (including program listings) contained herein.

Our Pragmatic books, screencasts, and audio books can help you and your team create better software and have more fun. Visit us at *https://pragprog.com*.

The team that produced this book includes:

Publisher: Andy Hunt
VP of Operations: Janet Furlow
Executive Editor: Dave Rankin
Development Editor: Adaobi Obi Tulton
Copy Editor: Jasmine Kwityn
Indexing: Potomac Indexing, LLC
Layout: Gilson Graphics

For sales, volume licensing, and support, please contact *support@pragprog.com*.

For international rights, please contact *rights@pragprog.com*.

ISBN-13: 978-1-68050-645-7
Book version: P1.0—April 2020

For Julie, Sofia, Eva, and Angelo—

you are life and joy

Contents

Part II — Fleshing Out the System

Part III — Tools of the Trade

Acknowledgments

I may have pushed a lot of buttons on keyboards to write this book, but I owe its fruition to the efforts of so many others. A whole lot of thank yous are in order.

To my Heavenly Father for life, my savior Jesus Christ for hope, and the Holy Ghost for peace. Thank You for rescuing a soul so rebellious and proud as mine, and may I live a life that extends to all others the love and grace You've extended to me.

To Mom and Dad, thank you for all the lessons you've taught me. To my brother Denis, I couldn't imagine how a brother could have done a better job than you did.

To my friends and coworkers who have had to endure me talking about this for 2+ years. We can finally have a meeting where I don't bring up my book.

To Adrian Bilauca, Damien Del Russo, Dave Copeland, Ben Marx, and Adam Jasiura for being technical reviewers of this book. You gave of your time and expertise with no expectation of reward. When I compare the early drafts to what your feedback guided me to, well, that's why books go out to reviewers. You delivered, and I and all the readers are in your debt.

To Jesse Riggins, for being a technical reviewer, a friend, and a fellow learner of microservices-based architectures through the years. It's been wonderful bouncing ideas off you, and goodness, I hope we get to work together again!

To Scott Bellware and Nathan Ladd, I have met few people as knowledgeable and as generous as you both. Thank you for the work you do in the Eventide community and in our profession. Scott, it was pure serendipity that led me to a TDD talk of yours at the LoneStarRuby Conference, a talk that permanently altered how I approach software development. Nathan, I've never had the pleasure of meeting you in person, and I'm so glad you made it. I aspire to become as good at my craft as you both are.

To Todd Pickell, thank you for taking that phone call that one day and telling me to go speak at meetups. You probably had other things to do, and I truly appreciate that gift of your time.

To Brian MacDonald, thank you for coming to OpenWest in 2017, staying to talk to me after that session, and encouraging me to write a pitch. I had no idea what an amazing and life-changing ride this would become.

To my editor, Adaobi Obi Tulton, the highest thanks are in order. I don't have the hubris to claim that I've been the most difficult author you've ever worked with, but I'm certain you've had easier projects. You are excellent at what you do, and if this book provides value to its readers, I don't think it would have without your excellent guidance. Thank you for talking me down from the ledge of discouragement, and thank you for saving this text from my attempts to be clever. Readers, if any of you ends up writing your own book for PragProg, ask for Adaobi!

To my dear children, Sofia, Eva, and Angelo, this book has cost a lot of memories of playing together that we might have otherwise had. Thank you for bearing with me and even being excited about this project. It's finally done! You are three of the most wonderful human beings I have ever met. It is an honor to know you and a blessing beyond words to get to be your father. Your imaginations and sense of wonder remind me constantly of how great a gift each day is. I love you, and I couldn't be prouder of you. Now let's go play!

To my love and companion, Julie. In alphabetical order you are beauty, charm, compassion, devotion, grace, inspiration, intelligence, and wit. I still remember the day you tripped me on my way out of class and how I toilet papered your desk in response—a greater love story has never been told. It is a privilege to be married to you. Thank you for putting up with me all these years, and thank you so much for the many nights and weekends of flying solo so that I could write. This book is as much a result of your effort as it is of mine, if not more. *Je t'aimais, je t'aime, et je t'aimerai.*

Finally, to you, the reader. I hope that you've learned a thing or two and that this book helps you in your endeavors. Thank you for reading.

Introduction

Here's the deal, y'all—software is easy to write, but it's hard to change.

If you're reading this book, then chances are you can write code. Maybe you're a software developer, a technical lead, an architect, or a CTO. You've shipped web-based applications that have provided a lot of business value to the people who paid you to do that. *You're good at what you do*, but something keeps happening with your projects, where productivity slows down despite spending more money and hiring more people. You want to learn how to fix that, and maybe you've heard about microservices and are wondering how to build them.

Telling a Tale of a Different Kind of Keyboard

So let's digress into a story about something that at once is what many adults wish to have spent more time practicing and what children often dread: the piano. I never really learned the piano, but I did learn one song well enough that I was asked to play it in a church group. The song is called "A Poor Wayfaring Man of Grief," and really liking it, I figured I needed to know how to play it. I can look at a staff and figure out what the notes are, but I can't do that fast enough to read the music and press the corresponding keys in real time.

So I set about memorizing the song. One. Beat. At. A. Time.

I put my fingers for both hands in place for the first beat and played it, removed my fingers from the keys, and then without looking at the music put them back and played that first set of notes. Then I read the second set and basically played a game of Simon[1] until I had memorized the song.

And I did. I could reproduce the notes. But woe was me when I made mistakes halfway through the song! It was a bit like typing a password. When you goof on entering a password, you generally have to start over.

---

1. https://en.wikipedia.org/wiki/Simon_(game)

One day a friend of mine offered to teach me piano properly. We sat down, and she observed my playing. She was gracious in how she let me know, "If you're ever going to play this instrument, you're going to have to unlearn a lot of things."

There's a technique to piano. For example, if you're walking your left hand up the keys, you'll play notes from your pinky to your thumb. When it's time to go to higher notes, your middle finger slides over to the right of your thumb, and it makes for an elegant trip up to the higher pitches. As an understatement, I did not discover this technique when I was memorizing that song. Folks who do learn good technique can work an amazing art.[2] What these other folks do is closed to me until I pay the price of unlearning.

Learning microservices-based architecture was and continues to be a similar process of unlearning. You're likely skilled in Model-View-Controller (MVC) frameworks that model systems in terms of Create-Read-Update-Delete (CRUD) operations. Maybe you've used frameworks like Ruby on Rails or Django.

But you keep running into a productivity wall. It becomes extremely difficult to add features and fix bugs. You've changed frameworks and you've changed languages. Is every project fated to hit this point where every enhancement is excruciating?

The answer to that question is a resounding "NO!"

What This Book Is

This is a hands-on tutorial. In this book, you're going to build a system according to a different set of principles—ones that will allow you to build systems where your productivity will not come to an encumbered halt. You're going to build *microservices*, focused units of autonomous functionality.

Chapter 1, You Have a New Project, on page 3 introduces the project you're going to build, and we'll take a crack at it using the traditional CRUD-based approach, seeing how it paints us into a corner. Following that, in Chapter 2, Writing Messages, on page 25 we'll unmask the monolith, and you'll see why most writing on microservices misses the point. We'll conclude this part of the book by writing code to interact with a piece of technology called a message store—a database optimized for storing asynchronous messages. These messages will form the basis of your architecture.

---

2.   https://www.youtube.com/watch?v=9fAZIQ-vpdw

With the fundamentals in place, you'll leverage this message store to add features to your system by building microservices and other autonomous components. You'll send emails (Chapter 9, Adding an Email Component, on page 133) and even transcode videos (Chapter 10, Performing Background Jobs with Microservices, on page 157). Along the way, the architecture you implement will allow you to slice and dice the same data in varied and interesting ways.

Once the bulk of the system is in place, in Chapter 12, Deploying Components, on page 195, you'll deploy your microservices-based system into the wild. In Chapter 13, Debugging Components, on page 207 you'll learn how this message-based architecture helps you keep a health system running. You'll even get exposure to how this architecture alters how you test your system in Chapter 14, Testing in a Microservices Architecture, on page 231.

What This Book Isn't

This is a hands-on tutorial, not a reference book or *The Definitive Guide*™ to microservices. There are topics we won't cover in detail. In Chapter 15, Continuing the Journey, on page 241, the final chapter, we call out some of these topics, and you'll have pointers on how to continue your learning.

This isn't a book about flashy technology. You're going to use PostgreSQL,[3] a world-class relational database, and that's about as exciting as the tools get. The excitement, instead, is in the principles.

Separating Principles from Implementations

This is the book that I wish had been written years ago when I first started learning service-based architecture. Finding information on high-level principles is pretty easy, but there weren't any hands-on tutorials. But by getting so low-level in this book, my biggest fear is that you interpret this particular implementation as microservices gospel. The details here serve only to show what the principles might look like in practice.

Using This Book

The chapters in the book build on top of one another. In Chapter 1, you start writing a project that we add to as we go throughout the book. I can't imagine a reading order other than "each chapter in order" that makes sense. Maybe I'm lacking in imagination, but that's my recommendation to you.

---

3. https://www.postgresql.org

As you're reading through the code, I can't stress highly enough the value of creating your own project folder, creating each file, and typing its contents yourself. Is that tedious? Possibly. But it's tedium with a purpose. Reading code is nice, but I want to get the concepts in this book into your brain, and typing code will do so much more of that transfer than merely reading. In addition, you should also be sure to complete the exercises in the chapters.

Using Node.js

For better or for worse, we use JavaScript and the Node.js runtime to implement our system. The principles we cover absolutely transcend programming languages, but bringing them down to the mundane requires implementing them in *something*. We use Node.js because it's a fine language when you stay away from its warts—which we do—and because most developers who have written code to run on the web can at least grok JavaScript.

Strapping In

Well, then—let's buckle our seat belts and get rolling. I'm glad you're along for the journey.

Part I

Fundamentals

You just got hired as part of a crack team to build the web's next-generation learning platform. We're going to tackle it in a way that you're probably not accustomed to—with autonomous microservices. You've probably heard something about microservices before, but what we do here is likely going to feel very, ah, different.

So we're going to start with the fundamentals. What are the downsides to how we've always built things, and why would we want to change? Having answered that, we get into the basic pieces of what makes a system microservices based.

CHAPTER 1

You Have a New Project

Congratulations! Today is your day. You've got a new project to get underway. A site full of videos; users to please—a system that will make future changes a breeze.

You're going to build Video Tutorials, the next-gen internet learning sensation. Content creators will publish videos, and the rest of the users will level up from watching those videos.

Some features of this system, like user registration and authentication, will seem familiar. Some features may be new, like transcoding videos. Through it all, rest assured that you have a top-notch business team to work with. They'll be busy discovering the benefits that our users want, and your job is to build a system that will support this platform for decades to come. Pieces of that system will necessarily evolve, so supporting that long-term change is going to be our main focus.

Kicking Off Video Tutorials

Let's start by getting the husk of this project off the ground. Our business team wants to support content creators by slicing and dicing video viewing metrics in all sorts of ways—some which they haven't even identified yet. The first metric they care about is a global count of video views.

Since we don't actually have any video content yet, we can just simulate video views with a button click. We're going to build enough server to serve a page like the screenshot on page 4. There's a button to click to simulate having viewed a video. To get this working we need:

- A basic project structure
- An HTTP route to GET this page
- An HTTP route to receive POSTs from the award-winning button

Let the fun begin.

Building the Bones

As mentioned in the book's introduction on page xviii, our code samples are all in Node.js. It's a fine platform for evented architectures, and probably more importantly, if you've done web development, you can probably at least grok what is going on when you read JavaScript. In the *Application* layer—the layer of the system that users interact with—we use a library called Express[1] to route requests to the functions that handle them. This isn't a book specifically about programming in Node.js, but in case you're unfamiliar with Express, it's worth a little ink to introduce it.

Express is a "fast, unopinionated, minimalist web framework for Node.js," and we use it to map URLs to functions that handle them and to render HTML in response. We certainly could use single-page apps, but we want to keep the focus on microservices rather than JavaScript UI frameworks.

Our first job is to build a simple Express server, and an Express server is made up of some configuration, some middleware, and some routes:

first-pass/src/app/express/index.js
```
const express = require('express')
const { join } = require('path')

const mountMiddleware = require('./mount-middleware')
const mountRoutes = require('./mount-routes')

① function createExpressApp ({ config, env }) {
```

---

1. https://expressjs.com/

```
❷  const app = express()

   // Configure PUG
❸  app.set('views', join(__dirname, '..'))
   app.set('view engine', 'pug')
❹  mountMiddleware(app, env)
❺  mountRoutes(app, config)

   return app
}
module.exports = createExpressApp
```

❶ A typical Node.js file defines a top-level function and exports it. createEx-pressApp is that top-level function for this file, and we export it at the very bottom. Its return value is a configured Express application.

To configure that Express application, this function receives some config-uration. config has references to the rest of the pieces of our system, and env has all the environment variables our program was started with. If you're just dying to dive into these exciting files, they're at code/first-pass/src/config.js and code/first-pass/src/env.js, respectively, and we'll work through them on page 7.

❷ This instantiates the Express application. Now we configure it.

❹ This is where we mount middleware into the Express application. Middle-wares are functions that get run on an incoming HTTP request and have the chance to do various setup and side effects before we get to the func-tion that ultimately handles said request. As an example, we'll use a middle-ware to ensure users are authenticated on certain routes in Chapter 8, Authenticating Users, on page 119.

❺ HTTP requests come into a server with a given URL, and you have to tell an Express server what to do for a given URL. That's what mounting the routes is for. You give Express a URL pattern and function to call to handle requests that go to that URL pattern. The file implementing this function is at code/first-pass/src/app/express/mount-routes.js. We don't have any routes quite yet, since we're just building the bones of the system right now, but we'll add our first route on page 11 when we go to load the home page shown before on page 4.

That's the main structure of an Express application, and we won't have to touch this file for the rest of the project. We will add middlewares as we con-tinue though, so that's where we turn next.

Mounting Middleware

Here is the start of our middleware:

```
first-pass/src/app/express/mount-middleware.js
Line 1   const express = require('express')
-        const { join } = require('path')

-        const attachLocals = require('./attach-locals')
5        const lastResortErrorHandler = require('./last-resort-error-handler')
-        const primeRequestContext = require('./prime-request-context')
-        function mountMiddleware (app, env) {
-          app.use(lastResortErrorHandler)
-          app.use(primeRequestContext)
10         app.use(attachLocals)
-          app.use(
-            express.static(join(__dirname, '..', 'public'), { maxAge: 86400000 }))
-        }

15       module.exports = mountMiddleware
```

Middlewares in Express are functions that we run as part of the request/response cycle and that for the most part aren't meant to actually handle the request. We require three of our own, starting at line 4. Then we define the dependency-receiving function mountMiddleware that is also exported at the very end of the file. It receives app, the Express application, and env, our environment variables. We won't use the environment variables until Chapter 8, Authenticating Users, on page 119.

To actually mount a middleware, we call app.use, passing in the middleware function in question. We mount the first middleware, lastResortErrorHandler, at line 8. We follow this with primeRequestContext and attachLocals, ending the function with Express's built-in middleware. express.static serves static files. We use that for the CSS and JavaScript files we serve for the browser UI.

Let's write those custom middlewares we just included, starting with prime RequestContext:

```
first-pass/src/app/express/prime-request-context.js
const uuid = require('uuid/v4')

function primeRequestContext (req, res, next) {
  req.context = {
    traceId: uuid()
  }

  next()
}

module.exports = primeRequestContext
```

This middleware's job is to set up values that we'll want on every request. For now we use it to generate a traceId for each and every request. Even in Model-View-Controller (MVC) apps that model state as Create-Read-Update-Delete (CRUD) operations, having a traceId is a nice thing. We'll attach it to log statements so that we know which log statements belong together. We put these values onto req.context to namespace them all to a single property on req. We don't want to pollute the req object that Express hands us with a multitude of keys.

Next is attachLocals:

```
first-pass/src/app/express/attach-locals.js
function attachLocals (req, res, next) {
  res.locals.context = req.context
  next()
}

module.exports = attachLocals
```

We're rendering all of our UI on the server. This middleware makes the context we set up on the request available when rendering our UI.

Finally, there's lastResortErrorHandler:

```
first-pass/src/app/express/last-resort-error-handler.js
function lastResortErrorHandler (err, req, res, next) {
  const traceId = req.context ? req.context.traceId : 'none'
  console.error(traceId, err)

  res.status(500).send('error')
}

module.exports = lastResortErrorHandler
```

This is an error-handling middleware, identified by having four parameters in its signature. When nothing else manages to catch an error during a request, we at least catch it here and log it. We will be more sophisticated than this in our error handling—this is just our last resort.

With the middleware in place, we can dive into config and env.

Injecting Dependencies

We use a technique called dependency injection[2] in this system. Quickly stated, you can sum up dependency injection as "passing functions the things they need to do their job." This is in contrast to "having functions reach into the global namespace to get what they need to do their job." Dependency

---

2. https://www.youtube.com/watch?v=Z6vf6zC2DYQ

injection doesn't have anything to do with microservices, but it is how the code in this book is structured.

So, enter code/first-pass/src/config.js, and let's set up its shell:

```
first-pass/src/config.js
function createConfig ({ env }) {
  return {
    env,
  }
}

module.exports = createConfig
```

That sure doesn't do much yet. We'll flesh it out on page 15 once we've finished with the home page application.

Next, let's write the file that ingests the runtime environment variables we'll use:

```
first-pass/src/env.js
module.exports = {
  appName: requireFromEnv('APP_NAME'),
  env: requireFromEnv('NODE_ENV'),
  port: parseInt(requireFromEnv('PORT'), 10),
  version: packageJson.version
}
```

This isn't the entire file, so check out the rest of it when you can. requireFromEnv is defined in the part that isn't printed here, and it checks if the given environment variable is present. If not, it exits the program and tells us why. When critical settings aren't present, we want to know about that ASAP.

What we've done here is locate every place where we read from the runtime environment in this one file. We don't have to wonder where we get environment settings from, and things that depend on environment settings don't realize that they do. This also isn't microservices-specific and is just the convention we use in this project.

We start with a few values. appName is a cosmetic name given to our running system. env tells if we're running in development, test, production, or whatever other environment we care to run. port is the port our HTTP server will listen on. version doesn't strictly originate from the environment, as we pull it out of the package.json file this project has (every Node.js project has a package.json).

Okay, with a barebones server built, let's start this puppy:

```
first-pass/src/index.js
① const createExpressApp = require('./app/express')
const createConfig = require('./config')
const env = require('./env')
```

```
② const config = createConfig({ env })
  const app = createExpressApp({ config, env })
③ function start () {
    app.listen(env.port, signalAppStart)
  }

  function signalAppStart () {
    console.log(`${env.appName} started`)
    console.table([['Port', env.port], ['Environment', env.env]])
  }

  module.exports = {
    app,
    config,
    start
  }
```

❶ Starting here we require the functions for building our Express app and config, as well as pulling in the environment.

❷ Then we instantiate config and the Express app.

❸ Finally, we define the start function that will be called to start the system. For now it calls the Express app's start function, passing it the port we want the HTTP server to listen on (env.port) and a callback function (signalAppStart). This latter gets called when the HTTP server is listening, and it logs some of the settings from the environment. It's nice to have confirmation the server is running.

Lastly, we just need some code that calls this start function:

first-pass/src/bin/start-server.js
```
const { start } = require('../')

start()
```

It simply requires the file located at code/first-pass/src/index.js, the one we just wrote. It pulls out the start function and calls it.

Earlier we mentioned that every Node.js project has a package.json file at its root, and ours is no exception. A package.json file defines a key named "scripts", which are commands you can run using the npm command-line tool. If you have one called "start-dev-server", you can run it with npm run start-dev-server. Ours does define a script named "start-dev-server":

```
{
  "scripts": {
    "start-dev-server": "nodemon src/bin/start-server.js --color",
  }
}
```

nodemon[3] is a library that watches for changes to code files and then reruns the command passed to it. We tell it to run the file at src/bin/start-server.js, so every time that we make a change to the source code, it will restart the server for us.

Taking the Server for a Spin and Starting the Database

If you look in the package.json file, you'll also see that it defines dependencies and devDependencies. The former are other packages of Node code that we rely on in all situations, whereas the latter lists packages we use only in development. Both are installed when you run npm install, so do that now.

At this point, you can actually run this server. To do so, you'll need to have your PostgreSQL database set up. If you're comfortable doing that on your own, then by all means do so.

However, you can also use Docker,[4] which is what the rest of this book will assume. To use Docker, you'll need to install it, and we punt to the Docker docs[5] to explain how to do that for your platform. Then, in each code folder there is a docker-compose.yaml, which contains the necessary Docker configuration to run the databases for that folder. You can start the databases by running docker-compose rm -sf && docker-compose up. Go ahead and do that now.

If you do use your own PostgreSQL installation, you'll need to make the DATABASE_URL value match your database's setup in .env in the project's root directory.

Assuming that you have your database running, from the command line in the project's root folder, simply run npm run start-dev-server, and you should get output similar to the following:

```
$ npm run start-dev-server

> microservices-book@1.0.0 start first-pass
> nodemon src/bin/start-server.js --color

[nodemon] 1.17.5
[nodemon] to restart at any time, enter `rs`
[nodemon] watching: *.*
[nodemon] starting `node src/bin/start-server.js --color`
Video Tutorials started
```

---

3. https://nodemon.io/
4. https://www.docker.com/
5. https://docs.docker.com/v17.09/engine/installation/

(index)	0	1
0	'Port'	3000
1	'Environment'	'development'

Congratulations! You have an Express server running. Sure, it responds to exactly zero routes, but no one said you were *done*. Just that, you can start the system, and that's a milestone worth celebrating. Now we can get that incredible home page delivered to our users.

Serving the Home Page

Let's build your first application in this system—the home page application. Adding an application is a three-step process:

1. Write the application on page 11.
2. Inject its dependencies and add it to config.js on page 15.
3. Mount the application in our Express instance on page 17.

So, for step 1, the question is, what is an application supposed to do? Applications will handle user input and display screens to the user. The first sure sounds like HTTP handlers, given that this is a web-based system. For the second, what do those screens need to contain? From our earlier requirements on page 3 we know that we're going to need to show view counts. Those counts will have to come from somewhere, and let's just say now that's going to come from a database. So, we'll need to run some queries.

Let's write the basic structure of an application:

first-pass/src/app/home/index.js
```
Line 1  const camelCaseKeys = require('camelcase-keys')
        const express = require('express')

        function createHandlers ({ queries }) {
     5    return {
          }
        }

        function createQueries ({ db }) {
    10    return {
          }
        }

        function createHome ({ db }) {
    15    const queries = createQueries({ db })
          const handlers = createHandlers({ queries })
```

```
      const router = express.Router()

20    router.route('/').get(handlers.home)

      return { handlers, queries, router }
   }

25 module.exports = createHome
```

First of all, notice createHome at line 14. All of our system components, including this application, will export a top-level, dependency-receiving function. config.js uses these functions to configure the system components. This application needs access to the database where it will read the video counts it's going to display, so it receives db, a Promise resolving to a connection to that database.

ES6 Object Shorthand Notation

If you're not familiar with how JavaScript has changed over the past few years, some of the syntax here may look funky. For example, createHome, receives { db } as its arguments.

That function signature is saying that it expects to receive a plain old JavaScript object with a db key. db will be introduced as a variable in the createHome's scope, and it will reference whatever the passed object's db referenced.

This might be a good time to visit Appendix 1, ES6 Syntax, on page 249 for a quick primer if you're not yet aware of the newer JavaScript syntax.

---

createHome then uses this db reference to call createQueries, which builds the database query functions it needs. The queries are then passed to createHandlers which builds the HTTP handlers it needs. These handlers are connected to an express.Router. For example, at line 20 it mounts handlers.home at this router's root path.

The function finally returns an object containing the handlers, queries, and router. That object constitutes the instantiated application that will get attached to the system config in config.js, and if you recall when we built the Express application on page 4, the mountRoutes function there will mount what we build here into the main Express application as shown in the figure on page 13.

Let's finish building the home application so that we can see how the pieces all connect. The first step is to build the HTTP handler a user hits when they request the home page:

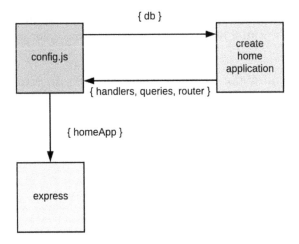

```
first-pass/src/app/home/index.js
function createHandlers ({ queries }) {
  function home (req, res, next) {
    return queries
      .loadHomePage()
      .then(viewData =>
        res.render('home/templates/home', viewData)
      )
      .catch(next)
  }

  return {
    home
  }
}
```

The job of an HTTP handler is to take an incoming request, extract the input from it, pass the input to whatever does the actual work, and then render a response. This handler's job is to show a screen with the global video view count and a button to simulate having watched a video.

Showing that page doesn't require any query params or a POST body, so the handler calls queries.loadHomePage to load the view count. That comes back in the homePageData variable, which we pass to res.render along with the Pug[6] template we want to render. Pug is an HTML templating language similar to HAML in Ruby, if you've ever used that. We'll only use its most basic features, so check out its documentation if you want to dive deeper.

---

6. https://pugjs.org/api/getting-started.html

In any case, the template file is located at code/first-pass/src/app/home/templates/ home.pug. We won't print it here—it just contains some basic markup to render the page.

The catch at the end of the chain is so that if there's an error, Express's next function handles it for us.

And that's it for the handler. We need to write that query function now:

```
first-pass/src/app/home/index.js
function createQueries ({ db }) {
  function loadHomePage () {
    return db.then(client =>
      client('videos')
        .sum('view_count as videosWatched')
        .then(rows => rows[0])
    )
  }

  return {
    loadHomePage
  }
}
```

This application only has one query, namely loadHomePage. This function's job is to return all the data we need to render the home page. We use a library called knex[7] for our database interaction. It's a *query builder*, and it provides nice JavaScript functions for building queries rather than writing raw SQL. There's nothing wrong with raw SQL, and sometimes we'll use it because we can't express a query with knex's JavaScript functions.

In any case, to get the data we need, we call db.then to resolve the database Promise and get the client connection. With that client, we run a simple query against a table named videos. Among its other columns, videos has a view_count column that tracks view counts for each video. We ask knex to sum all the view_counts and to name the result videosWatched. When we get the rows, we extract the first one.

You may be wondering where this mysterious videos table came from. In addition to providing query builder functionality, knex also provides database migrations.[8] Database migrations are a way to capture the evolution of your database schema in code. We'll create all our database tables through migrations, and let's start with videos:

---

7. https://knexjs.org/
8. https://knexjs.org/#Migrations

```
first-pass/migrations/20190426220729_create-videos.js
exports.up = knex =>
  knex.schema.createTable('videos', table => {
    table.increments()
    table.string('owner_id')

    table.string('name')
    table.string('description')
    table.string('transcoding_status')
    table.integer('view_count').defaultsTo(0)
  })

exports.down = knex => knex.schema.dropTable('videos')
```

A knex migration defines two functions, up and down. The up function is called when you apply a migration to the current schema. Our current schema does not have the videos table in it, so we call knex.schema.createTable, passing it the name we want and a callback function.

This table probably makes you feel right at home. We're going to have videos in the system, so we make a table named videos. And it has on it everything that it means to be a video. table.increments() adds the familiar auto-incrementing id column. The name and description columns hold display information about the videos, while transcoding_status will get used when we start transcoding videos. view_count, of course, held the data that we were after.

And boom! You just wrote the first application in this project! The next step is to connect this application to the running system.

Connecting the Home Page Application

Let's head over to config.js and pull the home page application into the system:

```
first-pass/src/config.js
Line 1  const createKnexClient = require('./knex-client')
     -  const createHomeApp = require('./app/home')
     -  function createConfig ({ env }) {
     -    const db = createKnexClient({
     5      connectionString: env.databaseUrl
     -    })
     -    const homeApp = createHomeApp({ db })
     -    return {
     -      // ...
    10      db,
     -      homeApp,
     -    }
     -  }
```

Lines 1 and 2 pull in the functions to create our database interaction code and the home application you just wrote, respectively. Using the databaseUrl from env, we instantiate our database interaction code at line 4. Since you haven't written that yet, you can imagine it to be simply the most amazing database interaction code. Ever. Or think of it as a simple wrapper on top of knex that we'll flesh out two paragraphs from now.

Next, at line 7 we make an instance of the home application, and like you saw on page 11, that needs a reference to the database. So we pass it db. And then finally at line 11, we add it to the config's return object.

Okay. The. Best. Database. Code. Ever:

first-pass/src/knex-client.js
```
Line 1  const Bluebird = require('bluebird')
        const knex = require('knex')

        function createKnexClient ({ connectionString, migrationsTableName }) {
    5     const client = knex(connectionString)

          const migrationOptions = {
            tableName: migrationsTableName || 'knex_migrations'
          }
   10
          // Wrap in Bluebird.resolve to guarantee a Bluebird Promise down the chain
          return Bluebird.resolve(client.migrate.latest(migrationOptions))
            .then(() => client)
        }
   15
        module.exports = createKnexClient
```

Maybe "thin wrapper over knex" was the more accurate description. Again, this file exports a dependency-receiving function—that's createKnexClient at line 4. Its job is to return a Promise that resolves to a functioning database connection.

Using Bluebird Promises

 Node supports Promises natively, but the Bluebird library,[9] adds some nice extensions that we're going to use. We'll call those out when we get to them.

Using the connectionString config passed to us, we instantiate a knex instance at line 5. This is what we'll return, but before we tell the rest of the system that the database is ready to go, we need to make sure that the database has our schema in it.

---

9. http://bluebirdjs.com/docs/getting-started.html

On line 7 we construct some options to pass to knex's migration functionality. knex keeps track of which migrations it has run in a table, and we give callers the option to specify the name of that table. This will be useful when we get to Chapter 12, Deploying Components, on page 195. If the caller didn't supply a custom name, we'll use the same default that knex uses.

Finally, at line 12 we run the migrations using the migrationOptions from before. client.migrate.latest() invokes knex's migration functionality and applies that migration you wrote on page 15. We wrap this in Bluebird.resolve to guarantee that the Promise going forward from this point is a Bluebird Promise rather than the native implementation.

When the migrations are done, we just return client, which is our knex instance. This is the value that the home application uses in the query functions you wrote on page 14.

The final step is to mount the application into Express.

Mounting the Home Application into Express

Head back to the file where we mount all of the routes in Express:

```
first-pass/src/app/express/mount-routes.js
function mountRoutes (app, config) {
  app.use('/', config.homeApp.router)
}
```

All we do is get the homeApp out of config and then mount its router at the very root. That seems like a good place for a home page.

And that's it! You've set up the home application, and if you start the server—npm run start-dev-server—you can navigate to http://localhost:3000 and just imagine what it would be like watching all these videos that our content creators are going to upload. All the learning!

Building the Record Views Application

Okay, now that you've imagined the equivalent of earning a PhD, let's get about the business of collecting those view analytics. The button we'll use to simulate views is already on the screen, and if you inspect the Pug template at code/first-pass/src/app/home/templates/home.pug, you'll see that it submits to /record-viewing/12345. The 12345 is a fake video ID, but the /record-viewing path is where we'll mount the application that records viewing videos.

Let's write that application:

first-pass/src/app/record-viewings/index.js

```
const express = require('express')

function createActions ({
}) {
  return {
  }
}

function createHandlers ({ actions }) {
  return {
  }
}

function createRecordViewings ({
}) {
  const actions = createActions({
  })
  const handlers = createHandlers({ actions })

  const router = express.Router()

  router.route('/:videoId').post(handlers.handleRecordViewing)

  return { actions, handlers, router }
}

module.exports = createRecordViewings
```

Let's dive right in at line 14 where we set up the dependency-receiving function. At this point, we're not quite sure what those are going to be, so let's continue.

This application is going to have what we'll call *actions*. Actions are the actual business code. This is in contrast to HTTP handlers that translate between HTTP and our actual business code. The actions will receive some dependencies as well, but we have to discover what they are first, so let's keep going.

An application is going to handle HTTP routes, so at line 18 we have handlers. They'll use the actions, so we pass them in.

Next, we instantiate an express.Router and then mount a handler at /:videoId. This endpoint receives requests to recording video viewings, so handleRecordViewing is a good name for the endpoint's handler. Let's go ahead and write that handler:

first-pass/src/app/record-viewings/index.js
```
function createHandlers ({ actions }) {
  function handleRecordViewing (req, res) {
    return actions
      .recordViewing(req.context.traceId, req.params.videoId)
      .then(() => res.redirect('/'))
  }

  return {
    handleRecordViewing
  }
}
```

There is going to be an action named recordViewing, and it'll do the work of recording the view. This handler's job is to get out of the incoming request everything we need to record the viewing. That's two pieces of data, namely the request's traceId (we set up the generation of trace IDs back on page 6) and the ID of the video that was viewed. That's embedded in the request path, and that's why the route we mounted this handler at has the leading colon. /:videoId told Express, "Hey, when someone calls us here, take whatever is at this point in the URL and attach it to req.params.videoId." When recording that succeeds, we just redirect the viewer's browser to the home page.

Before we write that action, let's mount the application into Express:

first-pass/src/app/express/mount-routes.js
```
function mountRoutes (app, config) {
  app.use('/', config.homeApp.router)
➤ app.use('/record-viewing', config.recordViewingsApp.router)
}
```

Straightforward. Just call app.use, mounting it at /record-viewing off the application's root path. Now we connect it to the system config in config.js (and we're only printing here the parts added for this application):

first-pass/src/config.js
```
Line 1  // ...

  const createRecordViewingsApp = require('./app/record-viewings')

5  function createConfig ({ env }) {

    // ...
    const recordViewingsApp = createRecordViewingsApp({ db })

10    return {
      // ...
      recordViewingsApp
    }
  }
```

Basically, just require the application (line 3), instantiate it (line 8), and add it to the return value (line 12).

Recording State Changes

Okay, we left the record viewings application on page 19 having written the HTTP handlers. The one that we wrote called actions.recordViewing. Now we're going to write that action and record the viewing:

first-pass/src/app/record-viewings/index.js
```
function createActions ({
  db
}) {
  function recordViewing (traceId, videoId) {
  }

  return {
    recordViewing
  }
}
```

This puts a shell in for that function. Let's discuss what this function needs to do.

Its job is to alter system state to reflect that a video has been viewed. We're also doing this in the context of providing a global count of all videos watched.

We already have a database table that could hold this data—you wrote the migration for it on page 15. You *could* simply update the view counts in this action. That would give us the data we need for the global view count. If you're used to MVC CRUD, then this approach might feel very natural.

But, and you probably anticipated some complication with this, what if we wanted to pay content creators based on these view counts? What if we later discovered an error in how we were recording those views? If *all* we have is current counts, we've lost the information we'd need to recalculate.

What if we wanted to see trends in viewing a video over time? This model has already discarded the data we'd need to do that. We could make a new table, say video_views, that stores a record for every time that a video is viewed, something like:

id	video_id	timestamp
1	aa635954-c5d8-4302-bd4a-6e04e5b7f432	1414281600000
2	aafd028a-d209-4ba2-b6f5-85531216c72b	783302400000

We're getting there, but now it's kind of weird having view counts stored on the videos table as well as in this hypothetical table. Furthermore, what if we had shipped to production with only the videos table and then later decided to add video_views? Simply put, we would have been hosed. Sure, we'd have the table, but what data would be in it? We'd only be able to populate it with data from that point moving forward.

If we had shipped to production with the video_views table, when the requirement to see trends came along, we could have said, "Oh, we totally have all the data we need, and from the beginning of the site." I'd much rather say that than, "Oops. We threw away all that data without considering if it would be needed."

But as much of an improvement as we have here, it's *still* lacking. What if we wanted to verify that a view was legitimate before recording it? That seems kind of important if these view counts are the basis of *sending actual money* to content creators. What if that verification took longer than what we're willing to put into a request/response cycle? What if we wanted to signal to other parts of the system that they have work to do whenever a video is viewed? video-views would sort of work for both, but in the case of the latter, it's kind of a specialized, one-off approach. Could we find a more general pattern?

Lastly, what if—*and this is the "What if...?" motivating the entire book*—we wanted to keep the notion of capturing a view completely separate from anything else that we might do with the fact that a video was viewed? Would it reduce your mental load to only have to worry about one thing at a time? What if you could evolve how you recorded views without worrying about how that might break any downstream analysis of said views? Do you think you might be able to deliver value faster if you didn't have to carry in your working memory every place in the system that videos are used? With the videos table from before, you sort of have to. We're one stinking model into this project, and MVC CRUD has *already* coded us into a corner. Can't we do better?

Charting a New Course

If you've built web apps before, chances are that you're used an MVC CRUD architecture that was something like this:

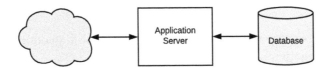

Requests came in from the web, and you had an application server fronting a database to handle them. Using this architecture, we coded our way into a corner before we had finished even a single feature. If showing a view count on the home page were all this project was ever going to do, the MVC CRUD architecture would be a sensible choice. But as Tom Hardy's character Eames in the Christopher Nolan film *Inception* said, "You mustn't be afraid to dream a little bigger."

We're going to do something different with this project. As you've likely gathered from the title of this book, we're going to build a microservices-based system. Rather than model our data as rows in relational databases or documents in document databases, we'll model our data by storing the *state transitions themselves*. Rather than having different parts of the system communicate implicitly by reading from our database, the different parts will communicate through an explicit contract. These two changes will be the basis of how we'll build a system that will be fit to live for decades, even if individual pieces are able to come and go.

As we go along, we're following an architecture like the following:

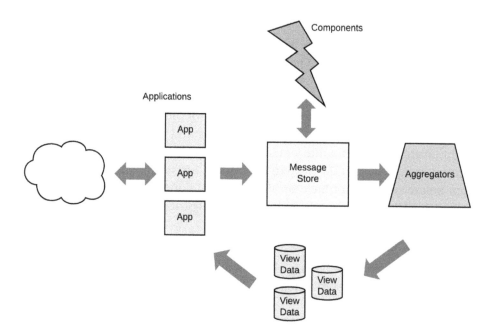

Every system is going to have its unique pieces, but in general they fall into one of five categories:

Applications

We built a couple of these in this chapter. If you've done MVC CRUD, then everything you built is properly understood as an Application. They have the HTTP endpoints and are what our end users interact with. The operate in a request/response mode, providing immediate responses to user input.

Components

Autonomous Components are doers of things. A Component encapsulates a distinct business process. They operate in batch mode, processing batches of messages as they become available.

Aggregators

Aggregators *aggregate* state transitions into View Data that Applications use to render what end users see. As with Components, they also operate in batch mode, processing batches of messages as they become available.

View Data

View Data are read-only models derived from state transitions. They are not authoritative state, but are *eventually consistent* derivations from authoritative state. As such, we don't make decisions based on View Data, hence why it's called *View* Data. In this book we'll use PostgreSQL tables for our View Data, but truly, they could be anything from generated static files to Elasticsearch[10] to Neo4j.[11]

Message Store

At the center of it all is the Message Store. The state transitions we're using as authoritative state live here. It is at the same time a durable state store as well as a transport mechanism. In this book, we'll use message-db,[12] an offering from The Eventide Project.[13]

You'll notice that this list didn't include the word "Service." 'Tis a troubled word that carries a lot of baggage. Much like the secret ingredient discussed in the "Fry and the Slurm Factory" episode of *Futurama*, the word "Service" has unfortunately come to represent whatever your imagination wants it to mean. "Service" can refer to anything running on a computer, and in most writing on the internet, what it precisely refers to has become quite clouded. Following the language of the Eventide Project,[14] we'll choose instead the word "Component" to highlight that we're dealing autonomous units of functionality that

---

10. https://www.elastic.co/

11. https://neo4j.com/

12. https://github.com/message-db/message-db

13. https://eventide-project.org/

14. http://docs.eventide-project.org/core-concepts/services/components.html

model a single business concern. There will be a few places where we still say "service" because it reads better. For example, "microcomponent" doesn't work so well.

The arrows in the diagram indicate how data moves through the system. It generally begins with end users sending requests to Applications. Applications write messages to the Message Store in response to those requests. Services pick up those messages, perform their work, and write new messages to the Message Store. Aggregators observe all this activity and transform these messages into View Data that Applications use to send responses to users.

This structure is going to feel bizarre at first. But chapter by chapter, as you flesh out the pieces, you'll see how a system made of autonomous components enables you and your team's long-term productivity. Hopefully, you'll have some fun along the way too.

What You've Done So Far

You put your web application development skills to use and laid the foundation for Video Tutorials, the next-gen web learning sensation that is about to take the world by storm. We'll remove the videos table as we continue building in upcoming chapters, but the rest of the structure is solid.

Speaking of videos table, here's a fun exercise. In this book we're going to allow users to upload videos, have other users watch those videos, track those viewings, comment on videos, and show screens to let users update video metadata. Can you truly come up with a single representation of videos that will work for all those cases? Will that single model scale? You're free to start with the videos table if you like, or you can start from scratch.

This chapter ends with a bit of a cliff hanger—how are we going to record these video viewings in a way that doesn't slowly strangle our productivity in the long run? According to the system map on page 22 what we built in this chapter was an Application, and Applications write messages to a Message Store. So guess what you're going to build next? That's right, you're going to build a Message Store. The anticipation is likely driving you mad.

We are in bondage to the law in order that we may be free.

> Marcus Tullius Cicero

CHAPTER 2

Writing Messages

When last we left our intrepid hero, the maw of the monolith was closing around. As if in a bad version of *Groundhog Day*, teeth bearing the stench of a thousand years were about to lay waste to an exciting greenfield project, and another iteration of the horrific loop was about to begin.

But in that darkest moment, when hope itself had failed, yet one light still shone. Our hero summoned the wisdom of software design principles, unmasked the monster, and restored, let's say, justice to the land.

That's pretty much the tale people will tell of your efforts in building Video Tutorials. Tongue less in cheek, in this chapter you are going to unmask the monolith. It turns out "monolith" doesn't just mean "code that's hard to work on." A monolith does tend to be difficult, and you're going to uncover why that is so that you can prevent that great darkness from claiming yet another project. Eternal glory awaits.

Unmasking the Monolith

Software is easy to write, but hard to change. MVC CRUD frameworks lead you to monolithic architectures, which optimize for writing. Those quick results they deliver come at the cost of adding a great deal of coupling into your project.[1] Coupling is the enemy of change. Coupling is what makes it impossible to make a change in subsystem A without fear of breaking subsystem B, C, and D. If you rename that column in your users table, well, hopefully you've cleared your calendar for the weekend.

That's fine if you're prototyping *applications*, but it's a sandy foundation for long-lived systems. Recall our system map (see the figure on page 26) from the previous chapter.

---

1. https://en.wikipedia.org/wiki/Coupling_(computer_programming)

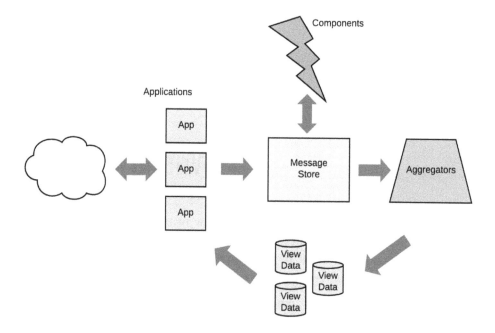

Applications are just one part of an overall system. There are also Components, Aggregators, and View Data to build and maintain. If you don't remember what these different pieces are and what they do, refer back to our list on page 22.

But what is the heart of a monolith's coupling? What is it that makes something a monolith? Is it a question of language? Framework? Database? Codebase size? Monorepo vs. polyrepo? How many servers the system is running on?

Depending on where you land when searching in the blogosphere, those might be posed as the essential questions. Or you might read that "microservices" means "stuff running on different machines." Or Docker. Surely, if you use Docker, you're dealing with microservices. Right? Right?

You landed here though, and you're going to learn all throughout this book that while those questions are important, none of them has any bearing as to whether or not something is a monolith. You can build a service-based system with Rails, and you can certainly build monoliths with Docker. *A monolith is a data model and not a deployment or code organization strategy.*

Trying to Compress Water

Remember the videos table from the previous chapter?

It has a mere six columns: id, owner_id, name, description, transcoding_status, and view_count. Do these pieces of data really all belong together? Do they represent a single thing? Can you imagine a single operation that simultaneously requires all six pieces of data? How many different concerns are represented here?

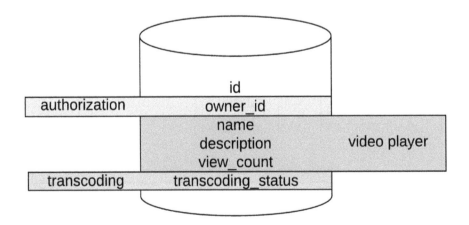

owner_id is useful if we're trying to make sure that someone trying to do something to this video is allowed to—authorization. But how does that help us when putting the video in the video player that other users will see? It would be nice to see the owner's actual name there, but this table doesn't even have that information. Finally, transcoding_status has nothing to do with either of those. Transcoding a video happens in the background, and if a video isn't ready for viewing, why would it show up at all for users who aren't the owner?

The thing represented by this table is an *aggregation* of many different concerns. Which means that any changes to this table could potentially break each of those concerns. This will happen every time you rely on a *canonical data model*[2]—the one representation of a system entity to rule them all and in the darkness bind them. You can try to force these data together, in the same way that you can try to compress some measure of water. It can be done, but only at the cost of considerable energy. That's because they don't want to be together.

This data model *is* the monolith, and no change of language, framework, or deployment strategy can fix that. Nor does the blogosphere's general advice in these situations.

Extracting "Microservices"

When you hit your productivity wall, the blogosphere is going to tell you to Just Extract Microservices.™ Okay. Here's our fledgling system with a hypothetical users concern added to the mix:

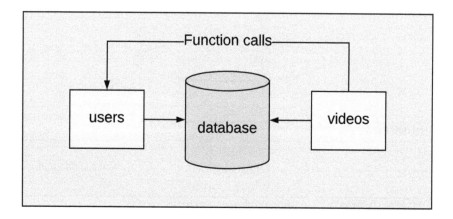

All of these pieces being in the green box represents that their running on the same server. users and videos are run-of-the-mill MVC "models" that have a table of the same name inside of the big, honkin' database sitting in the middle of it all. videos, of course, makes function calls to this users "model" to

---

2.   https://www.innoq.com/en/blog/thoughts-on-a-canonical-data-model/

get data about users. Imagine this project scaling to all sorts of "models," and then we hit the all-too-common "we can't work on this anymore, so we print our resumes and go find another job."

Or desperate to make it better we try to implement the blogosphere's advice and just extract the users and videos "microservices":

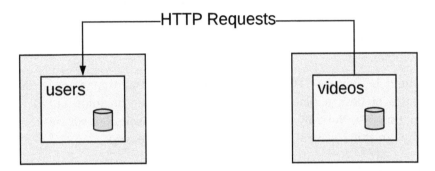

More green boxes, more problems. We've paid a price here. Two servers. Two databases. Those function calls from before? They're HTTP calls now. It's okay to pay a price to receive value, but what value did we receive here?

Absolutely nothing.

The data model *has not changed.* And what's worse, if this so-called "users" service goes down, it's bringing the so-called "videos" service down with it because "videos" *depends on* "users." "Videos" now has two reasons to fail. BOO!

What you have in that image is not microservices.

It is in every aspect still a monolith, only it is distributed now—a *distributed monolith.* Every aspect of working on this system will be more difficult than it was before. Your operational costs just went up (!). What you used to be able to do with a JOIN in a database you have to re-implement in app code (!!). You now need expensive tooling and orchestration to make this work even in development (!!!).

Simply putting a database table behind an HTTP interface does not produce a service, micro or otherwise. So what does?

Defining Services

The defining characteristic of microservices is *autonomy.* Nice word, but what does it mean in this context?

First of all, let's get back to calling them Components. Good. Now, Components don't respond to questions. We have things we ask questions of in software. They're called "databases," and the process of asking them something is called "querying." Even if you stick a database behind HTTP, it's still a database, architecturally speaking.

Components don't ask questions of anything else. If they did, they would *depend* on that thing and would no longer be autonomous. If you have to connect to something else to get data to make a decision, then you are not autonomous.

You might be saying, "That's all well and good, but that sounds like the properties of both a black hole and a white hole—no information in, no information out. Not only a paradox, but entirely useless in software." There is a way, and that way is through *asynchronous messages*.

Getting Components to Do Things

Asynchronous messages are what make service-based architectures possible. We'll just call messages from here on, but they come in two flavors: *commands* and *events*.

Commands are *requests to do something*. Maybe that's transferring some funds, or maybe that's sending an email. Whatever the desired operation is, commands are merely *requests*. The Component that handles a given command chooses whether or not to carry it out.

Components produce *events* in response to commands. Events are records of *things that have happened*. That means whatever they represent, it's already done. You don't have to like it, but you do have to deal with it.

Commands and events, collectively messages, are moved around in the system via *publish-subscribe*, or pub/sub for short.[3] In pub/sub, publishers publish data, and they're not sure who subscribes to it. Subscribers similarly don't know who published the information they consume.

When you write a Component, as you will in Chapter 9, Adding an Email Component, on page 133, you document which commands your Component handles as well as which events your Component publishes. With those messages defined, interested parties can request your Component do something and can also respond to the events your Component publishes.

---

3.   https://en.wikipedia.org/wiki/Publish–subscribe_pattern

Representing Messages in Code

So what does a message look like? We can represent them as JSON objects:

```
{
  "id": "875b04d0-081b-453e-925c-a25d25213a18",
  "type": "PublishVideo",
  "metadata": {
    "traceId": "ddecf8e8-de5d-4989-9cf3-549c303ac939",
    "userId": "bb6a04b0-cb74-4981-b73d-24b844ca334f"
  },
  "data": {
    "ownerId": "bb6a04b0-cb74-4981-b73d-24b844ca334f",
    "sourceUri": "https://sourceurl.com/",
    "videoId": "9bfb5f98-36f4-44a2-8251-ab06e0d6d919"
  }
}
```

This is a command you'll define in Chapter 10, Performing Background Jobs with Microservices, on page 157.

At the root of this object we have four fields:

id

Every message gets a unique ID, and we use UUIDs for them.

type

A string and something you choose when you define your messages. When we said earlier that events represent things that have happened, it's the type that tells us what that thing that happened was. And in the case of commands, the type tells us we want to have happen.

metadata

An object that contains, well, metadata. The contents of this object have to do with the mechanics of making our messaging infrastructure work. Examples of fields we'll commonly find in here include traceId, which ties messages resulting from the same user input together. Every incoming user request will get a unique traceId, and any messages written as part of that user request will get written with that request's traceId. If there are any components that write other messages in response to those messages, then those messages will have the same traceId. In that way, we can easily track everything that happened in the system in response to a particular user request. We'll put this into action in Chapter 13, Debugging Components, on page 207, which deals with debugging strategies. We will also commonly have a userId string, representing the ID of the user who caused the message to be written.

data

A JSON object itself, and the "payload" of the event. The contents of a message's data field are analogous to the parameters in a function call.

You can tell that this event is a command because the type is in the imperative mood. This is a convention we will always follow. Since a command is a *request* to do something, its type is in the imperative mood. This is in contrast to the event that might get generated in response to this command:

```
{
  "id": "23d2076f-41bd-4cdb-875e-2b0812a27524",
  "type": "VideoPublished",
  "metadata": {
    "traceId": "ddecf8e8-de5d-4989-9cf3-549c303ac939",
    "userId": "bb6a04b0-cb74-4981-b73d-24b844ca334f"
  },
  "data": {
    "ownerId": "bb6a04b0-cb74-4981-b73d-24b844ca334f",
    "sourceUri": "https://sourceurl.com/",
    "videoId": "9bfb5f98-36f4-44a2-8251-ab06e0d6d919"
  }
}
```

Notice the type on this event is in the past tense. That's because events are things that have already happened.

Naming Messages

Giving types to our messages is the most important of the engineering work we'll do. As we add features to our system, we'll use messages to represent the various processes the system carries out. The preceding messages come from the video cataloging process we'll build in Chapter 10, Performing Background Jobs with Microservices, on page 157.

We come up with types for the messages in collaboration with our company's business team. Message types are named after the business processes they represent. Furthermore, we select types using language familiar to experts in the domain we are modeling. This is not something we can do alone as developers.

If we were modeling banking, we might have messages like TransferFunds, AccountOpened, and FundsDeposited. We absolutely will not have types that contain "create," "update," or "delete." We're purging that CRUD from our vocabulary.

Storing State as Events

Up to this point, this concept of commands and events may be familiar. You may have already used technology such as Apache Kafka[4] to have components communicate via events. We're going to take it further though.

You may receive a command like PetPuppies, a command that should never be rejected. When a command is processed, the output is one or more events, such as PuppiesPet. If we wanted to know whether or not the puppies have been pet, how could we tell? Take a moment and think about it...

All we'd have to look for is that event. Instead of treating the messages as transient notifications, discarding them when we're done, we *save* them. Then we can constitute and reconstitute current state or state at any point in time to our heart's content. This is *event sourcing*—sourcing state from events.

If you've done MVC CRUD apps, then you're probably used to receiving incoming requests and then updating one or more rows in a database. At any given point, you were storing the *current state* of your system, having discarded all knowledge of how the system got into that state. Because we're already going to use messages to communicate between portions of our system, why not keep them around? Then we could use the events to know what the state of our system is now, and at any point in the past.

Storing Messages in Streams

One last note about messages before we begin writing them. When we start writing messages on page 36, we'll organize them into what we call *streams*. Streams group messages together logically, usually representing an entity or process in your system. Within a stream, messages are stored in the order they were written.

For example, Video Tutorials users will have an identity. We'll explicitly model that identity in Chapter 6, Registering Users, on page 83. All the events related to a particular user's identity will be in the same stream, and those are the only events that will be in that stream. Using the naming conventions of the Eventide Project,[5] a Ruby toolkit for building autonomous microservices, we call this type of stream an *entity stream*. We use UUIDs[6] as identifiers in our system, specifically version 4 UUIDs, and so a natural name for one of these user identity streams would be identity-81cb4647-1296-4f3b-8039-0eedae41c97e.

---

4. https://kafka.apache.org/
5. http://docs.eventide-project.org/core-concepts/streams/stream-names.html
6. https://en.wikipedia.org/wiki/Universally_unique_identifier

While any part of the system is free to *read* the events in such a stream, a property we'll use in Chapter 8, Authenticating Users, on page 119, an entity stream only has a single writer.

Here is a pair of such identity streams:

Stream: identity-cd5cb686-e841-4ade-9d4f-dd7baaac2dc6

Registered	AccountLocked	AccountUnlocked

Stream: identity-b6da5cea-f7aa-40ec-b4f7-c788501ff91d

Registered

There are other kinds of streams, though. If all goes as planned, Video Tutorials will have more than one user, each with a stream of the form identity-UUID. Every event in such an entity stream is also part of the identity *category stream*. To get the category stream that an entity stream belongs to, just take everything to the left of the first dash. So for identity-81cb4647-1296-4f3b-8039-0eedae41c97e, identity is the category. The identity category stream contains every *event* written to every identity in our system.

We talked about commands on page 30, and commands are also written to streams. They aren't written to entity streams, though—they are written to *command streams*. In the case of this identity Component, we'll write to streams of the form identity:command-81cb4647-1296-4f3b-8039-0eedae41c97e. This is an *entity command stream*, and it only contains commands related to a particular entity. What is the category of this stream? Is it the same as the entity stream from before? Again, to get a category from a stream, take everything to the left of the first dash. For this entity command stream, that gives us identity:command, which is not the same as identity. So no, entity streams are not in the same category as entity command streams.

Streams, like messages, don't get deleted. Messages are added to them in an append-only manner.

Now, if there's anything we can take from the 1984 *Ghostbusters* film, crossing the streams is Bad™ and continued abstract talk about streams will likely lead to that. Now that we have the basics of messages, let's get to a concrete example and resolve the cliffhanger we started on page 20.

Defining Component Boundaries

Stream boundaries are Component boundaries. If we have a stream category such as identity, what we're saying is that there's going to be a single Component authorized to *write* to streams in the identity category. Those are Component boundaries. Similarly, if we have command streams in the category identity:command, only that same Component is authorized to handle those commands. These strict rules are part of avoiding monoliths. In a monolith, anyone can add columns to the users table and make updates to its rows. Not so in our architecture! The lack of these boundaries are why we can't just Extract Microservices™ from a monolith. As you'll see when we look at distributing our system in Chapter 12, Deploying Components, on page 195, it's precisely these boundaries that allow us to extract things.

Sometimes, although not in this book, a Component will own more than one entity. This is rare, and it also doesn't break our rule in the previous paragraph. A category has a single owner, even on the rare occasions that a particular owner happens to own another category.

Recording Video Views

How are we going to record that a video was viewed? Since we're not going to just use an MVC CRUD-style database table, it stands to reason that we're going to write a message. Should that be an event or a command?

Questions are best answered by going back to fundamental principles. In our initial talks with the business team, one of the longer-term (read: outside the scope of this book) visions is to have users buy memberships to see premium content, and the creators of that content would get paid based on how many times their videos were viewed. So we know an event eventually needs to be written, and since we're recording that a video was viewed, VideoViewed seems like a good type for this kind of event.

The next question then, who writes that event? Should the record-viewings application write events directly, or should it write commands that some Component picks up and handles? We previously discussed on page 33 how a given event stream is populated by one and only one writer. So far, it could go either way.

Let's say that we have the application write the events and that it writes to streams of the form viewingX, where X is a video's ID. Are we capturing the necessary state? Check. Is there only a single writer to a given stream? Check. So far so good.

What if we wanted to run potential video views through some sort of algorithm to detect fake views before committing them to system state? Obviously none of *our* users would ever do that, but, you hear stories. Investors like to know we've addressed this kind of thing, and content creators would want to know the view counts are legit.

That seems like a bit much to put into a request/response cycle and something that we would want to put into a Component. That Component would currently do nothing besides receiving, say RecordVideoViewing commands, and writing VideoViewed events. We don't need to support this right now, so why take on that extra burden?

The only reason to do so would be if this choice affects long-term maintainability. Does it? If we had the application write the viewed events and later decided to move this into a Component, what would we need to change?

1. Refactor the Application to write a command to a command stream rather than an event to an event stream.

2. Write the Component.

We'd have to do step 2 anyway, and step 1 doesn't sound that hard. If we were doing this CRUD style, we might have had to set up a different API to call into with the video view. We'd have the same issue where verifying the view takes too long to put into a request/response cycle, so that API would likely have done some sort of background job. When it's done with the verification, maybe it would make another call into our application to record the result of that verification? Or we modify our application to pull from a different database? Or we directly couple our application to that API via a shared database table? Those all sound like messes from a design perspective, let alone the operational concerns of having to make two network hops. With a pub/sub flow that stores state as events and makes sure a given event stream only has a single writer, we're able to proceed confidently in the short term without setting ourselves up with a costly refactoring later.

Let's not worry about the Component right now and just have the Application record video viewings. We'll get to our first Component soon enough in Chapter 6, Registering Users, on page 83.

Writing Your First Message

Okay, when we left the record-viewings application, we were in the function that would record that a video was viewed. Here's where we left off:

first-pass/src/app/record-viewings/index.js

```
function createActions ({
  db
}) {
  function recordViewing (traceId, videoId) {
  }

  return {
    recordViewing
  }
}
```

We decided on page 35 that we'll use VideoViewed events to record video views. We'll write these events to streams of the form viewing-X, where X is the video's ID. So all we need to do in this function is build the event we're going to write and then write it to the Message Store:

The Code Directory Has Changed

From this point going forward in the book, the code is in the code/video-tutorials/ folder.

If you're using Docker for the database, be sure to stop the container for the first-pass folder and switch to code/video-tutorials and re-run docker-compose rm -sf && docker-compose up.

---

video-tutorials/src/app/record-viewings/index.js

```
function createActions ({
❶  messageStore
}) {
  function recordViewing (traceId, videoId, userId) {
❷    const viewedEvent = {
      id: uuid(),
      type: 'VideoViewed',
      metadata: {
        traceId,
        userId
      },
      data: {
        userId,
        videoId
      }
    }
❸    const streamName = `viewing-${videoId}`

❹    return messageStore.write(streamName, viewedEvent)
  }
  return {
    recordViewing
  }
}
```

❶ First of all, notice that we've taken out the reference to the db and replaced it with a messageStore reference. We're writing an event and not updating a row in a videos table.

❷ Then we construct the event. It's just a plain old JavaScript object that can be serialized to JSON. You'll notice the fields we mentioned on page 31. There isn't that much to an event.

❶ Next, we construct the name of the stream that we're going to write this event to.

❹ Finally, we actually call messageStore.write to write the event. That function takes the streamName that we want to write to and the message we want to write.

There's one last change we need to make in this file. In the top-level function we also need to change the db reference to messageStore:

video-tutorials/src/app/record-viewings/index.js
```
function createRecordViewings ({
  messageStore
}) {
  const actions = createActions({
    messageStore
  })
  // ... rest of the body omitted
}
```

The top-level function receives messageStore and passes it along to actions.

(Re)configuring the Record-Viewings Application

And we also have a change to our configuration to make. We need to pull in the Message Store, instantiate it, and pass it to the record-viewings application:

video-tutorials/src/config.js
```
Line 1  // ...
        const createPostgresClient = require('./postgres-client')
        const createMessageStore = require('./message-store')
        function createConfig ({ env }) {
     5    const knexClient = createKnexClient({
            connectionString: env.databaseUrl
          })
          const postgresClient = createPostgresClient({
            connectionString: env.messageStoreConnectionString
    10    })
          const messageStore = createMessageStore({ db: postgresClient })

          const homeApp = createHomeApp({ db: knexClient })
          const recordViewingsApp = createRecordViewingsApp({ messageStore })
```

```
15    return {
        // ...
        messageStore,
      }
    }
```

Line 2 requires the code that will create our database connection *to the Message Store*, and line 3 requires our Message Store code. We set up the database connection at line 8 by giving it the connection info we get from the environment. We'll add that to env.js and .env is just a moment. Line 11 then instantiates the Message Store by passing it the postgresClient reference. Line 14 passes messageStore to instantiate the recordViewingsApp, and then we add messageStore to the config function's return value at line 17.

A quick change in src/env.js:

```
video-tutorials/src/env.js
module.exports = {
  // ...
  messageStoreConnectionString:
    requireFromEnv('MESSAGE_STORE_CONNECTION_STRING')
}
```

And be sure to add the corresponding value to .env:

```
MESSAGE_STORE_CONNECTION_STRING=
  postgres://postgres@localhost:5433/message_store
```

Make sure to put that on a single line. So, good to go, right?

Hanging a Lantern

In showbiz, when writers call attention to glaring inconsistencies, that's called "hanging a lantern on it." We have one, ah, slight problem. We don't actually have the Message Store code yet. Let's punt that to the next chapter because this one is already pretty long, and we've covered a lot in it.

What You've Done So Far

You unmasked the monolith. You learned that monoliths are data models and that they speed up the near term at the expense of the long term by introducing high levels of coupling. You also learned that the most commonly recommended methods for dealing with this coupling don't actually do anything to address the coupling.

Then you got your feet wet with the basics of message-based architecture. Messages are what make autonomous microservices possible, and autonomouse microservices are what make long-term productivity possible. This was no small amount of learning.

Taking those principles then, you came back to our problem at hand—how do we record video views without writing ourselves into an inescapable corner? You learned about streams and concluded the chapter by writing a VideoViewed event to a stream in the viewings category. You stepped into a whole new world.

Aside from building the mechanics of the Message Store, which we'll start in the next chapter, being able to analyze business processes and model them as messages is the most important skill you can acquire. That's where the real engineering is done. To that end, choose some workflow that exists in the project you're currently working on. Instead of thinking of it in CRUD terms, can you model it as a sequence of events? Strike create, update, and delete from your vocabulary, and state what your current project does in terms that non-developers would use. Does it get you thinking differently about the project? Does it reveal holes in your understanding?

Lanterns are great and all, but we need something to store our messages. As we continue the journey to record video views and display the total view count on the home page, our next step is to go from mythical Message Store to actual Message Store. You may find it mundane, or you may find it exciting. Regardless of which, you'll find it in the next chapter.

CHAPTER 3

Putting Data in a Message Store

Imagine a house without plumbing. Such a dwelling might be fun for the occasional rustic experience, but there are several reasons why it wouldn't be desirable in the long term. A Message Store is kind of like the plumbing in a microservices-based system, only in contrast to a house's plumbing, we, um, want to keep the stuff it moves around.

You've started Video Tutorials, and you learned the interface for writing data to a Message Store. Now you're going to connect to a real Message Store and actually write that data. We're going to use Message DB,[1] the PostgreSQL-based Message Store implementation from the Eventide Project.[2] By the end of this chapter, you will have written the code we'll use to leverage Message DB's write capabilities. This will give you a deeper understanding of the pub/sub architecture we're implementing and better equip you to design microservices-based systems.

Defining Requirements

Simply put, a Message Store needs to provide two things with regard to writing messages:

- Persist append-only streams of immutable messages
- Provide *optimistic concurrency control*[3] on those streams

If you're tired of developing software and are looking for an experience painful enough to convince you to quit, you technically could use something as simple as a flat text file with a little code sprinkled on top to model a Message Store.

---

1. https://github.com/message-db/message-db
2. https://eventide-project.org
3. https://en.wikipedia.org/wiki/Optimistic_concurrency_control

Now, as Jeff Goldblum's character in *Jurassic Park* mused, just because one *could* do a thing does not mean one *should*, but hey, the option is there.

We'll choose a different path, though, and we'll use a Message Store built on top of a relational database, specifically PostgreSQL. RDBMSs are tried-and-true, battle-hardened technology. You'll write a sprinkle of code on top, and we'll close the chapter with the ability to write messages to the Message DB.

Fleshing Out Message Structure

In Chapter 2, Writing Messages, on page 25, we showed some example messages. That's what they look like *before* being written to the Message Store. The act of writing them adds some additional fields:

streamName

> A string and the name of the stream this event belongs to. We discussed the importance of streams and how they're named on page 33.

position

> This is used for optimistic locking, a method for dealing with concurrent writes. It denotes a particular message's position within its stream. The Message Store will generate these values.

globalPosition

> Just as position records a message's position within its stream, globalPosition records a message's position within the entire Message Store. This field enables real-time consumption of messages, which you'll get to in Chapter 5, Subscribing to the Message Store, on page 65. The Message Store will generate these values as well.

time

> This captures *when the message was written to the Message Store*. This is about the mechanics of messaging, and if your message needs to capture a time for domain reasons, put that in the data field. For example, if you were modeling credit card payments, you'd want to model when that payment becomes effective, which isn't necessarily the same data that the corresponding message is recorded. Once again, the Message Store will generate these values.

Both commands and events will have these fields, since they only differ by whether or not the type is imperative or past tense. You'll also never put commands in the same stream as events, but the storage mechanism can't tell the difference.

Surveying Message DB

As mentioned earlier, Message DB is built on top of PostgreSQL. It's a lot simpler than you might expect a piece of messaging infrastructure to be. It boils down to a single messages table[4] with some indexes[5] and user-defined functions[6] that we use to interact with the table rather than querying against the messages table directly. We won't walk through all of the code making up the Message Store itself, but let's do inspect the messages table:

```
CREATE TABLE IF NOT EXISTS message_store.messages (
  id UUID NOT NULL DEFAULT gen_random_uuid(),
  stream_name text NOT NULL,
  type text NOT NULL,
  position bigint NOT NULL,
  global_position bigserial NOT NULL,
  data jsonb,
  metadata jsonb,
  time TIMESTAMP WITHOUT TIME ZONE DEFAULT (now() AT TIME ZONE 'utc') NOT NULL
);

ALTER TABLE
  message_store.messages
ADD PRIMARY KEY (global_position) NOT DEFERRABLE INITIALLY IMMEDIATE;
```

This table has columns for all the fields we'll find on our messages. Our job in the rest of this chapter is to write the JavaScript code we'll use to write messages to this table.

Scaffolding the Message Store Code

Let's get started by laying out the bones of our Message Store code. Like all of our submodules, we'll have a top level that receives dependencies and uses those dependencies to configure itself:

```
video-tutorials/src/message-store/index.js
const createWrite = require('./write')
function createMessageStore ({ db }) {
  const write = createWrite({ db })
  return {
    write: write,
```

We start the Message Store by requireing a file that doesn't exist yet but that we will write immediately after the scaffolding here—the file that contains the logic for actually writing to the Message Store.

---

4. https://github.com/message-db/message-db/blob/master/database/tables/messages.sql
5. https://github.com/message-db/message-db/tree/master/database/indexes
6. https://github.com/message-db/message-db/tree/master/database/functions

Next, we define createMessageStore, the top-level, dependency-receiving function that initializes the Message Store. It receives an object it will use for connecting to the PostgreSQL instance where the Message Store is installed. We then pass that db to createWrite to set up the write functionality just before returning. Yes, scaffolding isn't very interesting, so let's set up that database connection.

Connecting to Message DB

Message DB is Just PostgreSQL™, so connecting to it is the same as connecting to PostgreSQL. Now, we've been using knex for our database connections up to this point because we were writing our own schema migrations. Message DB ships with a schema that we won't touch, so we don't need knex for that. We'll just use the pg package,[7] a lower-level interface into PostgreSQL. Let's write the wrapper code for dealing with this library that we punted on last chapter on page 38:

```
video-tutorials/src/postgres-client.js
const Bluebird = require('bluebird')
const pg = require('pg')

function createDatabase ({ connectionString }) {
❶  const client = new pg.Client({ connectionString, Promise: Bluebird })

❷  let connectedClient = null

   function connect () {
     if (!connectedClient) {
       connectedClient = client.connect()
         .then(() => client.query('SET search_path = message_store, public'))
         .then(() => client)
     }

     return connectedClient
   }

❸  function query (sql, values = []) {
     return connect()
       .then(client => client.query(sql, values))
   }

❹  return {
     query,
     stop: () => client.end()
   }
}

module.exports = createDatabase
```

---

7. https://node-postgres.com

The file exports a function that takes a connectionString so that it knows how to connect to the PostgreSQL instance where the Message Store lives. It then:

❶ Instantiates a database connection.

❷ Message DB installs its machinery in a message_store schema inside of its PostgreSQL database. So, when we actually connect to the database, using client.connect, we immediately follow that with a query that sets the search_path on that connection to include this message_store schema. If that didn't make any sense, this callback makes it so that the queries we issue to the Message Store work.

❸ Defines a query function. We'll have the rest of our code couple to this function rather than coupling directly to the pg.Client interface. We won't have complicated query patterns, and this simple query interface will suffice. We call our connect function to make sure the we've established the connection and set up the search_path properly.

❹ Then we return query and a stop function. This latter we use in test so that we can terminate our test process when all of the tests have run.

Now that we have the database connection, we can write the write function.

Writing write

Let's start by examining the write_message[8] function signature that the Eventide schema provides:

```
CREATE OR REPLACE FUNCTION write_message(
  _id varchar,
  _stream_name varchar,
  _type varchar,
  _data jsonb,
  _metadata jsonb DEFAULT NULL,
  _expected_version bigint DEFAULT NULL
)
```

This is a user-defined function and is the write interface that Message DB gives us. From this, we can tell that when writing a message, we supply the id, streamName, type, data, and metadata properties. The last parameter this function receives, _expected_version, is used when we're implementing optimistic concurrency control later in this chapter under Adding Optimistic Concurrency Control to Our Writes, on page 47. Our job then is to write a function that

---

8. https://github.com/eventide-project/postgres-message-store/blob/master/database/functions/write-message.sql

receives a message and then calls this user-defined function with the values
from that message. Let's start with the bones of the function:

```
video-tutorials/src/message-store/write.js
const writeFunctionSql =
  'SELECT message_store.write_message($1, $2, $3, $4, $5, $6)'
function createWrite ({ db }) {
  return (streamName, message, expectedVersion) => {
    if (!message.type) {
      throw new Error('Messages must have a type')
    }

    const values = [
      message.id,
      streamName,
      message.type,
      message.data,
      message.metadata,
      expectedVersion
    ]

    return db.query(writeFunctionSql, values)
  }
}

module.exports = createWrite
```

❶ First, we're going to call the write_message user-defined function, so let's
capture the SQL we'll use in a variable here. The series of arguments with
dollar signs in front of them are how we pass variables safely to a query
using the pg library. When we get to the actual query call in just a moment,
we'll pass an array of values, and those dollar sign values correspond to
positions in that array of values.

❷ Next, for this function to, ah, function, we need a database connection.
createWrite receives that database connection, returning the actual function
that will do the writing.

❸ The function that actually does the writing takes three arguments,
namely the streamName we're writing to, the actual message we're writing,
and expectedVersion, which again we use for optimistic concurrency control
and which we'll ignore until Adding Optimistic Concurrency Control to
Our Writes, on page 47.

❹ Now, messages must have a type. The Message Store will bark at us if we
don't supply one, so we might as well bark first and return a less cryptic
error than what PostgreSQL will give us if try to use a null value where
one is not allowed.

❺ Next, we assemble the array of values we mentioned a few points up. If you check carefully, the order of these values matches the order of the parameters that the write_message user-defined function expects.

After completing these steps, we conclude by calling db.query to actually invoke write_message. Note that we return the result of that call, a Promise that resolves when the call has completed. And just like that we've handled simple writes.

Adding Optimistic Concurrency Control to Our Writes

In the last section we wrote code that, come hell or high water, will put messages in the Message Store. But sometimes, we'll need a more delicate touch.

Messages have a position property that orders a message within its stream. Streams have versions, and their version is equal to the maximum position value of all the messages in that stream. Note that we're talking about the position property and not the globalPosition property, which orders messages in the whole Message Store.

A thorough treatment of concurrency is beyond the scope of this book, although we will touch on it lightly later in the book on page 242. But for now, imagine if we had two instances of a component writing to the same stream. We must ensure that writes assuming a certain state of the stream only proceed if the state of that stream hasn't changed between the moment the decision to write is made and when the write actually occurs.

For example, suppose that our two instances are processing bank transactions, recording deposits. If a command to credit an account with $5 is being handled by two instances at the same time, each is going attempt to write a Deposited event. Getting two of those events from a single command would be, how to say it, "career limiting"? So, what we want is for those writes to be able to say, "Hey, write this message to the this stream, but only if the stream is still at version 3." That's exactly what the expectedVersion parameters lets us do.

Eventide handles the mechanics of enforcing the expectedVersion, and in the case of a conflict, the Promise that db.query returns will be rejected. We'll get an error from the database. It isn't good form to pass raw database errors around, so we're going to write code to intercept the error and normalize it.

First, at the top of the file we need to pull in an error type and define a regular expression:

```
video-tutorials/src/message-store/write.js
const VersionConflictError = require('./version-conflict-error')
const versionConflictErrorRegex = /^Wrong.*Stream Version: (\d+)\)/
```

VersionConflictError is defined in code/video-tutorials/src/message-store/version-conflict-error.js. We won't print it here, but it's just a basic error that captures the name of the stream we were trying to write to, the actual version of the stream when we tried writing, and the version we were expecting. versionConflictErrorRegex matches the database error we'll get in the event of a version conflict, and it also lets us extract from that error what the stream's actual version was. Let's put these two values to use:

video-tutorials/src/message-store/write.js

```
return db.query(writeFunctionSql, values)
  .catch(err => {
    const errorMatch = err.message.match(versionConflictErrorRegex)
    const notVersionConflict = errorMatch === null

    if (notVersionConflict) {
      throw err
    }

    const actualVersion = parseInt(errorMatch[1], 10)

    const versionConflictError = new VersionConflictError(
      streamName,
      actualVersion,
      expectedVersion
    )
    versionConflictError.stack = err.stack

    throw versionConflictError
  })
```

Picking up right after the db.query call and attaching a catch handler to the return Promise, we:

❶ First, attempt to match the error we got to versionConflictErrorRegex. Why, you ask? Well, the database is perfectly capable of throwing errors that aren't from version conflicts. So, we have to make sure we're handling a version conflict. If not, then just rethrow whatever error it was, and let nature take its course.

❷ Now that we know we have a version conflict, we get the actual version out of the database error.

❸ Then we instantiate the instance of VersionConflict error and throw it. That way, the error processing above this function will have a normalized and informative error to work with rather than a raw database error.

And that wraps up writing to the Message Store. With this function in place and the Message Store interface defined, the config code you wrote on page 38 will start working and the parts of the system that need to write to the Message Store will now be able to.

"Can't Kafka Do All of This?"

I hear that question a lot when it comes to event sourcing. Kafka is a message broker, and it as well as other message brokers are fine pieces of technology. You might be wondering why we can't just use something like Kafka to store the messages instead of Eventide. Kafka—so hot on resumes right now—is particularly is well-suited to handling large numbers of events and moving them around.

Kafka can be configured to retain messages indefinitely, can be used to access events that have previously been processed (necessary for projections), *and* supports the concept of topics. At first blush, topics seem a whole lot like streams.

One problem is that Kafka expects a set of topics that are defined *in advance*. In an event-sourced system, we can't know what streams are needed in advance. For example, if we model user identities by giving them their own event stream, we'd have to know in advance about every user who would ever sign up for our system. This requirement is problematic at best.

Furthermore, we weren't done with our write code until we could handle concurrent writes with optimistic concurrency. Kafka does not have this capability[9] at this point in time, and the issue is also listed as a "Minor" priority. That prioritization is correct. As Scott Bellware put it, Kafka is a buffer and not a Message Store.[10] Its priorities shouldn't be those of a Message Store.

Kafka and other message brokers are fine pieces of technology, but they aren't designed with the requirements of event sourcing in mind. They also introduce new ops requirements, unknown failure modes, and other complications. Those are fine prices to pay if you gain enough value. But message brokers offer no benefits over PostgreSQL, something we're already using anyway.

What You've Done So Far

You started this chapter with code that pretended to write messages to a Message Store. You now have code that actually will. Kudos!

In the book's introduction on page xvii we talked about principles vs. implementations. We're using Eventide's Message Store, and you'd need some

---

9.   https://issues.apache.org/jira/browse/KAFKA-2260
10.   https://twitter.com/sbellware/status/1068209924512145408

pretty decent scale before it wouldn't handle your needs. But there are others. Greg Young's EventStore[11] is an example of one.

Go read about some other Message Stores—the things they do differently, the things they do the same. If you're particularly ambitious, you could build the rest of this book using one of those!

Our current goal is still to be able to record video views and display the global count of videos watched on the home page. We're finally capturing those views into a durable location, but as awesome as events are, they look *nothing* like the data we need to display that global count. Now that we've got the data *in* the store, how do we get it back *out* and in a useful shape?

That's exactly what the next chapter is about, so make sure you're buckled in because it's your humble author's favorite part of this whole architecture.

---

11. https://eventstore.org/

CHAPTER 4

Projecting Data into Useful Shapes

Tell me how many times this dream has played out for you. You've snapped your fingers and now you have your dream job. There you are, heading in to your first day of work. This is it! Your. Dream. Job. You look down at the nameplate on your office door, and what title does it say just below your name?

Auditor.

What? You haven't had this dream? Well, neither have our users. So while storing all of our application state as a linear log of what has happened sounds pretty amazing, how do we turn that log into a user interface that isn't just a linear log of everything that has happened in our system? How do we make it *not* just look like an audit trail?

When I first got into microservices and the idea that autonomous Components don't ask or answer questions, it was this very question that held me back from embracing this architectural style. It took me about a year for it to click. But you're likely a bit quicker on the uptake.

Let's check out our system architecture again (see the figure on page 52).

So far we've written an Application in Chapter 1, You Have a New Project, on page 3 and Chapter 2, Writing Messages, on page 25, and we wrote some Message Store interaction in Chapter 3, Putting Data in a Message Store, on page 41.

This chapter is all about Aggregators, the pieces in our system that transform events from an auditor's dream to things that everyone can enjoy. It answers the question, "Now that we have all this recorded state, what do we do with it? How do we turn these events into screens for our users?" Message stores are fantastic for writing data, but they are exceptionally bad for rendering screens to users. The data just isn't in the right shape.

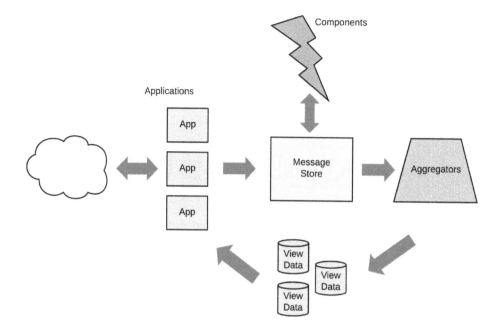

Our site will need to display all kinds of screens to our users, and it's in this chapter that you'll learn how to turn our append-only logs of immutable events into structures that make for fast querying and display to users. In fact, when we get to Chapter 13, Debugging Components, on page 207, you'll even take the various events generated throughout the project and build additional views *from the same data*. This concept of writing data in one shape and reading it in one or more other shapes is known as *Command-Query Responsibility Segregation*, or CQRS for short.

Let's do this.

Handling Events

An Aggregator's existence is define by a two-step process:

1. Receive an event.
2. Handle it by updating View Data somewhere.

In our case, we're only going to use PostgreSQL tables for View Data, but as you'll learn, we're not limited to only relational tables.

(Re)Introducing the RDBMS

Okay, so technically we used a relational database when writing to our Message Store in Chapter 3, Putting Data in a Message Store, on page 41. That was optimized for *writing* data. In this chapter we're going to build tables optimized for *reading* data. You won't find third normal form[1] tables here. Those are optimized for writing. What if we could build our database schema in such a way that every screen only required querying for *a single row*? Let's start with a migration to define the schema we're going to write to:

```
video-tutorials/migrations/20180303013723_create-pages.js
exports.up = knex =>
  knex.schema.createTable('pages', table => {
    table.string('page_name').primary()

    table.jsonb('page_data').defaultsTo('{}')
  })
exports.down = knex => knex.schema.dropTable('pages')
```

Two columns, and one of them is a JSON blob. The idea is that there are some mostly static pages on our site. The home page is an example. We want to get the data for these pages with a single query and no joins.

To that end, this migration creates a two-column table that houses key–value pairs. The keys are the strings in the page_name column, and the values are jsonb objects that default to the empty object but that will be filled out with the data needed to render the pages they represent. For example, the home page might have home and { "videosWatched": 42, "lastViewProcessed": 24 } for page_name and page_data, respectively. videosWatched is the number of videos watched, and lastViewProcessed is how we handle idempotence. It is the id of the last message incorporated into the View Data. So if we see a message with a lower number or equal number, then we know that the View Data already incorporates that message.

Writing Your First Aggregator

Since this is the first Aggregator, here is the basic shape of one:

```
video-tutorials/src/aggregators/home-page.js
function createHandlers ({ queries }) {
  return {
  }
}
```

---

1. https://en.wikipedia.org/wiki/Third_normal_form

```
function createQueries ({ db }) {
  return {
  }
}

function build ({ db, messageStore }) {
  const queries = createQueries({ db })
  const handlers = createHandlers({ queries })
  return {
    queries,
    handlers,
  }
}

module.exports = build
```

Our Aggregators handle messages, so they have handlers. They also interact with a database, so they have queries. There is a top-level function, which we name build that receives dependencies, namely db and messageStore, references to the database and the Message Store, respectively. The top-level function passes them to the queries and handlers. This shape is not a hard-and-fast rule for Aggregators in general, but is what most of our Aggregators will have.

With that shape in place, let's write our message handlers.

Handling Asynchronous Messages

Message handlers are functions that receive a message and *do something*. For Components that'll mean carrying out some state-changing business function. For Aggregators that means updating a View Data.

We define an autonomous component's message handlers as a JavaScript object whose keys are the message types the component handles. This Aggregator needs to handle VideoViewed events, and when we get one, we want to increment the global watch count by 1. So let's write that first handler:

```
video-tutorials/src/aggregators/home-page.js
function createHandlers ({ queries }) {
  return {
    VideoViewed: event => queries.incrementVideosWatched(event.globalPosition)
  }
}
```

createHandlers receives the queries from the top-level function, and returns an object with key VideoViewed, whose value is a function that takes an event and delegates the appropriate action to queries.incrementVideosWatched. At a glance, we can tell how this Aggregator handles this event, and that's good.

Let's write that query function:

```
video-tutorials/src/aggregators/home-page.js
function incrementVideosWatched (globalPosition) {
  const queryString = `
    UPDATE
      pages
    SET
      page_data = jsonb_set(
        jsonb_set(
          page_data,
          '{videosWatched}',
          ((page_data ->> 'videosWatched')::int + 1)::text::jsonb
        ),
        '{lastViewProcessed}',
        :globalPosition::text::jsonb
      )
    WHERE
      page_name = 'home' AND
      (page_data->>'lastViewProcessed')::int < :globalPosition
  `

  return db.then(client => client.raw(queryString, { globalPosition }))
}
```

Oof. That's a gnarly query if you're unfamiliar with PostgreSQL jsonb columns, but we can work through it. It has the same structure as any UPDATE query you've worked with before:

```
UPDATE
  pages
SET
  -- the jsonb part
WHERE
  page_name = 'home' AND
  (page_data->>'lastViewProcessed')::int < :globalPosition
```

It's doing an UPDATE against the pages. It SETs something that we ignore until next paragraph, and it only does it on rows WHERE certain criteria are met. Those criteria are first that the page_name column equals home. Second, we're going to go into the page_data json and make sure its lastViewProcessed property, which we'll explicity treat as an integer, is less than the globalPosition of the event we're handling.

Now, what in tarnation are we SETting? It's actually two calls to PostgreSQL's jsonb_set[2] function. jsonb_set works similarly to JavaScript's Object.assign that we use throughout the book. Let's consider the inner call first:

---

2. https://www.postgresql.org/docs/11/functions-json.html

```
jsonb_set(
  page_data,
  '{videosWatched}',
  ((page_data ->> 'videosWatched')::int + 1)::text::jsonb
),
```

The first argument page_data means we're operating on the page_data column. This is likely *not* a surprise since this is a two-column table, and the other column is not a jsonb column. We're setting a property on the object stored in this column. What property? That's the second argument, {videosWatched}.

Now, what value are we going to set it to? Take the videosWatched property of the page data column, page_data ->> 'videosWatched', and cast it to an integer. PostgreSQL doesn't know that this is an integer property, so we tell it that it is by adding ::int, getting us to (page_data ->> 'videosWatched')::int. Then add 1 to it, or (page_data ->> 'videosWatched')::int + 1.

Next, we have to do some more casting because this column stores jsonb and not integers. Unfortunately, we can't convert directly from integers to jsonb, so we first cast it all to text, ((page_data ->> 'videosWatched')::int + 1)::text, and then finally from text to jsonb, ((page_data ->> 'videosWatched')::int + 1)::text::jsonb. Equivalent JavaScript would be:

```javascript
const pageData = {
  videosWatched: 0,
  lastViewProcessed: 0
}
const videosWatchedUpdate = {
  videosWatched: pageData.videosWatched + 1
}
const result = Object.merge({}, pageData, videosWatchedUpdate)
```

Now, here's the isolated outer call:

```
jsonb_set(
  result_of_inner_call,
  '{lastViewProcessed}',
  :globalPosition::text::jsonb
)
```

It is similar, only instead of starting with the value in page_data, we start with the value that results from updating the videosWatched count. The return value of the inner call becomes the starting point for the second call. This time we're updating the lastViewProcessed property, and we're setting it to the globalPosition of the event we're processing. But again, we have to cast it to text and then again to jsonb. There are a lot colons in that last argument, so here's a visual breakdown of them shown in the figure on page 57.

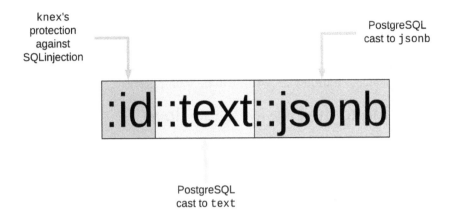

We have :globalPosition because of knex—we'll bind that to the value of the event's globalPosition. Then there's ::text to get to text and finally ::jsonb to get to jsonb.

Getting Idempotent with It

If you were casually reading along up to this point, this is a heads-up that what we're about to say is possibly the most important topic when working with microservices. We're going to talk about *idempotence*.

The word "idempotence" literally means "same power,"[3] and the idea is that if a function is idempotent, there are only two states that matter—it having been called zero times, and it having been called one or more times. Additional calls have no additional side effects.

This is as important to microservices as oxygen is to you, dear reader. Messaging. Systems. Fail. You *will* see the same message more than once, and it is physically impossible to guarantee exactly-once delivery. As software developers, we build our abstractions in the sky, but ultimately all of our programs execute on physical hardware. So, *you* as the consumer of messages in a message-based architecture must account for the fact that you'll eventually see the same message more than once. You must write idempotent message handlers. Go idempotent, or go home, as they say.

This handler is idempotent because of the way the increment query is written. Notice the WHERE clause. Every event the Aggregator processes will go through this query, and the query only updates rows whose lastViewProcessed property is less than the id of the current event. So, if we see an event a second time, lastViewProcessed will be equal to or greater than said event, and the query

---

3. https://en.wikipedia.org/wiki/Idempotence

becomes a *no-op*.[4] Call it as many times as you want, we're only going to increment the count once for a given message.

As we write additional Aggregators and start branching into Components, we'll see other idempotence patterns. It isn't always as simple as it was here, but every message handler we write will be idempotent.

Connecting to the Live Message Flow

Now that we have an Aggregator, we need to hook it up to the live flow of messages. An Aggregator is meant to be constantly running, picking up messages more or less as they occur. To hook this one up to that flow, we head back to the top-level function:

```
video-tutorials/src/aggregators/home-page.js
function build ({ db, messageStore }) {
  const queries = createQueries({ db })
  const handlers = createHandlers({ queries })
  const subscription = messageStore.createSubscription({
    streamName: 'viewing',
    handlers,
    subscriberId: 'aggregators:home-page'
  })

  function init () {
    return queries.ensureHomePage()
  }

  function start () {
    init().then(subscription.start)
  }

  return {
    queries,
    handlers,
    init,
    start
  }
}
```

Line 4 calls messageStore.createSubscription, which doesn't exist yet. We'll write that in the next chapter, Chapter 5, Subscribing to the Message Store, on page 65. For now, we know it as a function that takes three things:

- A streamName to subscribe to. When you hook into the live flow of messages, you do so by observing a specific stream, particularly a category stream.

---

4. https://en.wikipedia.org/wiki/NOP

- handlers to handle (in an idempotent manner!) the messages on that stream. As we said on page 54, we represent handlers as a JavaScript object whose keys are the message types we handle.

- A globally unique subscriberId. When we write the subscription code in Chapter 5, Subscribing to the Message Store, on page 65, we'll use streams to record how far along in the flow of messages a given subscription is. The name of that stream is partially derived from this subscriberId, which is why they must be globally unique.

Merely creating a subscription doesn't actually start the flow of messages, however—that's what the start function at line 14 is for. We're taking the convention that every autonomous component must expose a start function to actually begin its polling cycle. We don't want that cycle to start in test, for example.

This start function has one piece of work to do before releasing the message hounds. queries.incrementVideosWatched, which you wrote on page 55, assumes that the row it's going to update exists. This assumption is a lot easier than checking to see if it exists every time we process a message, but it does mean we need to put that row in place. So, start calls init, which in turn calls queries.ensureHomePage:

```
video-tutorials/src/aggregators/home-page.js
function ensureHomePage () {
  const initialData = {
    pageData: { lastViewProcessed: 0, videosWatched: 0 }
  }

  const queryString = `
    INSERT INTO
      pages(page_name, page_data)
    VALUES
      ('home', :pageData)
    ON CONFLICT DO NOTHING
  `

  return db.then(client => client.raw(queryString, initialData))
}
```

This function sets up what this row looks like before we've seen any messages and then inserts it into the database using ON CONFLICT DO NOTHING. We'll insert this row exactly once, no matter how many times we start this Aggregator.

Congrats! You just wrote your first Aggregator. You took the flow of VideoViewed events and turned it into a View Data that the home page application can use. You could make up additional aggregations, and in fact, the exercises at the end of this chapter include a challenge to do that. This is where message-based architectures become particularly interesting. You can slice and dice the same source data into whatever shape is required. And since you were saving all that source data, you can do this going all the way back to when you first turned the system on.

Okay, break time is over, we still have a little work to do to connect this the running system.

Configuring the Aggregator

We need to pull this Aggregator into config.js and modify src/index.js so that it calls the Aggregator's start function. config.js first, then start:

```
video-tutorials/src/config.js
// ...
const createHomePageAggregator = require('./aggregators/home-page')
function createConfig ({ env }) {
  // ...
  const homePageAggregator = createHomePageAggregator({
    db: knexClient,
    messageStore
  })
  const aggregators = [
    homePageAggregator,
  ]
  const components = [
  ]
  return {
    // ...
    homePageAggregator,
    aggregators,
    components,
  }
}
```

We start by requireing the Aggregator. Then inside of createConfig we instantiate it by passing it the db and messageStore reference that were instantiated in code represented by the ellipses—we won't keep reprinting the configuration from previous chapters. The we set up an array named Aggregators and put home-PageAggregator in it. We'll use this array to start all of our Aggregators. Since we're here in the file, we also make a similar array for components. It's empty for now because we won't write our first Component until Chapter 6, Registering Users, on page 83. Lastly, we add homePageAggregator, aggregators, and components to config's return object.

Now that these pieces are configured, we can start this Aggregator in src/index.js:

```
video-tutorials/src/index.js
function start () {
  config.aggregators.forEach(a => a.start())
  config.components.forEach(s => s.start())
  app.listen(env.port, signalAppStart)
}
```

To the app.listen call that starts the Express application, we added a couple of lines to start all the Aggregators and Components. config.aggregators.forEach loops over the aggregators array we set up in config.js and calls each Aggregator's start function. It does the same thing for components, which at this point is empty.

And just like that, you have an Aggregator that is configured to connect to the live flow of messages and aggregate a View Data the home page Application can use to show the global videos watched count.

Having the Home Page Application Use the New View Data

Speaking of the home page application, it currently isn't using our Aggregator's output. Let's fix that:

```
video-tutorials/src/app/home/index.js
function createQueries ({ db }) {
  function loadHomePage () {
    return db.then(client =>
      client('pages')
        .where({ page_name: 'home' })
        .limit(1)
        .then(camelCaseKeys)
        .then(rows => rows[0])
    )
  }

  return {
    loadHomePage
  }
}
```

We just need to modify the loadHomePage query. Instead of querying the mono-lithic videos table, we're going to query the special-purpose pages table. We want the one where page_name is equal to home. Notice how there was no sum-mation to do, no joins. We built laser-focused View Data to serve this partic-ular page. If we have other View Data needs, we can build them using all the same events, and the home page Application won't have to change one wit. That's the power of autonomy.

Coming to Terms with Data Duplication

With all this talk of multiple aggregations from the same source data, you may be thinking that sounds like a lot of duplicated data. What developers have not had the mantra "Thou shalt not duplicate data" hammered into them? Surely, we sin against everything our profession has taught us!

It *is* important to not duplicate data, but what that really means is do not duplicate the authoritative source of truth. We can make as many aggregations as we want precisely because they are not the *source* of truth. The events in the Message Store are. As the diagram here illustrates, we can aggregate as much as we like:

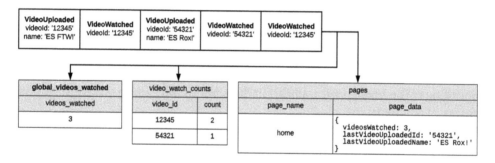

Those are three equally valid representations derived from the same, single source of truth.

Traditional MVC also duplicates derivations. Joins and multiple queries assembled to render responses are just derivations of whatever your write model is. The difference is that in traditional MVC, you constantly repeat generating those derivations with every request. We know exactly what the home page needs, and since events are immutable and append-only, once an event is applied, our derivations cannot change until a new event arrives. So why bother reconstructing our home page view on every request?

Now this doesn't mean that what we did with the home Application is always the right way to aggregate data—only a detailed system analysis can reveal that. But when we've separated writes and reads and shed the assumptions that MVC makes, we find we have a lot of powerful tools at our disposal that were previously off-limits.

What You've Done So Far

Welcome to the wonderful world of CQRS. Up to this point you had append-only streams of events but no clear way to turn that into what the home page

Application needed to fulfill the requirement of showing a global videos watched count. Now you've learned how to do that, and in so doing have unleashed one of the biggest superpowers this architecture can provide.

You also learned about idempotence. You're going to encounter that word *a lot* in this book. As light-hearted as we can be with corny pop culture references throughout the rest of this project, there is none of that when it comes to idempotence. To make light of idempotence is to fail at our task.

To really drive that point home, modify queries.incrementVideosWatched in code/video-tutorials/src/aggregators/home-page.js and remove the bit of the WHERE clause that made the handler idempotent. Run the project and click the button a few times. Then, stop the project and restart it. Notice how the counts go up even though no new videos were watched. Now imagine that instead of aggregating view counts, this were a service performing seven-figure wire transfers. #IdempotentLife

Also, given what you learned here, how might you write an Aggregator that counts how many videos a particular user has watched? Or how about the number of times a particular video has been watched? How would you shape your target View Data? You can use the home page Aggregator you wrote as a template for starting a new Aggregator.

We have the engine set up, now we just need to put the gas in it. In the next chapter we'll augment the Message Store code to support subscriptions, which will get messages flowing into our Aggregators. Let's get us flowing to the next chapter.

CHAPTER 5

Subscribing to the Message Store

I heard a story while taking a French class once about a royal advisor talking to the king about the development of the printing press.

"I have some good news and some bad news, your majesty," the advisor said.

"The good news first," the king replied.

"Books *are* everywhere."

"The bad news, then?"

"No one knows how to read, Sire," the advisor lamented.

You have enough Message Store code to write state as append-only streams of immutable events. We don't yet have any way get the messages back out. The books are there, but no one is continuously reading them.

That's what you're going to fix in this chapter, building the mechanism that components will use to subscribe to the Message Store. Hopefully polling does not offend your software design sensibilities because that's what the solution is based on. But for accepting polling, you get a robust way for various subscribers to see messages as they're written. That enables communication between components in the system, all while keeping those components autonomous. And autonomous components will help you maintain high levels of productivity and sanity.

Sketching the Subscription Process

The subscription code falls into three categories:

- Managing the current read position on page 68
- Fetching and processing batches of messages on page 69
- Orchestrating the subscription on page 71

The subscription code will use the Message Store for all of its data storage so you'll get more practice writing to and reading from the store.

Before diving into these categories, let's tour the basic shape of the subscription code. It's found in video-tutorials/src/message-store/subscribe.js:

```
video-tutorials/src/message-store/subscribe.js
const Bluebird = require('bluebird')
const uuid = require('uuid/v4')

const category = require('./category')

function configureCreateSubscription ({ read, readLastMessage, write }) {
}

module.exports = configureCreateSubscription
```

This outer function receives as dependencies the functions from the Message Store we'll use to implement subscriptions. read retrieves all the messages in a given stream and is how subscribers get their batches of messages to process, whereas readLastMessage and write are for managing read position. You'll write read and readLastMessage in this chapter, and you wrote write in Chapter 3, Putting Data in a Message Store, on page 41.

This function returns a function that actually builds the subscription. Let's add the shell of this second function:

```
video-tutorials/src/message-store/subscribe.js
function configureCreateSubscription ({ read, readLastMessage, write }) {
❶   return ({
      streamName,
      handlers,
      messagesPerTick = 100,
      subscriberId,
      positionUpdateInterval = 100,
      tickIntervalMs = 100
    }) => {
❷     const subscriberStreamName = `subscriberPosition-${subscriberId}`

      let currentPosition = 0
      let messagesSinceLastPositionWrite = 0
      let keepGoing = true
❸     return {
        loadPosition,
        start,
        stop,
        tick,
        writePosition
      }
    }
  }
}
```

❶ These are the parameters that code setting up a subscription passes in. Here's what they mean:

streamName   Consumers subscribe to a stream, and this is the name of that stream. We always subscribe to category streams. Turn back to the explanation on page 33 if you need a refresher on the differences between stream types.

handlers   An object whose keys are message types and whose values are functions that receive a message as the sole parameter (e.g., { VideoViewed: function (event) { }). This object defines which messages the subscription cares about.

A property of these handlers that CANNOT BE OVERSTATED ENOUGH![1] is that they must be idempotent. An idempotent function is one where calling it once or calling it a thousand times makes no difference. Every time we write a subscription handler in this book, we absolutely must, no questions asked, consider idempotence. Why? Because we have no guarantees that we'll only handle a given message once. Networks fail, and until we can reinvent the physical laws of the universe, we'll have to settle for idempotence.

messagesPerTick   The maximum number of messages to process in one polling loop. Defaults to 100, and not every subscription needs the same value.

subscriberId   Consumers identify themselves with this argument. This will become part of how read position is stored, so it must be globally unique across all subscriptions.

positionUpdateInterval   A subscription will write its position to the Message Store after processing this many messages.

tickIntervalMs   When a subscription queries for new messages to process and finds none, it will wait this number of milliseconds before querying again. A lower number means more queries, but it also means handling messages closer to real time. Different components can have different frequencies.

❷ Now set up a few bookkeeping variables. subscriberStreamName builds the stream name this subscription will use to persist its read position. Do you see why a globally unique subscriberId is needed? Also, components can

---

1.   Here are some more exclamation points to really stress the point: !!!!!!!!

subscribe to multiple streams, and each subscription needs a unique subscriberId.

currentPosition tracks the last message processed, and messagesSinceLastPosition-Write tracks how many messages have been processed since the last time the subscription wrote its position to the store. The polling loop code uses keepGoing to know if it should keep polling.

❸ This inner function ultimately returns an object full of functions, and this is that object. We spend the rest of this chapter writing the functions returned in this object.

Managing the Current Read Position

Imagine you're a Component subscribing to some category stream in the system. This is the sort of thing you could make a Halloween costume out of. Now imagine that you're just booting up. The first thing you need to do is load your last committed read position.

What do you know about your committed read positions? First, you know that they're stored in a stream whose name is in subscriberStreamName, so the position will be in a message. How's that for dogfooding the Message Store? Second, you know you only write to this stream every positionUpdateInterval messages, so when you're first getting started, you won't actually find any written position in the store. Also, you're just appending to this stream the now-current read position, meaning the last message in this stream is the only one you need. Did the outer function above receive a way to retrieve the last message in a stream?

You'll load the read position with the function loadPosition:

```
video-tutorials/src/message-store/subscribe.js
function loadPosition () {
  return readLastMessage(subscriberStreamName)
    .then(message => {
      currentPosition = message ? message.data.position : 0
    })
}
```

It uses the received readLastMessage function to read the last message from the subscriberStreamName stream. then if it found such a message, it sets currentPosition to the position property of that message's data. Otherwise, we're starting from 0.

Next up, after we process each message, we have to do some bookkeeping and check to see if it's time to commit the read position. Enter updateReadPosition:

```
video-tutorials/src/message-store/subscribe.js
function updateReadPosition (position) {
  currentPosition = position
  messagesSinceLastPositionWrite += 1

  if (messagesSinceLastPositionWrite === positionUpdateInterval) {
    messagesSinceLastPositionWrite = 0

    return writePosition(position)
  }

  return Bluebird.resolve(true)
}
```

It receives position, which will be the globalPosition of the message that was just processed and sets currentPosition to that value. Since it just processed another message, that means messagesSinceLastPositionWrite needs to go up by one, and finally it checks to see if it has processed positionUpdateInterval messages since the last time it wrote to the read position. If so, then it calls writePosition to go ahead an write this new position:

```
video-tutorials/src/message-store/subscribe.js
function writePosition (position) {
  const positionEvent = {
    id: uuid(),
    type: 'Read',
    data: { position }
  }

  return write(subscriberStreamName, positionEvent)
}
```

This function also receives the position of the last processed message and constructs an event to record that position. We use events of the type Read—past tense, sounds like "red"—to track these positions. Then we write the event to the subscriberStreamName stream. We don't include any metadata because there is no meaningful traceId or userId we could use here. And that does it for managing the read position. Next up is fetching and processing the messages.

Fetching and Processing Batches of Messages

You'll write the function for reading messages from a stream on page 75. It'll default to reading messages from position 0, but it will accept a fromPosition parameter to let you read from a different position in the stream. Right now is when we use that parameter:

```
video-tutorials/src/message-store/subscribe.js
function getNextBatchOfMessages () {
  return read(streamName, currentPosition + 1, messagesPerTick)
}
```

To get the next batch, you just delegate to read using the streamName, currentPosition + 1, and messagesPerTick values—currentPosition + 1 because the Eventide function that queries for the next batch of messages uses >= in the global_position conditional in its WHERE clause:

```
CREATE OR REPLACE FUNCTION get_category_messages(
  category varchar,
  "position" bigint DEFAULT 1,
  batch_size bigint DEFAULT 1000,
  -- ...
)
-- ...
    SELECT
      -- ...
    FROM
      messages
    WHERE
      category(stream_name) = $1 AND
      global_position >= $2';

  -- ...
```

We want the messages *after* the last one we processed. Of course, once you have a batch, you'll need to process it:

```
video-tutorials/src/message-store/subscribe.js
function processBatch (messages) {
  return Bluebird.each(messages, message =>
    handleMessage(message)
      .then(() => updateReadPosition(message.globalPosition))
      .catch(err => {
        logError(message, err)

        // Re-throw so that we can break the chain
        throw err
      })
  )
    .then(() => messages.length)
}
```

This one is a bit more involved, but the basic flow is that for each message, you process it and then update the subscription's read position to be the position of the message you just processed. And if there was an error, log it.

We handle one message at a time, and that's why we use Bluebird.each.[2] It takes an array and function that will return a Promise for each member of the array, but it doesn't go on to the next element until the previous one resolves. What do we want to do with each message? Call handleMessage and then call updateReadPosition

---

2. http://bluebirdjs.com/docs/api/promise.each.html

with the message's globalPosition. If there's an error, log it using logError, a function we won't print here, but you can imagine what it does. When the batch is done, return how many messages got processed. The subscription's polling cycle will use that count to know if it should poll again immediately or wait tickIntervalMs before polling again.

You wrote updateReadPosition on page 69, so you just have handleMessage to write:

```
video-tutorials/src/message-store/subscribe.js
function handleMessage (message) {
  const handler = handlers[message.type] || handlers.$any

  return handler ? handler(message) : Promise.resolve(true)
}
```

How to actually handle the messages is what the caller supplied with handlers. It isn't the subscription's job to know what messages mean. It *is* the subscription's job, though, to call those handler functions. A subscriber might not have a handler for each message type we retrieve here, so the first step is to see if it did supply a definition. If so, we return the result of calling that handler with the message.

Most of the time a subscriber is going to specify exactly which message types it handles, and it does that by the keys on the handlers object. In very rare cases that we won't explore until Chapter 13, Debugging Components, on page 207, a subscriber will just want to see all types of messages. In those cases the subscriber would supply an $any handler. This is similar in spirit to the default case in a switch statement, and just like with a switch, a specific handler will take priority over the more generic $any.

If the handlers object has neither a specific handler or an $any, we just return a Promise resolving to true. If there is no handler function, then doing nothing is how we properly handle the message.

And that's it for fetching batches of messages and processing them. Nice work! Now that we have all these useful functions, you just need to orchestrate calling them.

Orchestrating the Subscription

Orchestrating the flow is kind of fun, and you'll see a, ah, clever use of JavaScript mechanics. There are two main functions, and a couple of helpers. One of the main functions orchestrates calls to getNextBatchOfMessages and processBatch. We'll call this function tick. The other main function orchestrates calls to tick, only doing so when it's time to poll again. We'll call this function poll. Let's go through everything in the order it would all be called.

First, the polling cycle doesn't begin right when a subscriber instantiates a subscription. This is by design—we don't want our tests to actually start a polling cycle, for example. So there's a start function the outside world will call to start the subscription, which you put into the home page Aggregator on page 58. start's implementation is not very exciting:

video-tutorials/src/message-store/subscribe.js
```
function start () {
  // eslint-disable-next-line
  console.log(`Started ${subscriberId}`)

  return poll()
}
```

It gives a console message that the subscription is starting and then calls poll. We'll no doubt be asked to present papers at academic conferences about this kind of breakthrough.

It's probably worth mentioning there's a stop function as well:

video-tutorials/src/message-store/subscribe.js
```
function stop () {
  // eslint-disable-next-line
  console.log(`Stopped ${subscriberId}`)

  keepGoing = false
}
```

It sets that keepGoing flag to false, which matters to poll, the function you will write next:

video-tutorials/src/message-store/subscribe.js
```
async function poll () {
  await loadPosition()

  // eslint-disable-next-line no-unmodified-loop-condition
  while (keepGoing) {
    const messagesProcessed = await tick()

    if (messagesProcessed === 0) {
      await Bluebird.delay(tickIntervalMs)
    }
  }
}
```

This function uses JavaScript's async/await functionality, and the particulars of that are out of scope for this book. Mozilla has some great material worth reading,[3] but the quick version is that async/await lets you write asynchronous code syntactically as if it were synchronous. This is the only place

---

3. https://developer.mozilla.org/en-US/docs/Web/JavaScript/Reference/Statements/async_function

in the book we'll use this because your humble author believes that Promise chains in the style we'll use them in this book generally reveal intent more clearly than async/await. However, for poll, a Promise chain would muddy the waters.

poll is defined with the async keyword before the function keyword. The first thing to do is await the call to loadPosition. We don't want to continue until the subscription knows its starting position. It could of course always start from 0, since all message handlers MUST BE IDEMPOTENT!, but if the category we're subscribing to has 1,000,000 messages in it, that's a lot of wasted idempotence checking. Said another way, recording and retrieving the read position is a performance optimization and has nothing to do with correctness.

Once we have the read position loaded, then we start a potentially infinite (gasp) loop. "An infinite loop in a single-threaded execution environment sounds like a bad idea," hopefully comes to your mind. Normally it would be, but bear with it. The very next thing we do is await a call to tick. This is going to prevent the code from moving to the next line before a tick of the polling cycle completes, but because of how Node.js operates, it doesn't mean that the entire execution will block. The calls to tick will have calls to databases, command-line programs, and possibly HTTP calls, depending on the handler. We will not block execution.

Once the tick completes, if we processed any messages, we'll immediately fall through for another pass. If not, we'll wait for tickIntervalMs milliseconds before trying again. Of course, if keepGoing ever becomes false, the loop stops.

Now let's write tick:

```
video-tutorials/src/message-store/subscribe.js
function tick () {
  return getNextBatchOfMessages()
    .then(processBatch)
    .catch(err => {
      // eslint-disable-next-line no-console
      console.error('Error processing batch', err)

      stop()
    })
}
```

As we said earlier, tick orchestrates getting batches of messages and then processing them. It's literally a call to getNextBatchOfMessages and then funneling them into processBatch. And if there's an error, log it before calling stop. We're not going to bother trying to automatically recover from an error. If something goes wrong at this level, we want human attention on it.

And that's the subscription flow! To get this working, we just need to implement readLastMessage and read in the Message Store.

Reading the Last Message in a Stream

All of our read functions will sit in a file that exports a dependency-receiving function that captures the database connection. Let's write that shell now:

video-tutorials/src/message-store/read.js
```
function createRead ({ db }) {
  return {
  }
}

module.exports = exports = createRead
```

It receives the db and returns... something. Let's define that something.

Eventide provides a function to get the last message from a stream.[4] It's signature is as follows:

```
CREATE OR REPLACE FUNCTION get_last_stream_message(
  stream_name varchar
)
```

It just takes a stream name. Here's some JavaScript to wrap that for our project:

video-tutorials/src/message-store/read.js
```
const deserializeMessage = require('./deserialize-message')

const getLastMessageSql = 'SELECT * FROM get_last_stream_message($1)'
function createRead ({ db }) {
  function readLastMessage (streamName) {
    return db.query(getLastMessageSql, [ streamName ])
      .then(res => deserializeMessage(res.rows[0]))
  }
  return {
    readLastMessage,
  }
}
```

First off, at the top we define getLastMessageSql to hold the SQL snippet we call. Then we receive the streamName and feed it into db.query along with the getLastMessageSql. We then pass the first result to deserializeMessage, a function we haven't yet written. Let's rectify that:

---

4.   https://github.com/eventide-project/postgres-message-store/blob/master/database/functions/get-last-message.sql

```javascript
function deserializeMessage (rawMessage) {
  if (!rawMessage) {
    return null
  }

  return {
    id: rawMessage.id,
    streamName: rawMessage.stream_name,
    type: rawMessage.type,
    position: parseInt(rawMessage.position, 10),
    globalPosition: parseInt(rawMessage.global_position, 10),
    data: rawMessage.data ? JSON.parse(rawMessage.data) : {},
    metadata: rawMessage.metadata ? JSON.parse(rawMessage.metadata) : {},
    time: rawMessage.time
  }
}

module.exports = deserializeMessage
```

The Message Store is a PostgreSQL database, and idiomatic RDBMSs tend to use snake_casing. Also, position and global_position come back as strings, and we need them as numbers. So, we just pluck out the fields from rawMessage, converting as necessary.

It's important to note that this function does not work on *category* streams, which is fine because we won't have a need to get the last message from a category stream.

Reading a Stream's Messages

Now let's get the messages in a particular stream. We're going to support three classes of streams, namely, entity, category, and the $all stream. As a refresher, entity streams are usually named something like identity-721304b9-8ece-4c1c-aaed-efad4886023d—a category followed by a UUID. The events in this example entity stream are also in the identity category stream. $all is a stream containing every message in the store.

Eventide provides us with functions for entity and category streams. We'll write our own query for the $all stream when we get to Chapter 13, Debugging Components, on page 207.

Stream Type	SQL Snippet
Category	SELECT * FROM get_category_messages($1, $2, $3)
Non-category	SELECT * FROM get_stream_messages($1, $2, $3)

With that in mind, let's write read:

video-tutorials/src/message-store/read.js

```
const getCategoryMessagesSql = 'SELECT * FROM get_category_messages($1, $2, $3)'
const getStreamMessagesSql = 'SELECT * FROM get_stream_messages($1, $2, $3)'
function createRead ({ db }) {
  function read (streamName, fromPosition = 0, maxMessages = 1000) {
    let query = null // <callout id="co.messageStore.read.bookkeeping />
    let values = []
    if (streamName.includes('-')) {
      // Entity streams have a dash
      query = getStreamMessagesSql
      values = [streamName, fromPosition, maxMessages]
    } else {
      // Category streams do not have a dash
      query = getCategoryMessagesSql
      values = [streamName, fromPosition, maxMessages]
    }

    return db.query(query, values)
      .then(res => res.rows.map(deserializeMessage))
  }
  return {
    read,
    readLastMessage,
  }
}
```

❶ First, let's capture the SQL we need to call either the category or entity stream read functions. We'll choose which one to use in the body of the function.

❷ Next, we get to the read function. It takes three parameters: the streamName to read from; a starting position, fromPosition, that defaults to 0; and a maximum number of messages to return, maxMessages, that defaults to 1,000. If a stream has more than 1,000 messages you'll either have to supply a bigger number there—not recommended—or handle pagination.

❶ Before we issue the query, we need to determine which SQL snippet between getCategoryMessagesSql and getStreamMessagesSql to use. We also have a values array to hold the arguments we'll pass to the query. For both getCategoryMessagesSql and getStreamMessagesSql, we'll pass all three parameters this function takes, but for $all, we'll leave off the streamName.

❸ Now we're figuring out which type of stream we have. If streamName has a dash, then we're dealing with an entity stream and choose getStreamMessagesSql as the query and all the arguments we received as the values.

❹ However, if we didn't get a dash, then we're dealing with a category stream and choose getCategoryMessages as the query.

❺ Then we finally issue the query and run the resulting messages through deserializeMessage.

And boom, we have a function for getting the messages from a stream. The last step in making the subscription process work is to connect the subscriptions and read functions to the Message Store's interface.

Adding the Read Functions to the Message Store's Interface

read and readLastMessage both sit inside a top-level dependency-receiving function that receives a db reference. Let's open code/video-tutorials/src/message-store/index.js and pull these functions in:

```
video-tutorials/src/message-store/index.js
const createRead = require('./read')
const configureCreateSubscription = require('./subscribe')
// ...
function createMessageStore ({ db }) {
  // ...
  const read = createRead({ db })
  const createSubscription = configureCreateSubscription({
    read: read.read,
    readLastMessage: read.readLastMessage,
    write: write
  })
  return {
    // ...
    createSubscription,
    read: read.read,
    readLastMessage: read.readLastMessage,
  }
}
```

The first step is to require the read functions we just wrote and the subscription code. Then in the body of createMesageStore, we instantiate read, followed by configuring createSubscription. We have to instantiate read first because two of its functions are dependencies of the subscriptions code. write also gets passed in to the subscription code. Finally, we add the read functions and createSubscription to the Message Store's return object, making these functions available to the rest of the system—for example, the home page Aggregator you wrote on page 53.

Starting the Server

With the subscriptions in place, we can now start the server and observe the flow of data through the system. The included docker-compose.yml file contains an entry for a Message DB instance. You are, of course, welcome to install Message DB directly into a PostgreSQL database by following the directions[5] Message DB provides. For the duration of this book, we'll assume you're using the Docker setup.

If your containers are not already running, you can start them with docker-compose up from code/video-tutorials. Then, in another console, run npm run start-dev-server. You should have output similar to the following:

```
Video Tutorials started
```

(index)	0	1
0	'Port'	3000
1	'Environment'	'development'

```
Started aggregators:home-page
```

Navigate to http://localhost:3000, and you'll be treated to the home screen and a "Record viewing video" button. You can click that button to simulate video views. The home page Aggregator will eventually pick up those events and increment the watch count. You'll likely have to reload the page to see its effects.

What You've Done So Far

You had Message Store code that could write messages, and now the autonomous components you'll write in this system have a means to automatically get new messages as they happen. Or at least close enough to "as they happen." You just turned the Message Store into not only a database but also a data *transport*. The Message Store is now an effective communication medium, enabling the pub/sub, decoupled architecture we're after. You achieved this by writing a polling mechanism that works for any of your components in this system.

Now, polling is to software architecture as a basic rice and beans meal is to cuisine. It isn't fancy and it won't get you featured at the latest architectural conferences, but it gets the job done in a reliable way. What could possibly be better than that? Spending countless ops hours supporting something more complicated with unpredictable failure modes? Not only is that not a

---

5.   https://github.com/message-db/message-db#installation

great way to spend your weekends, it wouldn't be fair to the folks that entrusted us to build this system.

To take your learning further, think about the tunable aspects of this subscription system. You can change the messages retrieved per tick, how often the subscription writes its read position, and how often it polls for new messages. How do different values for these settings affect performance? What kinds of functionality would need which values? For example, if you had a Component sending email, how close to real time does it need to be? If it can be relaxed, how might you change the defaults to have it run less frequently?

Let's have a look at the system architecture again:

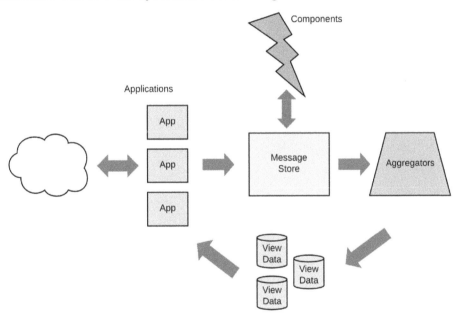

You now have a fully running message-based system! You've closed the loop on how data flows through it all:

1. Users trigger video views.
2. An Application picks them up and writes events in response.
3. An Aggregator builds View Data based on those events.
4. The Application uses that View Data to update the home page.

The only kind of piece you haven't built is, ironically, Components. Now that you have the whole flow in place, it's time to add your first Component. In the next chapter, you're going to build user registration for Video Tutorials. It's going to take an identity Component to do that. So what are we waiting for? Let's get on our way.

Part II

Fleshing Out the System

Now that we have the fundamentals down, we're going to apply them to fleshing out the rest of Video Tutorials. You're going to see how registration and authentication work. You'll add an email service. You'll build a system for transcoding videos that our users submit. You'll cap this part off with building UI that can handle the asynchronous nature of the system.

CHAPTER 6

Registering Users

If up to this point we had been writing banking software, we would have been doing a rather lousy job of it. You see, we've left the front door wide open. The whole two endpoints we have in our system do absolutely nothing to identify who is calling them.

In this chapter you're going to start adding user registration. Registration is a process, and we're going to see how we discover processes and capture them in domain messages. What events capture the steps of our process? What commands trigger those events? What Components emerge as owners of these messages, and how do we communicate the message contract to the rest of the world?

You'll also learn about data validation in an eventually consistent world. You're probably used to having an immediate response as to whether or not user-submitted data is valid, and maybe you've been wondering how to do that in the world of asynchronous messages. You'll learn strategies for just this very thing as you work through this chapter.

Here again is our system architecture (see the figure on page 84), but this time highlighting the portions we'll be working on in this chapter.

One last reminder, if you ever forget what the different portions of the architecture are, you can refer back to the list on page 22.

Our first step is to define our registration process by discovering the domain messages that represent it. An identity Component will emerge as the component in our software that owns these messages. With this Component's message contract defined, we'll build a register-users application that uses this contract and lets our users submit their registration requests.

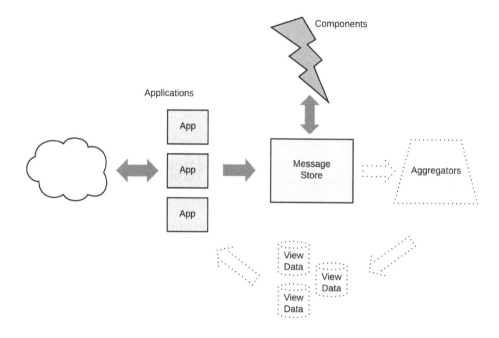

This process of discovering messages is where the real engineering work is done. Quite frankly, knowing how to discover and define messages is more important than code. Here we go!

Discovering Domain Messages

Whenever you add new functionality to a message-based system, the first step is discovering the domain messages that model the new functionality. Remember that we've traded implicit coupling in the database for an explicit communication contract captured in the events. Changes to this contract are difficult. They define communication between two or more components, and changing this contract necessarily propagates into any component using it. It's easier to change an explicit contract than it is to change a monolith's implicit contract, but we still want to get it as correct as possible at first.

What events do we need to store state? What commands and events can cause those events to occur? What entities emerge when we discover these messages? We've skipped over this process up to this point so that we could get comfortable working with events, but now it's time to learn how to discover and define them.

Starting with the Business Process

Before jumping into code, we need to understand the business process we're trying to capture in our system. Our goal is to answer questions like:

- What does our system do?
- What domain behavior are we trying to capture?
- What actions can users take?
- If our system were implemented with paper or spreadsheets, what discrete steps emerge?

We need to register users, and when they try to register, we'll tell them if they succeeded or not. Maybe they sent us an invalid email address; maybe they're trying to register with an email address that has already been used; or maybe something else. And of course, if they succeeded, we need to record that too. We'll also send them a welcome email, although we won't implement sending the email until Chapter 9, Adding an Email Component, on page 133.

Translating the Business Processes into Events and Commands

Think over all your CRUD experience that MVC frameworks pushed you into. You're used to thinking about application functionality in terms of managing records in a database. In that mindset you've likely modeled user registration as *creating* a user. Given that background and the fact that events are in the past tense, it might feel natural to define a UserCreated event. Let's examine that choice.

Recall how we said on page 32 that we're dealing with *domain* messages—messages that capture the actual process we're modeling. We're not writing software for ourselves. We're writing it for other people, so we have to take off our "software developer" hat and put on our "the rest of humanity" hat. Software developers are a rather small subset of all humans, and our craft requires thinking in ways that most people do not.

Most people don't think in terms of CRUD operations, and when we're trying to model domains to serve human beings, we want our systems to name things the same way that human beings name them. While all of our training tells us that registration is the same thing as *creating* a user, the rest of humanity likely thinks of this in terms of *signing up* or *registering*. We choose the latter, and we'll represent that a user has registered with a Registered event. That event comes into being in response to a Register command.

Notice how by naming the event Registered we could distinguish between when visitors come to the site and register vs. when system administrators cause new accounts to exist. That captures a lot more than just issuing a CREATE query against a database table. Indeed, in the rest of this book (and hopefully systems we write after!), we will avoid the CRUD verbs in all of our domain modeling.

Beating a Dead Horse

I promise no equines were harmed in the writing of this book, but let's call out a point that really highlights why domain events should not have CRUD verbs in them. Domain events are records of things that have happened. Consider the metaphysical claim you're making when you try to write a UserCreated event when a user registers for your website.

Your user was just *created*? *Really?*

Oh, somewhere a record in a database may get created as a result of a user registering, but if your users are really *created* at the moment they register, then (a) that's amazing that they can already type, and (b) you're likely going to have trouble with COPPA, the Children's Online Privacy Protection Act of 1998, at least in the United States.

Your users aren't getting created when they *register* for your application. They're registering. The domain event isn't an alias for a CRUD action—it's capturing the user's intent. So we'll say they're registering in our event names.

We may also have sad moments when users attempt to register with invalid information. That suggests a RegistrationRejected event.

Now, we only have one command and two events here, but can we identify an entity these messages are coalescing around?

These messages all have to do with identifying users. The act of registering is how we distinguish one of our users from the other billions of human beings on the planet—it's what makes them special to our system. That suggests an identity entity.

Dark days may arrive where users want to no longer have an account. In that case, they'll cause a CloseAccount command whose handling would result in an AccountClosed event.

We could represent identity entities with the state machine as shown in the figure on page 87.

In this chapter we'll only implement the registration portion. Locking accounts is an exercise at the end of Chapter 8, Authenticating Users, on page 119, while closing accounts is not something that we address in the book.

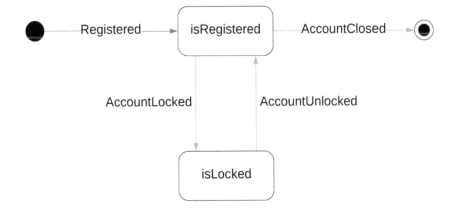

Fleshing Out the Identity Messages

Now that we've named the messages, we need to figure out what data they'll contain. Remember that *the events are the state of the system*. It won't be enough to simply say that a user has registered; we also need an email and password combo. We'll hash the password before writing these events as well because we're pros who care about our users.

Let's put this Component in a folder at video-tutorials/src/components/identity. Components provide definitions of their messages, and we'll handle that by writing a file named contract.md that documents what the Component does and the message contract the Component implements. We'll place that file in the same directory as each Component's code. We won't reprint those files in full here, but the identity Component's contract is found in code/video-tutorials/src/components/identity/contract.md. Do familiarize yourself with that file to know what questions it answers. This file will be the point of reference that applications and other Components use to write well-formed commands for the Component and to understand the messages the Component writes. Heck, it'll help you as you write the Component that implements that contract.

In any case, here is an example Register command:

```
{
  "id": "928a73ca-2925-42c9-974a-467cd96e0a44",
  "type": "Register",
  "data": {
    "userId": "46aa6e66-adf9-40d0-bfe0-ae8ed5b70892",
    "email": "user@example.com",
    "passwordHash":
      "$2b$10$IrxFcWAxwRQGcNbK5Zr03.aLvgFGSUSdeUGw860NXoz3Nm.PUlycS"
  }
}
```

If your system needs to collect other information at registration time, maybe a name, those would likely be included on this command as well. We're keeping registration simple, though.

When these are successful we'll write Registered events such as the following:

```
{
  "id": "10e23852-2725-4789-a4d2-4e0630b3a55d",
  "type": "Registered",
  "data": {
    "userId": "46aa6e66-adf9-40d0-bfe0-ae8ed5b70892",
    "email": "user@example.com",
    "passwordHash":
      "$2b$10$IrxFcWAxwRQGcNbK5Zr03.aLvgFGSUSdeUGw860NXoz3Nm.PUlycS"
  }
}
```

And for those cases when registration runs afoul of our business rules, we'll write RegistrationRejected events like these to streams in the identity category:

```
{
  "id": "ea0835d6-a073-4a25-aca9-db75c4c153f4",
  "type": "RegistrationRejected",
  "data": {
    "userId": "46aa6e66-adf9-40d0-bfe0-ae8ed5b70892",
    "email": "not an email",
    "passwordHash":
      "$2b$10$IrxFcWAxwRQGcNbK5Zr03.aLvgFGSUSdeUGw860NXoz3Nm.PUlycS",
    "reason": "email was not valid"
  }
}
```

A service also defines what stream a command must be written to, and again, that's defined in code/video-tutorials/src/components/identity/contract.md. In the case of Register commands, the identity Component states they should be written to streams in the identity:command category; for example, identity:command-2b9df609-276f-488a-bc88-3566c5f17dc6. This is a command stream dedicated to a particular entity, the identity whose registration we're trying to effect.

The events listed here will go to entity streams in the identity category. We'd find these events in a stream named identity-46aa6e66-adf9-40d0-bfe0-ae8ed5b70892. Note that identity and identity:command are two separate categories.

Examples from Other Domains

Just in case you need to build something other than exactly the same system we build in this book, let's get an idea of what events from other domains might look like.

If you're working on an e-commerce solution, you probably need to allow users to add items to carts, and also provide shipping and billing information. These are domain events. Maybe you'll then have ItemAddedToCart with a payload identifying the item and the price the item had at the time it was added.

Sometimes information that comes from a single screen might actually be hiding more than one event. I've seen single screens where I enter shipping and billing information. I'd be surprised if those were handled by the same Component, since they're very different functions. So maybe that type of screen implies at least two events—ShippingInformationProvided and BillingInformation-Provided.

You'll probably need to verify that billing information, so when you do that you might have BillingInformationVerified because it worked or BillingInformationRejected with some reason because the payment gateway said it didn't work.

After you've taken the order, maybe a particular item is out of stock, so there's an ItemNotFulfilled event. Or maybe it all worked and you have an OrderShipped event that contains tracking information.

If you were building a rental property management system, you might see events like MaintenanceIssueReported or MaintenanceIssueResolved. In inventory management you might see ProductReceived or InspectionFailed.

As we get more into this book dealing with video tutorials, we're going to see events like, VideoUploaded, VideoTranscoded, and VideoTranscodingFailed.

Be very granular! You're trying to capture *what happened* and reveal the intent of those changes. If it's something that modified your old MVC's database, it needs to be an event and possibly more than one. You might even have more than one type of event that could result in the same database operation because different intents can lead to the same result.

Adding Registration to Our System

Getting back to our system, let's figure out what work we need to do to get registration up and running. We already mentioned the identity Component. That doesn't technically exist yet, but we have its contract. With our architecture we can build against a contract even if if the backing Component doesn't exist.

Since registration originates from a web interface, we'll need an application to capture the registration data and issue Register commands as illustrated in the figure on page 90.

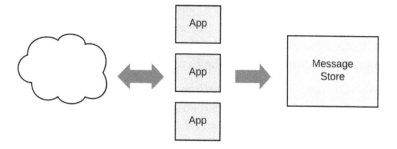

And that's it for registration. We won't need any aggregation until adding authentication in the next chapter (Chapter 8, Authenticating Users, on page 119).

Receiving User Input

We'll make a register-users application which will take user input and write a Register command to the Message Store. It'll have the same structure as the home application we saw on page 11.

This application will need to handle three different types of requests:

- Showing the registration form
- Showing a confirmation page after registration
- Receiving registration form submissions

First off, we show the registration form with:

```
video-tutorials/src/app/register-users/index.js
function createHandlers ({ actions }) {
  function handleRegistrationForm (req, res) {
    const userId = uuid()

    res.render('register-users/templates/register', { userId })
  }
  return {
    handleRegistrationForm,
  }
}
```

This handler just shows the registration form. The Pug for it is located at video-tutorials/src/app/register-users/templates/register.pug

Notice that we're generating a userId and passing that into the template. We want to generate identifiers as early as possible. This userId is included in the registration form as a hidden field.

Next, after a user registers successfully, we will show them a confirmation screen:

```
video-tutorials/src/app/register-users/index.js
function createHandlers ({ actions }) {
  // ...
  function handleRegistrationComplete (req, res) {
    res.render('register-users/templates/registration-complete')
  }
  return {
    handleRegistrationForm,
    handleRegistrationComplete,
  }
}
```

This handler renders the page we'll redirect users to after they register. It lets them know their request was received and invites them to log in. The cynical among us may also say that it gives a delay so that our asynchronous registration process feels less asynchronous, but we don't hire cynics on our team. You can see the Pug file for this screen at code/video-tutorials/src/app/register-users/templates/registration-complete.pug.

Turning Registration Requests into Commands

Finally, we have the handler that receives our users' registration requests:

```
video-tutorials/src/app/register-users/index.js
function createHandlers ({ actions }) {
  // ...
①  function handleRegisterUser (req, res, next) {
    const attributes = {
      id: req.body.id,
      email: req.body.email,
      password: req.body.password
    }

    return actions
      .registerUser(req.context.traceId, attributes)
②    .then(() => res.redirect(301, 'register/registration-complete'))
③    .catch(ValidationError, err =>
        res
          .status(400)
          .render(
            'register-users/templates/register',
            { userId: attributes.id, errors: err.errors }
          )
      )
④    .catch(next)
  }

  return {
    handleRegisterUser
  }
}
```

❶ Now we're getting to something interesting. This handler gets called when users submit the registration form. If you look at the Pug, you'll see that the HTML form on that page sends us three fields, namely id, email, and password. We use those to fields to build the object attributes that we pass to actions.registerUser along with the request's traceId.

We'll go through the action in just a second on page 92, but for now we handle three possible outcomes of this call: (a) the happy path, (b) it all blowing up because of incorrect user input, and (c) it all blowing up for reasons unknown.

❷ In the happy path, we redirect happy users to /register/registration-complete, where they'll see a message telling them they'll get an email confirmation of their happy registration.

❸ This catch handles the unhappy path were it was our users' fault. This form of a catch on a Promise chain is one of those Bluebird extensions we mentioned earlier on page 16. We can call catch and pass it a particular kind of error and a function. If the Promise chain throws, this catch handler will only get invoked if the thrown error is the same type as what we passed. In this case we're catching ValidationErrors, which we required near the top of the file and which actions.registerUser might throw. We can have as many of this style of catch as we'd like on a Promise chain, and as a preview, we'll see an example of that while working through authentication on page 126. Note too that we just reuse the userId in this case.

❹ Here we handle an unknown explosion. We take the noble course and punt. Dealing with the unknown isn't this handler's job, so we call next(err) so that some error-handling middleware can deal with it.

Let's look at that action now.

Superficially Validating User Input

Here's the registration action:

```
video-tutorials/src/app/register-users/index.js
function registerUser (traceId, attributes) {
  const context = { attributes, traceId, messageStore, queries }

  return Bluebird.resolve(context)
    .then(validate)
    .then(loadExistingIdentity)
    .then(ensureThereWasNoExistingIdentity)
    .then(hashPassword)
    .then(writeRegisterCommand)
}
```

This function relies on the mechanics of Promise chains to handle control flow, so all we have to do is declare the steps this action goes through. Each of those steps is a reference to a function we required at the top of the file. We start by first declaring context. Each of those functions takes a single parameter, which will be this context. Each step will return context, but possibly with modifications based on what the step does. They may also throw errors.

We start the chain with Promise.resolve(context) to lift ourselves into the Promise land, followed by a call to validate to validate user input. It would be nice to live in a world where users submit only correct information (our programs would certainly be shorter!), but that is unfortunately not this world. We validate that the user submitted the following:

- A password that is at least eight characters long
- A sufficiently complex password
- A valid email address
- An email address that has not already been used

We'll get to the fourth validation case on page 95, but the first three are trivial and are what Daniel Whitaker refers to as "superficial validation."[1] This type of validation does not involve the state of the system. An email without @ somewhere in it is not a valid email address, regardless of how many videos have been uploaded and watched, for example. That's also not a property unique to user identities in our system—there's an RFC that defines them.[2] Let's write this superficial validation:

video-tutorials/src/app/register-users/validate.js
```
const validate = require('validate.js')

const ValidationError = require('../errors/validation-error')

const constraints = {
  email: {
    email: true,
    presence: true
  },
  password: {
    length: { minimum: 8 },
    presence: true
  }
}
function v (context) {
  const validationErrors = validate(context.attributes, constraints)
```

---

1. http://danielwhittaker.me/2016/04/20/how-to-validate-commands-in-a-cqrs-application/
2. https://tools.ietf.org/html/rfc2822

```
     if (validationErrors) {
       throw new ValidationError(validationErrors)
20   }

     return context
   }

25 module.exports = v
```

This is a very focused file. The first thing to note is that we're using the validate.js library.[3] validate.js expects an object that defines the validation rules it checks for. We define such an object, constraints, at line 5. We like our emails to look like email addresses and not be blank, and we like our passwords to be at least eight characters long. A production site ought to enforce better password rules than that, and validate.js has ways to set up whatever you'd like. In fact, you don't even have to use validate.js. Since the validation is encapsulated in this function, the rest of the system doesn't care at all.

In any case, at line 16 we actually call validate.js, and it returns null if there were no errors. If there were errors, say the email address supplied was 'hi i am not an email lolz', we'd get back something like:

```
{ email: [ 'Email is not a valid email' ] } // Indeed it isn't.
```

The object's keys will match the keys of constraints, and the values will be arrays of strings, one string for each violated constraint. If a particular field had no problems, it won't show up in the error object.

If we got errors, we throw a ValidationError constructed with them. Otherwise we just return context unchanged. Congrats! Superficial validation done.

Now, ultimately a Component is responsible for enforcing its business rules, and it is sovereign over the event streams that it writes to. The validation we did here is not a substitute for that, and when we write the Component on page 110, we will duplicate the email check. So why did we bother with any validation here?

In the case of password length, the Component is only going to see a hash of the password, so it can't possibly tell what the plain-text password was. Unless we're running it on a quantum computer,[4] but seeing how those aren't yet offered by our deployment solution (which we get to in Chapter 12, Deploying Components, on page 195), here we are. As for validating the email address, that we could leave to the Component, but to do so would require a command→Component processes

---

3.   https://validatejs.org/
4.   https://en.wikipedia.org/wiki/Quantum_computing

command and writes event→Aggregator picks up event cycle, which would lead to some unpleasant UI work and a bad user experience for registration. We'll do an example of this kind of user interface in Chapter 11, Building Async-Aware User Interfaces, on page 173, but for now, we don't want to make people just coming to our site for the first time experience that.

Ensuring Uniqueness of Email Addresses

Next up is loadExistingIdentity, and this function is defined at:

video-tutorials/src/app/register-users/load-existing-identity.js
```
function loadExistingIdentity (context) {
  return context.queries
    .byEmail(context.attributes.email)
    .then(existingIdentity => {
      context.existingIdentity = existingIdentity

      return context
    })
}

module.exports = loadExistingIdentity
```

Following Eric Elliot's advice in his article "Mocking Is a Code Smell,"[5] this function does the single job of querying View Data for a record with the given email address. It doesn't check to see if it actually found one because that would be mixing I/O (the query) and branching business logic. This function's job is to simply issue the query, and attach the result to context. It gets access to the queries because we put them in the context when we started the Promise chain. Let's write queries.byEmail:

video-tutorials/src/app/register-users/index.js
```
function createQueries ({ db }) {
  function byEmail (email) {
    return db
      .then(client =>
        client('user_credentials')
          .where({ email })
          .limit(1)
      )
      .then(camelCaseKeys)
      .then(rows => rows[0])
  }

  return { byEmail }
}
```

---

5. https://medium.com/javascript-scene/mocking-is-a-code-smell-944a70c90a6a

This is probably a good time to look at the migration that creates the View Data that byEmail queries:

```
video-tutorials/migrations/20180623124103_create-user-credentials.js
exports.up = function up (knex) {
  return knex.schema.createTable('user_credentials', table => {
    table.string('id').primary()
    table.string('email').notNullable()
    table.string('password_hash').notNullable()

    table.index('email')
  })
}

exports.down = knex => knex.schema.dropTable('user_credentials')
```

It creates the user_credentials table, with columns id, email, and password_hash.

The actual check for an existing record occurs in:

```
video-tutorials/src/app/register-users/ensure-there-was-no-existing-identity.js
const ValidationError = require('../errors/validation-error')
function ensureThereWasNoExistingIdentity (context) {
  if (context.existingIdentity) {
    throw new ValidationError({ email: ['already taken'] })
  }

  return context
}

module.exports = ensureThereWasNoExistingIdentity
```

Again, this function has one job. If loadExistingIdentity had found a record using the supplied email address, it would have attached it at context.existingIdentity. So this function checks to see if there is anything at context.existingIdentity. If so, it throws a ValidationError, passing in an object of the same shape as we saw in the superficial validation on page 92.

Keep in mind that this check for a duplicate email used eventually consistent View Data. Records show up in user_credentials *after* we've written a Register command, *after* the identity Component (coming up on page 110) picks up that command and issues a Registered event, and *after* the Aggregator we'll write on page 120 picks up that event and writes it to the user_credentials View Data. We'll justify validating unique emails this way on page 99.

Finishing the Application

Back to actions.registerUser, we have two steps left. hashPassword and writeRegister-Command. Here is hashPassword:

```
video-tutorials/src/app/register-users/hash-password.js
const bcrypt = require('bcrypt')

// We could pull this out into an environment variable, but we don't
const SALT_ROUNDS = 10
function hashPassword (context) {
  return bcrypt
    .hash(context.attributes.password, SALT_ROUNDS)
    .then(passwordHash => {
      context.passwordHash = passwordHash

      return context
    })
}

module.exports = hashPassword
```

It uses bcrypt[6] to hash the password and attaches the hash at context.passwordHash.

Now that everything has checked out, we can finally write the command:

```
video-tutorials/src/app/register-users/write-register-command.js
Line 1  function writeRegisterCommand (context) {
   -      const userId = context.attributes.id
   -      const stream = `identity:command-${userId}`
   -      const command = {
   5        id: uuid(),
   -        type: 'Register',
   -        metadata: {
   -          traceId: context.traceId,
   -          userId
   10       },
   -        data: {
   -          userId,
   -          email: context.attributes.email,
   -          passwordHash: context.passwordHash
   15       }
   -      }
   -
   -      return context.messageStore.write(stream, command)
   -    }
   20
   -    module.exports = writeRegisterCommand
```

This looks like every time we've called messageStore.write before. We construct the command at line 4 using the data from context. Then we write it using the reference to the messageStore we put into context.

---

6. https://www.npmjs.com/package/bcrypt

Building the Register Application's Router

Now that the action is complete, let's bring all these pieces together to flesh out this application:

video-tutorials/src/app/register-users/index.js

```
function build ({ db, messageStore }) {
  const queries = createQueries({ db })
  const actions = createActions({ messageStore, queries })
  const handlers = createHandlers({ actions })

  const router = express.Router()
```
❶
```
  router
    .route('/')
    .get(handlers.handleRegistrationForm)
    .post(
      bodyParser.urlencoded({ extended: false }),
      handlers.handleRegisterUser
    )
```
❷
```
  router
    .route('/registration-complete')
    .get(handlers.handleRegistrationComplete)

  return { actions, handlers, queries, router }
}
```

```
module.exports = build
```

createRegisterUsers is our dependency-receiving function that we export at the end of the file. It receives db and messageStore, references to the View Data database and Message Store, respectively. It instantiates the queries, actions, and handlers we just worked through. It finally creates an express.Router. That router mounts our three handlers and does so on two different routes.

❶ The root route mounts two of the handlers. If we GET that route, we'll see the registration form. If we POST to it, then we're submitting the registration form, and our registration handler picks it. Notice the bodyParser middleware on that post declaration. Middlewares are functions that run before our handler functions and get access to the incoming request and outgoing response object. They're used to do things like logging or do transformations on the incoming request. This middleware does the latter, receiving the email address and password in the raw POST data and making them available as properties on a req.body object.

❷ On the /registration-complete route, a GET request returns the registration complete page. That's probably a shocker. Yes, it's true that if you directly type in that URL you'll also see the registration complete page. So, you could have fun reloading that page over and over again if you wanted to.

Lastly, we need to configure the register-users Application and mount it in our Express instance. First, configuring it:

```
video-tutorials/src/config.js
// ...
const createRegisterUsersApp = require('./app/register-users')
function createConfig ({ env }) {
  // ...
  const registerUsersApp = createRegisterUsersApp({
    db: knexClient,
    messageStore
  })
  return {
    // ...
    // ...
    registerUsersApp,
  }
}
```

Finally, we mount it in Express:

```
video-tutorials/src/app/express/mount-routes.js
function mountRoutes (app, config) {
  app.use('/', config.homeApp.router)
  app.use('/record-viewing', config.recordViewingsApp.router)
  app.use('/register', config.registerUsersApp.router)
}
```

We mount it at /register, and that wraps up the Application layer's involvement with registering users. Most of that likely looked like what you've done in MVC projects—our event-sourced microservices architecture didn't introduce the need to validate user input, for example. The only part of this process that's unique to event-sourced microservices is that at the end of validation we wrote a command rather than directly writing to a CRUD model.

If you make sure your Docker setup (docker-compose up) or other PostgreSQL instances are running and restart the server at this point (npm run start-dev-server) again, you can use the "Register" link in the upper right-hand side of the screen to navigate to the registration form and fill it out. If you use your favorite database viewer and the connection information in the .env file, you can find the command issued when this form is submitted.

Validating Eventually Consistent Data

While you are successfully recording user registration requests, we still haven't justified the decision to use the View Data to validate that the emails supplied during registration aren't duplicates, a direct contradiction of what we said on page 21 when first discussing the pieces of our architecture.

When making decisions like this, it's important to ask a series of questions because the truth is, there is no single, correct-for-all-systems answer. There isn't even a correct-for-all-kinds-of-data-within-the-same-system answer. There are always trade-offs, but if you're asking the right questions, you can get answers that work for your needs. Consider:

- How likely is the thing you're trying to prevent?
- How bad is it if the thing you're trying to prevent happens?
- Whose constraint is it, anyway?
- What does "correct" mean?

For the first question, refer back to that map of a microservices-based system:

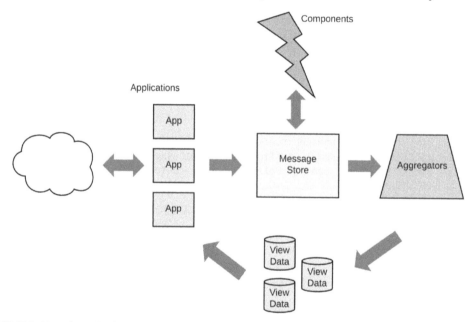

Validation has to live in one of those places. We used the Application and View Data to validate that email addresses used in registration haven't been used before, by issuing a simple query. This honored the uni-directional flow of data through the system and did not violate any of the rules of what Components are.

"Ah, but Ethan," you may say. "Isn't the View Data *eventually* consistent?"

You might be concerned that a situation like the following could arise:

1. User 1 sends a registration request with tricksie@example.com.

2. System checks user_credentials table and lets user 1's request through, writing the corresponding Register command.

3. User 2 sends a registration request with tricksie@example.com.

4. System checks user_credentials table and lets user 2's request through, writing the corresponding Register command.

5. identity Component picks up user 1's command, processing it and writing the Registered event.

6. identity Component picks up user 2's command, processing it and writing the Registered event.

7. The (as of yet unwritten) Aggregator processes user 1's event, inserting a row into user_credentials.

8. The (as of yet unwritten) Aggregator sees a Registered event with a duplicate email address, packs up shop, and moves to the mountains in a remote area.

Those points are completely accurate. But here's the thing—when we say "eventually consistent," we don't mean that when the request comes in, someone prints it out, ties it to a carrier pigeon, and sends the pigeon off to an out-of-state location where another worker will copy down the request and commit it to system state. We're talking about a pretty small window—on the order of milliseconds. Honestly, how likely is it that these two requests will come in? In this case, I would say "not very."

That might not be satisfying. You might be thinking along the same lines of Nassim Nicholas Taleb, who stated in an episode of EconTalk,[7] "in the presence of the probability of ruin, you will be ruined." Surely, if these two events get written, there's no recovery from that, right?

The thing is, getting these two events written isn't ruin. You'll see in Chapter 8, Authenticating Users, on page 119 that when someone logs in, we identify them with the *combination* of email and password. Suppose that the race condition occurs, and the Aggregator has just finished writing the first set of credentials. The table in question would contain the following:

id	email	password_hash
uuid-1	dup@example.com	$0meh4$h

Now the duplicate comes in, and it will have a different userId. We can already tell these two identities apart. We could add an additional column to the credentials table, something like needs_to_change_email. Then when the second event comes through, we set that to true. With some UI work we could then

7. http://www.econtalk.org/nassim-nicholas-taleb-on-rationality-risk-and-skin-in-the-game/

prompt this user to change email addresses. So even if we do get the same email address, we're not talking about catastrophe. That table would contain something like this:

id	email	password_hash	needs_to_change_email
uuid-1	dup@example.com	$0meh4$h	false
uuid-2	dup@example.com	$0me-other-h4$h	true

If you truly are in a situation where you RELLY CANNOT HAZ DUPLICATEZ!!!!, then what you're saying is it's a fundamental property of identities that no two of them have the same email address. Up to this point we've been treating the duplicate email addresses as an Application layer concern, that it's an annoyance to have two accounts with the same email address, but that no fundamental laws were violated. Accordingly, we put the validation in that layer. However, if unique email addresses are truly a fundamental property of identities, then it's up to the Component that owns identities to enforce that property.

A Component could go to the Message Store and look at every identity in the system and see if their current email address matches the one in this new registration command. If so, it would reject the command, maybe writing a RegistrationRejected event with an appropriate reason. That would be costly to do on the fly, so at startup time it might compile a list of used email addresses and stash that list in its own database table. No one else would be allowed to use that stash, of course, because that would violate the Component's autonomy. But it can do whatever it wants internally.

After consulting with our business team, we've decided that unique email addresses are not a fundamental property of identities. So we'll leave the uniqueness check in the eventually consistent Application layer. But this discussion does show why we don't want to rely on *View* Data to make decisions in our systems.

Coping with Trade-Offs

Are any of these solutions perfect? No. Software never is. There are only trade-offs. This particular case would actually be simpler in the immediately consistent world of a monolith because it makes no distinction between data and applications of that data. In exchange for that ease, you would lose the chance to consciously reason about and select an option that meets the needs of your system. Honest use of the system is not likely to encounter a problem here, and if it does, the resolution isn't too hard. As for bad-faith use of the system, well, don't be concerned about a 4@xor's user experience.

The last big question is about the definition of "correct." This varies case-by-case and is something that must be decided with the business team and domain experts involved on the project. For example, suppose you're an e-commerce store shipping physical goods. Physical goods have this weird property where you can't just conjure up copies of them out of thin air. (Weird, right? How do people deal with that?) You can't fulfill customer orders without actually having inventory.

You could use any of these strategies, but which one is right? If you can immediately tell that you're out of stock, do you really want to send your customers away to competitors? What if you don't have stock *now*, but you will tomorrow? What's the right strategy? Work with your business team. That's a good thing to do anyway.

What You've Done So Far

This has been one of most important chapters of this project. You just took a business requirement and turned it into a message-backed model. As a developer and designer of software systems, that is the crucial skill that you bring to the table. It'll take code to realize this design, of course, but it's knowing how to decompose requirements into logical steps that lets you know what code needs to be written in the first place.

Why not try doing some more domain decomposition? Think of some other process in your life, and discover the domain events that could model it in software. Maybe that's your morning routine, or maybe that's organizing a gathering. What distinct steps do you go through? Those are your events. Do some of them seem to cluster around any entities? What commands could users of your system use to kick off these steps? Don't sweat it too much if you're stuck at this point. The rest of this book is going to be all about doing this very exercise in many different contexts.

Registration did present some questions whose answers weren't straightforward. We met those questions with questions of our own that we'll need to ask if we're going to build a successful system.

As a review, those question were:

- How likely is the thing we're trying to prevent?
- How bad is it if the thing we're trying to prevent happens?
- Whose concern is it, anyway?
- What does "correct" mean?

We'll take these questions with us as we consider validation in future chapters.

With a well-defined message contract you were able to build a client of a Component without having actually built the Component itself. You're telling this identity Component what to do, even though it doesn't exist yet. If we had two teams working on this project, with the Component's contract defined, one team could immediately begin working on the client application while the other simultaneously worked on the backing Component. Proper boundaries let you do that sort of thing, and a message-based architecture helps you maintain those boundaries.

All that said, we don't have a second team building that backing Component. That's on us and is the topic of the next chapter. It's going to require one final change to the Message Store, and then we can declare "done" on user registration. We have some Register commands sitting in our Component's command stream—let's go handle them.

CHAPTER 7

Implementing Your First Component

If you've ever read L. Frank Baum's classic *The Wonderful Wizard of Oz*, then you're familiar with the trope of the man behind the curtain. The way we left things in the previous chapter is kind of like that, only we don't even have anything behind the curtain—it's good and empty there. The register-users application is writing commands, but no one is home processing them.

We'll fix that in this chapter. We're working in two places here:

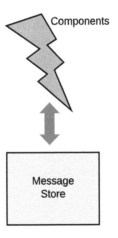

Components

Message
Store

We're going to implement the identity Component and start processing those Register commands. But handling them will require a little more from the Message Store. We have and will continue to go on and on about idempotence. Before processing a Register command, we need to make sure that we haven't already registered the user in question. For that to work we need a way to get the current state of an identity—not an eventually consistent state, but its state *right now*. So what say you to doing that right now?

Fetching a Stream's Current State

In Chapter 4, Projecting Data into Useful Shapes, on page 51, you built eventually consistent View Data. That means that while they'll eventually get current with everything that has been written in the system, there is no guarantee that at *any particular point in time* they represent the truth as best we know it. That works for View Data, but not so much for when you're trying to decide, say, whether or not to process the $10 million wire transfer. We need to know the state of an entity *right now*.

Entity streams are inherently without shape, since they're just append-only logs of immutable events. The log doesn't directly give the state of an entity. It's optimized for *writing* and not for reading. We need to shape that stream into something else.

Enter the Message Store's fetch function. This is the function that implements the event sourcing in our system. It takes the name of a stream where the entity state we care about lives and what we call a *projection*. To understand a projection, let's talk shadow puppets.

Think of the streams of data as the stream of light emanating from a flashlight. To make a shadow puppet you hold up your hands in various shapes. The light hits your hands and casts the desired shadow on the wall. From the same light, you can create different shadows by changing the position of your hands. Your hands are the projection, the thing that gives shape to the otherwise shapeless stream.

Let's implement fetch:

```
video-tutorials/src/message-store/read.js
function createRead ({ db }) {
  function fetch (streamName, projection) {
    return read(streamName).then(messages => project(messages, projection))
  }
  return {
    // ...
    fetch
  }
}
```

The streamName parameter tells us which stream contains the events we need. We pass that along to read, which you implemented on page 75, to get all those events. then we feed them into the project function, also passing in the projection that we received.

> **Commands Will Never Be Part of a Projection**
>
> We put commands and subscriber positions in streams as well as events, so you may wonder why we keep saying "events" here and not "messages." Projections are groups of functions that shape *state* into a useful form. Commands are not state. They are requests to change state, so we will never use a command type in a projection.

Let's write project now:

video-tutorials/src/message-store/read.js

```
Line 1  function project (events, projection) {
     2    return events.reduce((entity, event) => {
     3      if (!projection[event.type]) {
     4        return entity
     5      }
     6
     7      return projection[event.type](entity, event)
     8    }, projection.$init())
     9  }
```

Notice that project is outside the dependency-receiving function createRead. It's a pure function and doesn't interact with the Message Store at all. project's goal is to turn the array of events into a single value representing the entity we're projecting. To that end, it calls events.reduce. Array.prototype.reduce[1] takes a reducer function and a starting value. projection.$init is a function that returns the starting value of the reduction, answering the question, "What is this entity's value before we've applied any events to it?" So the starting value of the projection is the result of calling projection.$init. The reducer will get called once and in order for each event in events, and at each iteration it receives the current value of entity and the current event in the iteration. It must apply the event to entity and return the resulting value.

In addition to the $init key returning the entity's starting point, a projection must define a key–value pair for each event type that affects the entity. The key is the event type, and the value is a handler function that receives the current state of the entity and the event to apply. It then returns the entity's value now that the event has been applied.

Let's consider a concrete example to get the gist. We're working on our identity Component whose job it is to record user registrations. In the previous chapter on page 85, we discussed that an identity could be represented as a state machine with an isRegistered state as shown in the figure on page 108.

---

1. https://developer.mozilla.org/en-US/docs/Web/JavaScript/Reference/Global_Objects/Array/reduce

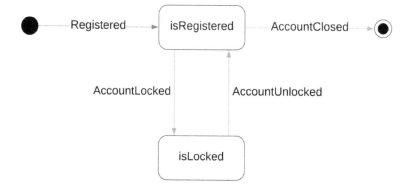

Again, we're ignoring both locking accounts and closing accounts for now, but it's the presence of a Registered event that transitions an identity from the starting state to the isRegistered state. Registered events also contain an email property in their data as defined by the contract.md file we wrote for this Component at code/video-tutorials/src/components/identity/contract.md.

So, we could project an identity like so:

```
video-tutorials/src/components/identity/load-identity.js
const identityProjection = {
  $init () {
    return {
      id: null,
      email: null,
      isRegistered: false,
    }
  },
  Registered (identity, registered) {
    identity.id = registered.data.userId
    identity.email = registered.data.email
    identity.isRegistered = true

    return identity
  },
}
```

The $init key function defines the starting state of this entity. If we have not applied any events, then an identity is an object with a null id and email and false for isRegistered.

Now, the only kind of event that affects this projection right now is a Registered event. So, we have the key Registered, matching the type of the event that we care about, whose value is a handler function that takes the current state of the identity and applies the Registered event, which we name registered. We apply registered to identity by copying the necessary properties out of registered.data to identity. We get the userId and email, assigning them to identity at id and email, respectively. We also set isRegistered to true because, again, finding a Registered event in the stream means that this identity has been registered. Finally, we return the updated identity:

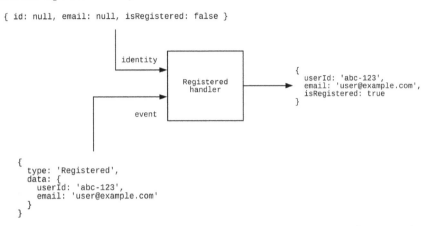

```
{ id: null, email: null, isRegistered: false }
```

```
identity

Registered
handler

event

{
  userId: 'abc-123',
  email: 'user@example.com',
  isRegistered: true
}

{
  type: 'Registered',
  data: {
    userId: 'abc-123',
    email: 'user@example.com'
  }
}
```

If there were other events to project, then identity, now with these updated fields, would be passed into the next handler. That handler would apply that next event to identity, returning the result, and so on and so forth. This is a simple projection, though, and we only care about one type of event... for now. Wouldn't it be a swell exercise at the end of the chapter to augment this projection to reflect AccountLocked events?

So with an understanding of a projection's shape, let's return to the project function:

video-tutorials/src/message-store/read.js
```
function project (events, projection) {
  return events.reduce((entity, event) => {
    if (!projection[event.type]) {
      return entity
    }

    return projection[event.type](entity, event)
  }, projection.$init())
}
```

It starts by calling reduce on the array of events, using projection.$init's return value as the starting value for the reduction. At line 3 it checks if projection did not define a handler for the given event.type. If there is no handler, then much like in an Aggregator, the correct way to handle the event is to make no change. We signal doing nothing by just returning entity as is. However, if there was a handler, then at line 7 we return the result of calling that handler with the current state of the entity and the new event. That handler again returns the entity with the event applied to it, and this return value becomes the input entity to the next handler if one needs to be called. Now we just need to connect fetch to the Message Store's interface:

```
video-tutorials/src/message-store/index.js
function createMessageStore ({ db }) {
  // ...
  return {
    // ...
    fetch: read.fetch,
  }
}
```

We hook it into the return value in the Message Store's main file, and we're done.

There is one limitation to our fetch function. Remember that read returns at most 1,000 messages when we don't tell it otherwise. This implementation of fetch will not support projecting streams with more than 1,000 messages. It is very unlikely that any particular stream will ever have more than that number, so we'll accept this limitation, and with good monitoring we'll know when and if we need to change this.

All right. The Message Store lets us project a stream now, and with that, you have finished implementing the rest of our Message Store interface code. You have lived as few dare to dream and have definitely earned a big "way to go," so "WAY TO GO!" Now it's time to write that first Component.

Joining the "I Wrote a Microservice" Club

Seven chapters into this book, and this is the moment you've been waiting for—your first Component! Here's to hoping you aren't underwhelmed.

We have two things to do with this Component. We need it to subscribe to where its commands will be, and we need it to handle those commands. Let's start with the top-level function this Component defines:

```
video-tutorials/src/components/identity/index.js
Line 1  function build ({ messageStore }) {
          const identityCommandHandlers =
            createIdentityCommandHandlers({ messageStore })
          const identityCommandSubscription = messageStore.createSubscription({
     5      streamName: 'identity:command',
            handlers: identityCommandHandlers,
            subscriberId: 'components:identity:command'
          })
          function start () {
    10        identityCommandSubscription.start()
          }
```

```
   -      return {
   -        identityCommandHandlers,
   -        start
  15      }
   -    }
   -
   -    module.exports = build
```

It sure seems a lot like an Aggregator at first blush. The first line defines the dependency-receiving function that we export at the end of the file. It receives a reference to the messageStore and sets up the identityCommandHandlers and an identityCommandSubscription. Like in an Aggregator, these handlers are message handlers, not the HTTP handlers you'd find in an Application.

The identityCommandSubscription subscribes to the identity:command category stream. Why that stream? Because that's what we decided on page 87 when we defined this Component's messages and recorded them in this Component's contract.md file.

As a polling component, this Component has a start function at line 9. We first saw this start function concept on page 58 when we wrote the home-page Aggregator. All Components and Aggregators in this book have a start function.

Handling Register commands

Next we handle the Register commands:

```
video-tutorials/src/components/identity/index.js
Line 1  function createIdentityCommandHandlers ({ messageStore }) {
   -      return {
   -        Register: command => {
   -          const context = {
   5          messageStore: messageStore,
   -            command,
   -            identityId: command.data.userId
   -          }
   -
  10          return Bluebird.resolve(context)
   -            .then(loadIdentity)
   -            .then(ensureNotRegistered)
   -            .then(writeRegisteredEvent)
   -            .catch(AlreadyRegsiteredError, () => {})
  15        }
   -      }
   -    }
```

This handler turns the command, a request to do something, into an event, an immutable piece of history. The first thing is to build a context at line 4 that will flow through the Bluebird pipeline. It has the messageStore, the command, and it pulls the identityId out of the command as well. In Chapter 9, Adding an

Email Component, on page 133, when we add email capabilities to this system, we'll have event handlers that need to call loadIdentity, so we can't assume the presence of a command in the context.

Remember, *we have no guarantees that we'll see messages only once.* We can't just assume that this is the first time we've handled this command. We have to make this handler idempotent.

Loading the Identity

How would you tell if this command has already been processed? The first step is to fetch the identity that would be recorded if the command had already been processed:

```
video-tutorials/src/components/identity/load-identity.js
const identityProjection = {
  // ... body omitted
}
function loadIdentity (context) {
  const { identityId, messageStore } = context
  const identityStreamName = `identity-${identityId}`

  return messageStore
    .fetch(identityStreamName, identityProjection)
    .then(identity => {
      context.identity = identity

      return context
    })
}

module.exports = loadIdentity
```

❶ First off we need to build the name of the stream where the identity's events would reside. We know how to build that name because the message contract in code/video-tutorials/src/components/identity/contract.md tells us how. Identities are found in the identity category, and we just tack the ID on to the end of that.

❷ Now that we have the identityStream, we fetch and project the identity, using the function you just wrote on page 106. We'll go through the projection in just a moment.

❸ Next, now that we have the identity, sourced from the events in the stream whose name we put into identityStreamName, we attach it to the context. We follow this pattern all throughout the project—a loadX function will attach X to context. After attaching it, we just return context so that the next part of the pipeline can do its job.

Now let's go through the projection again:

```
video-tutorials/src/components/identity/load-identity.js
const identityProjection = {
  $init () {
    return {
      id: null,
      email: null,
      isRegistered: false,
    }
  },
  Registered (identity, registered) {
    identity.id = registered.data.userId
    identity.email = registered.data.email
    identity.isRegistered = true

    return identity
  },
}
```

This is the same projection we used as an example when writing fetch on page 106. Projections turn streams of events into current-state entities. Like all projections in this book, it has an $init key, and the return value for that function is the state of the entity before applying any events to it. $init here tells us that before encountering any events, an identity has a null id and email and that its isRegistered property is false.

Next, it defines one event handler because there's only one event that affects this entity, namely Registered. The handler takes the running state of the identity as its first argument and the current event as its second argument. It assigns the userId and email from event.data, sets isRegistered to true, and returns identity.

Making the Command Handler Idempotent

Now that we've fetched the identity, the next step in the pipeline on page 111 is checking to see if we've already handled this command:

```
video-tutorials/src/components/identity/ensure-not-registered.js
const AlreadyRegisteredError = require('./already-registered-error')
function ensureNotRegistered (context) {
  if (context.identity.isRegistered) {
    throw new AlreadyRegisteredError()
  }

  return context
}

module.exports = ensureNotRegistered
```

> ### \|// Joe asks:
> ### ❤ Won't Running Projections Be Really Slow?
>
> Looping through every message in a stream every time we get a command…won't that grind our system to a halt?
>
> In practice, this ends up not being a problem. Computers are fast and are getting faster with each passing year. Also, if we've modeled our system correctly, it's unlikely that any particular entity stream—the type of stream we project—will have 1,000s of messages to project.
>
> That said, the main strategy in keeping projection times down is something called *snapshotting*. We won't implement it in this book, but we do discuss how it works on page 245.

All the function needs to do is see if the projected identity isRegistered. If so, we have already processed the command, so we throw an AlreadyRegisteredError —the handler's pipeline will turn that into a no-op. If not, just feed context through.

Writing the Registered Event

Referring back to the pipeline on page 111, if we've made it this far, then we haven't processed this command before, and we're good to go with processing it now. If we had chosen to do validation of the user's input in the Component, the validation would also be here. We didn't choose that, so all that's left is to turn Register commands into Registered events:

```
video-tutorials/src/components/identity/write-registered-event.js
function writeRegisteredEvent (context, err) {
  const command = context.command

  const registeredEvent = {
    id: uuid(),
    type: 'Registered',
    metadata: {
      traceId: command.metadata.traceId,
      userId: command.metadata.userId
    },
    data: {
      userId: command.data.userId,
      email: command.data.email,
      passwordHash: command.data.passwordHash
    }
  }
  const identityStreamName = `identity-${command.data.userId}`
```

```
    return context.messageStore
      .write(identityStreamName, registeredEvent)
      .then(() => context)
}

module.exports = writeRegisteredEvent
```

This function constructs the appropriate event, copying the relevant metadata and data from the command we pulled out of context. Then it's just a quick write of this event to identityStreamName, and boom, you're registering users.

Wiring the Identity Component into the System

To get this working, wire it into the system config:

```
video-tutorials/src/config.js
Line 1  // ...
   -    const createIdentityComponent = require('./components/identity')
   -    function createConfig ({ env }) {
   -      // ...
   5      const identityComponent = createIdentityComponent({ messageStore })
   -      const components = [
   -        identityComponent,
   -      ]
   -      return {
  10        // ...
   -        identityComponent,
   -      }
   -    }
```

Line 2 requires the Component's constructor. Line 5 instantiates the Component, injecting the messageStore dependency. With the Component instantiated, at line 7 we add it to the components array. Adding it to this array is what lets the system know it needs to call the Component's start function. Finally, we add the Component to the config's return value at line 11.

So, yeah, sorry if the first Component was underwhelming. Components themselves aren't really all that exciting. The overall architecture is, but the Components themselves are honestly kind of "meh." But at this point, you have now captured users registering for your system. This is a crucial feature in nearly every web-based system. And if you restart your server at this point, you will be able to see your Register commands being turned into Registered events.

Disambiguating "Projections" and "Replaying"

One final note before we close the chapter. Now that you're getting a solid foundation for building autonomous, message-based microservices, as you continue your learning, you're bound to come across other uses of the words "projection" and "replaying." Each word generally has one of two meanings.

What you did in this chapter, where you had a Component that needed the current state of an entity to decide how to handle an event, provides the first meaning of each. You *projected* the identity's events, sourcing its current state from those events. This can be understood as *replaying* the events, since you'll do this every time you get an event that operates on an identity. One of the most frequent questions out there is how do you *replay* events without redoing side effects? Clearly in this case there is no worry because projections *absolutely never trigger side effects*. A projection's handlers, as we use the term in this book, always and only return new copies of entities having applied a new event to them.

The second meaning of "project" is found in our Aggregators. Conceptually there isn't much different between our projections and Aggregators. Each is taking a append-only log and *projecting* them into some other shape. Components project over and over again as needed to handle messages, and Aggregators do this in an ongoing manner in near real time. We use a different term to clarify this temporal difference. Components project; Aggregators aggregate.

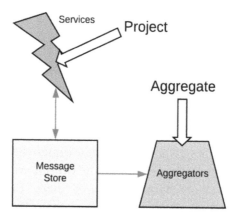

The second meaning of "replay" comes the fact that you can write a new Component or Aggregator well after you've started populating the Message Store with messages. They'll begin their subscription at the very first message in the Message Store and work their way to the present. That's exactly what happened in this chapter—you wrote the Component *after* an application was already writing commands to it.

How did you avoid reprocessing side effects in this case? The same way you always avoid reprocessing side effects. Here's a hint if it's not coming to mind: the answer starts with "idem" and ends with "potent." Imprint that word onto your soul.

Taking It Further

Suppose we had AccountLocked events. Here's an example:

```
{
  "id": "a1a1147f-41e8-4b8a-bc78-5a11af097f7e",
  "type": "AccountLocked",
  "data": {
    "lockedTime": "2019-12-25T07:00:00.123"
  }
}
```

Could you modify the identity projection in code/video-tutorials/src/components/identity/load-identity.js to account for this? What would the key be on the new handler? What would you have to add to the value returned by $init?

What You've Done So Far

Your first Component. How does it feel? Hopefully exciting. In the previous chapter you constructed a Component's message contract, and an application was able to use that contract even before the backing Component was in place. In this chapter you put that Component in place and were able to start processing messages that had already been written. Our system can now register users, which means we can get our user counts up and make the business team very happy when they're shopping around to investors.

You implemented an idempotent message handler. Your Component does this by fetching the current state of the entity it cares about and seeing if the message under consideration has already been handled. Its effect would be reflected in the projected entity. You'll use this pattern over and over again.

Now, having users register is great, but they still can't get into the system and do things. We need to authenticate them, and that's what we do next.

CHAPTER 8

Authenticating Users

Have you ever been to a U2 concert? Whatever you think of the band or its members, one can hardly argue that they haven't been a commercial success. Even though their concert tickets tend to have assigned seats, hordes of people will line up outside the venue hours before it opens.

If our site were a space in the physical world, that's pretty much what "outside" it would look like at this point. Unbelievable numbers of people have surely registered for our soon-to-conquer-the-webs site. However, they're sitting outside the door and still haven't found what they're looking for. It's time to let them in.

Authenticating users will be much simpler than registration was in Chapter 6, Registering Users, on page 83. We're working everywhere in our system except for the Components in this chapter:

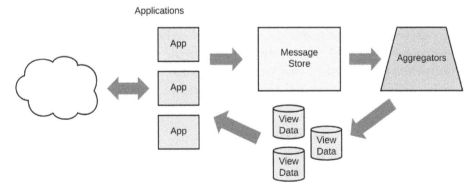

We have two goals:

- Aggregate the Registered events produced by the identity Component you wrote in Chapter 7, Implementing Your First Component, on page 105.

- Write an authenticate application to use the output of that Aggregator to authenticate users, defining any necessary messages around authentication.

Aggregating Registered Events

You've already built the machinery for capturing user registration—we just haven't done anything with the events. Now you'll build an Aggregator to turn those Registered events into View Data you can use for authentication. Its job is to turn Registered events into a queryable table.

Let's start with the top-level function:

```
video-tutorials/src/aggregators/user-credentials.js
function build ({ db, messageStore }) {
  const queries = createQueries({ db })
  const handlers = createHandlers({ queries })
  const subscription = messageStore.createSubscription({
    streamName: 'identity',
    handlers,
    subscriberId: 'aggregators:user-credentials'
  })

  function start () {
    subscription.start()
  }

  return {
    handlers,
    queries,
    start
  }
}

module.exports = build
```

Standard stuff. It receives db and messageStore references and instantiates queries, handlers, and a subscription. It subscribes to the identity category stream. Take a moment to think about why. Much like the apocryphal Willie Sutton answer when he was asked why he robbed banks,[1] we subscribe to that category because that's where the Registered events are. The identity Component's contract.md told us that.

Next up, the handlers for the Aggregator:

```
video-tutorials/src/aggregators/user-credentials.js
function createHandlers ({ queries }) {
  return {
    Registered: event =>
      queries.createUserCredential(
        event.data.userId,
```

---

1. https://en.wikipedia.org/wiki/Willie_Sutton#%22Sutton's_law%22

```
        event.data.email,
        event.data.passwordHash
      )
    }
  }
```

This Aggregator's only job is aggregate Registered events into authentication View Data, so we have a single handler for that event type. This handler merely delegates to queries.createUserCredential, passing the user's ID, email address, and hashed password, all of which came from the event's data. You will put a tear in your humble author's eye if at this point you're wondering how on earth this handler is idempotent. Fear not fellow traveler, the query function makes our handling of these events idempotent:

video-tutorials/src/aggregators/user-credentials.js
```
function createQueries ({ db }) {
  function createUserCredential (id, email, passwordHash) {
    const rawQuery = `
      INSERT INTO
        user_credentials (id, email, password_hash)
      VALUES
        (:id, :email, :passwordHash)
      ON CONFLICT DO NOTHING
    `

    return db.then(client =>
      client.raw(rawQuery, { id, email, passwordHash }))
  }

  return { createUserCredential }
}
```

This function performs an INSERT query to make a row for each user. We make this INSERT idempotent by adding an ON CONFLICT DO NOTHING clause. This table, defined on page 96, made the id column the primary key. If we were to see the same Registered event a second time, we would get a conflict on that primary key. Since we tell the database to DO NOTHING in that case, we effectively no-op, ensuring that our handling of this event is idempotent.

And that is the Aggregator. In this kind of architecture, each of the pieces remains focused and easy to reason about. We just need to connect this Aggregator to the system config:

video-tutorials/src/config.js
```
Line 1  // ...
    -   const createUserCredentialsAggregator =
    -     require('./aggregators/user-credentials')
    -   function createConfig ({ env }) {
    5     // ...
```

```
const userCredentialsAggregator = createUserCredentialsAggregator({
  db: knexClient,
  messageStore
})
const aggregators = [
  // ...
  userCredentialsAggregator,
]
return {
  // ...
  userCredentialsAggregator,
}
}
```

This is a familiar wiring job. First, require the constructor at line 2 and then instantiate the Aggregator at line 6. Then add the instance to the Aggregators array at line 12 so that the system knows to call its start function. Finally, add it to the configs return value at line 16.

Fantastic. That's it for this Aggregator. Let's authenticate those users.

Discovering the Authentication Events and Commands

Strictly speaking, we don't *need* any events to handle authentication. In Chapter 6, Registering Users, on page 83, we wrote a migration for View Data with emails and hashed passwords. We can just query that table and then track login status using cookies, JWTs,[2] or whatever. Authentication is also synchronous, so it doesn't involve any Components or require commands. This is why the term "auth service" is nonsensical. Authentication is a query, and autonomous services—the component we're building—don't respond to queries.

That said, there may still be interesting domain events around authentication. We may want to know how often users log in or if we're getting a lot of failed attempts. Maybe we need to lock those accounts. We don't really know yet, but we can still track the events.

Our two events will be UserLoggedIn and UserLoginFailed. These events originate from the authentication application you'll write in this chapter, so that application must define them. That definition lives in code/video-tutorials/src/app/authenticate/contract.md, and please go read that file. We only reproduce here examples of these events.

---

2. https://jwt.io/

Here's an example UserLoggedIn:

```
{
  "id": "40f969ec-d6ea-466e-beb5-d37543db162e",
  "type": "UserLoggedIn",
  "data": {
    "userId": "e90647af-8103-4fe9-ae1f-4766103cca54"
  }
}
```

You'll write these to streams of the form authentication-X, where X is the user's ID.

For UserLoginFailed events:

```
{
  "id": "a314d64f-6e4f-4a99-bfd4-5cf5afc52846",
  "type": "UserLoginFailed",
  "data": {
    "userId": "e90647af-8103-4fe9-ae1f-4766103cca54",
    "reason": "Incorrect password"
  }
}
```

These will go in the authentication category, just like UserLoggedIn events.

Sometimes a login attempt will fail, but we don't know who the user is. This is most likely because the submission used an email address that is not in our system. In that case we won't bother recording an event. This event wouldn't change our domain model. It's important system health information—it might reveal an attack on our system—but it isn't *domain information*. We're not writing a DDOS detection system. We'll log it in our server logs where monitoring systems would pick it up.

Letting Users in the Door

With all the bricks in place, we can add the authenticate Application. Node.js has good authentication libraries, such as Passport,[3] but we're not going to use them. Using one could be the topic of its own dedicated tutorial, and we want to keep the focus on microservices here.

In any case, let's dive into the authenticate Application. It needs to do three main things:

- Present a login form
- Log users out
- Handle login requests

---

3. http://www.passportjs.org/

As always, let's start with the top-level function:

video-tutorials/src/app/authenticate/index.js
```
function build ({ db, messageStore }) {
  const queries = createQueries({ db })
  const actions = createActions({ messageStore, queries })
  const handlers = createHandlers({ actions })

  const router = express.Router()

  router
    .route('/log-in')
    .get(handlers.handleShowLoginForm)
    // ...
    .post(
      bodyParser.urlencoded({ extended: false }),
      handlers.handleAuthenticate
    )

  router.route('/log-out').get(handlers.handleLogOut)

  return { actions, handlers, queries, router }
}
```

It receives references to the db and the messageStore. Like other Applications, it has queries, actions, HTTP handlers, and an express.Router.

We mount three endpoints total into the router. Let's work through each of these execution paths.

The first is a GET handler at the /log-in path. It's handled by handlers.handleShowLoginForm:

video-tutorials/src/app/authenticate/index.js
```
function handleShowLoginForm (req, res) {
  res.render('authenticate/templates/login-form')
}
```

As you probably figured, it renders the login form. We won't reproduce the Pug template for that form here, because it's just standard HTML, but if you're curious it's in video-tutorials/src/app/authenticate/templates/login-form.pug.

Let's skip down and see how the /log-out route works. When users GET that endpoint, we handle that with handlers.handleLogOut:

video-tutorials/src/app/authenticate/index.js
```
function handleLogOut (req, res) {
  req.session = null
  res.redirect('/')
}
```

It doesn't take many lines to log users out. We just set their session cookie to null and redirect them to the home page. You might be wondering what this session cookie business is. It comes from an npm package we use when setting up the Express app:

video-tutorials/src/app/express/mount-middleware.js
```
const cookieSession = require('cookie-session')
// ...
function mountMiddleware (app, env) {
  const cookieSessionMiddlware = cookieSession({ keys: [env.cookieSecret] })
  app.use(cookieSessionMiddlware)
  // ...
}
```

cookie-session[4] is an Express middleware that, well, manages session cookies. Our cookies get signed so that we can know their values are authentic, and to sign them we need a secret. That secret comes from the environment variables, and those are extracted in code/video-tutorials/src/env.js if you're curious. With env.cookieSecret, we instantiate an instance and store it in cookieSession Middleware.

Next, we mount it as one of the first things in the Express app. This middleware allows you to identify the users calling into our site. We mount it early to know as soon as possible who's making the request.

Back to the authenticate Application, now that you've completed rendering the login form and logging users out, let's log them in. Here is the router declaration for receiving login requests again:

video-tutorials/src/app/authenticate/index.js
```
router
  // ...
  .post(
    bodyParser.urlencoded({ extended: false }),
    handlers.handleAuthenticate
  )
```

Users attempt to log in by POSTing to the /log-in route. After mounting a bodyParser (we first saw bodyParser on page 98), this route calls handlers.handleAuthenticate:

video-tutorials/src/app/authenticate/index.js
```
function handleAuthenticate (req, res, next) {
  const {
    body: { email, password },
    context: { traceId }
  } = req

  return actions
    .authenticate(traceId, email, password)
```

---

4.   https://www.npmjs.com/package/cookie-session

```
②      .then(context => {
         req.session.userId = context.userCredential.id
         res.redirect('/')
       })
③      .catch(AuthenticationError, () =>
         res
           .status(401)
           .render('authenticate/templates/login-form', { errors: true })
       )
④      .catch(next)
}
```

There's a lot going on here, so let's break it down. handlers.handleAuthenticate has four parts:

❶ Extract the submitted email and password from the request body, and pass that into actions.authenticate, which we'll write right after this list.

❷ If that worked, the actions.authenticate call resolves to a context object that will have a userCredential.id property that happens to be the user's id. Stuff that into the session cookie by assigning its value to req.session.userId.

❸ If logging in failed because of an incorrect email or password, re-render the login form to show the errors to the user. We won't tell users which one was wrong because then 4@xors could use the login form to sniff for email addresses.

❹ It might have failed for some other reason, so if it did, we punt.

That first part is where it's interesting, so let's write that action function:

video-tutorials/src/app/authenticate/index.js
```
function authenticate (traceId, email, password) {
  const context = {
    traceId,
    email,
    messageStore,
    password,
    queries
  }

  return Bluebird.resolve(context)
    .then(loadUserCredential)
    .then(ensureUserCredentialFound)
    .then(validatePassword)
    .then(writeLoggedInEvent)
    .catch(NotFoundError, () => handleCredentialNotFound(context))
    .catch(CredentialsMismatchError, () =>
      handleCredentialsMismatch(context)
    )
}
```

It receives the user-supplied email and password and builds a context to flow through a Promise chain. That chain first visits loadUserCredential, which queries for a user credential record matching the email. Here is the code for that:

```
video-tutorials/src/app/authenticate/load-user-credential.js
function loadUserCredential (context) {
  return context.queries
    .byEmail(context.email)
    .then(userCredential => {
      context.userCredential = userCredential

      return context
    })
}

module.exports = loadUserCredential
```

It's a loadX function, and our convention is that a function with a name like this loads something and attaches it to the context. This function is no exception. It uses the Application's queries.byEmail to find a user credential with a matching email address and attaches it at context.userCredential. For this to work, we'll of course need that query function:

```
video-tutorials/src/app/authenticate/index.js
function byEmail (email) {
  return db
    .then(client =>
      client('user_credentials')
        .where({ email })
        .limit(1)
    )
    .then(camelCaseKeys)
    .then(rows => rows[0])
}
```

This query loads from user_credentials a record with a matching email.

After loadUserCredential we need to ensure we found a user credential—can't authenticate a user if the user's record doesn't exist:

```
video-tutorials/src/app/authenticate/ensure-user-credential-found.js
const NotFoundError = require('../errors/not-found-error')
function ensureUserCredentialFound (context) {
  if (!context.userCredential) {
    throw new NotFoundError('no record found with that email')
  }

  return context
}

module.exports = ensureUserCredentialFound
```

If there was no matching user credential record, it throws a NotFoundError, which will propagate back to the action. However, if there was a user credential record, just return context.

Back to the action, the next step is to make sure the password matched. That happens in:

```
const bcrypt = require('bcrypt')

const CredentialMismatchError =
  require('../errors/credential-mismatch-error')
function validatePassword (context) {
  return bcrypt
    .compare(context.password, context.userCredential.passwordHash)
    .then(matched => {
      if (!matched) {
        throw new CredentialMismatchError()
      }

      return context
    })
}

module.exports = validatePassword
```

We use bcrypt again, this time to compare the given password to the one stored in the record. If it didn't match, throw a CredentialMismatchError, which gets handled back up at the action level. If the password matched the stored record's password, then just pass through context unchanged.

The action's last step is to record the login. That happens in writeLoggedInEvent:

```
function writeLoggedInEvent (context) {
  const event = {
    id: uuid(),
    type: 'UserLoggedIn',
    metadata: {
      traceId: context.traceId,
      userId: context.userCredential.id
    },
    data: { userId: context.userCredential.id }
  }
  const streamName = `authentication-${context.userCredential.id}`

  return context.messageStore.write(streamName, event)
    .then(() => context)
}

module.exports = writeLoggedInEvent
```

Similar to the writeX functions you've done so far, here you just build a User-LoggedIn event. You can find the user's id in actionContext.userCredential—loadUserCredential put that in place earlier on page 127. Then construct the stream it goes to, following the decision we made earlier in this chapter, on page 122. Then write the event to the messageStore and pass back context.

If this is the execution path the login request followed, then the action will return back to the handler at this point. We do have two error handlers on this Promise chain, though, and they handle the two errors we might have deliberately thrown while authenticating the user.

The first handles NotFoundErrors, by calling handleCredentialNotFound and passing in context. When you call then on a Promise, the function you give receives whatever the last resolved value in the chain was as its argument. Sadly, catch calls don't work that way. They only pass in the error that was caught. In this case we don't actually care about the error, but we do want the context in our catch handler. Rather than just passing a reference to handleCredentialNotFound—again, like we can with thens—we pass an anonymous function that calls handleCredentialNotFound with the context.

Here is handleCredentialsNotFound:

```
video-tutorials/src/app/authenticate/handle-credential-not-found.js
const AuthenticationError = require('../errors/authentication-error')
function handleCredentialNotFound (context) {
  throw new AuthenticationError()
}

module.exports = handleCredentialNotFound
```

Authentication requests can fail because of using an email address that doesn't exist or from using the wrong password with an otherwise valid email. We don't show users the difference between these because then malicious ones would be able to figure out what emails are in our system and which aren't. So, we take the concept of a missing credential and normalize it to a more generic AuthenticationError suitable for the HTTP layer.

Finally, we also handle CredentialsMismatchErrors by calling handleCredentialsMismatch and passing context to it.

Here is handleCredentialsMismatch:

```
video-tutorials/src/app/authenticate/handle-credential-mismatch.js
const AuthenticationError = require('../errors/authentication-error')
function handleCredentialMismatch (context) {
  const event = {
    id: uuid(),
    type: 'UserLoginFailed',
```

```
    metadata: {
      traceId: context.traceId,
      userId: null
    },
    data: {
      userId: context.userCredential.id,
      reason: 'Incorrect password'
    }
  }
  const streamName = `authentication-${context.userCredential.id}`

  return context.messageStore.write(streamName, event).then(() => {
    throw new AuthenticationError()
  })
}

module.exports = handleCredentialMismatch
```

Again, a very focused function. Its job is to write the UserLoginFailed event and transform the specific error into a generic one for the HTTP layer. Just like with the last error handler, we don't actually know which user (or if it even was a user) typed in the incorrect password, so we set userId to null. reason reflects the password mismatch. This time, however, since we did find a user credential record, we do know which user is affected by this failed login. So we write the event to that user's authentication stream. If you later implement account locks based on some number of incorrect tries, these are the events you'll key off of. Finally, we throw an AuthenticationError.

Wiring the Application to the Rest of the System

As with all of our Applications, we have the two-step dance of wiring it into the system config and then mounting it in Express. First the config:

video-tutorials/src/config.js
```
Line 1  // ...
        const createAuthenticateApp = require('./app/authenticate')
        function createConfig ({ env }) {
          // ...
     5    const authenticateApp = createAuthenticateApp({
            db: knexClient,
            messageStore
          })
          return {
    10        // ...
            authenticateApp,
          }
        }
```

Again, its require the constructor (line 2), instantiate (line 5), and add it to the return value (line 11).

Lastly, we need to mount the authenticate Application in Express:

video-tutorials/src/app/express/mount-routes.js
```
function mountRoutes (app, config) {
  app.use('/', config.homeApp.router)
  app.use('/record-viewing', config.recordViewingsApp.router)
  app.use('/register', config.registerUsersApp.router)
  app.use('/auth', config.authenticateApp.router)
}
```

Just plunk it at /auth off the root, and that's a wrap on authenticating users. If you were to run the server, register a user, and then log in with that user, you could use your browser's development tools to see the session cookie:

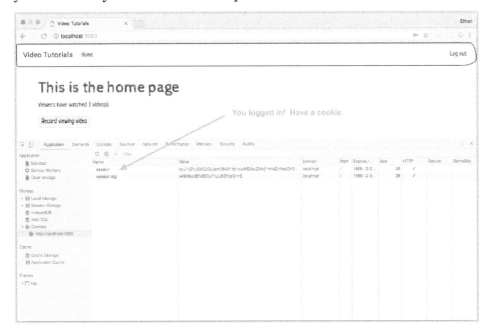

Using Third-Party Authentication

We obviously rolled our own password-based authentication system here, but an increasing trend—and the highly recommended approach in a real-world system—is to use third-party identity management from Facebook, Google, Auth0, or others. How do you think one of those would fit into your system? They end up redirecting users' browsers to our server with special information in the URL. How can you use that, and how does that play into our event strategy?

What different domain event might you use to distinguish between a user registering with an email and password vs. one of these third-party providers? Is that distinction needed? Would you have a different event for logging in with a third-party provider vs. logging in with a username or password?

What You've Done So Far

Good work! User identity is one of the most common and fundamental aspects of any system, and even though you're building this one with a very different architecture than what you're likely used to, that hasn't stopped you from getting users into your system. Hopefully a couple of things stand out here. The first is that there are portions of an asynchronous, event-based system that feel very familiar. Those parts are likely going to all be around reading data. It really isn't any different. The second flows from the first—do you see how the idea of an "auth service" is a bit of a misnomer? Authentication is simple a query against View Data. Repeat the mantra "we don't read data out of Components."

Earlier on page 85 we showed an identity entity model that could support locking accounts. In this chapter you've collected all the data you would need to actually implement that. As an exercise, you might try to do so. What rules govern locking? Number of failed login attempts? Do they have to be within a certain time frame? Who will be able to issue the UnlockAccount command? What Component would handle that? If you put it in the identity Component, it's okay to make a second subscription there. Just be sure to have start call the second one as well.

In any case, now that you can authenticate users, you'll probably want to communicate with them via email. They'll want to know about new videos, and maybe we want to have them confirm their email address as part of registration. Sending email is our very next topic, and we'll see how in an autonomous services architecture adding this additional feature can be 100 percent contained to the Component implementing it.

So get ready to spam the heck outta—err, send relevant and useful email—to your users!

CHAPTER 9

Adding an Email Component

As a kid, I once had a youth leader who said something to the effect, "If you love people, give them paper handouts." I think a very similar rule applies to users of the websites we build. If we love them, we should send them email. Lots of it too. We want to thank them for joining, let them know when their videos have reached certain view milestones, and inform the content creators of all the sweet payouts they're going to receive. Maybe you have a new puppy, and if you do, your users really need to see that. The more the better. And that's exactly what you're going to learn how to do in this chapter.

At this point in the journey you've seen how components in an evented architecture communicate with one another. You've handled commands and events and even built a very simple Component. In this chapter you're going to see some of the payoff of this learning.

I remember when I first started sending email in my MVC days. I was using Ruby on Rails, and Rails provided life-cycle hooks for "model" objects. One of them let you tap into when a row was first saved into the database, and it was a common practice at the time to hook the email sending code into this life cycle. It sort of made sense. Creating a new row in the users database surely meant that a user had just registered? Right?

Well, no, it didn't. Why on earth would we couple writing a row to a database with sending an email? What do these operations have to do with one another? That type of coupling makes change difficult.

In this chapter you'll send registration emails to our users without touching the existing handling of Register events. Now, sorry to disappoint, but you're not going to literally send emails by the end of this chapter, unless you're doing the suggested exercises. Why? We don't want to make this book about configuring Component with an email provider. We're going to use a library

(SPOILER ALERT: nodemailer) that has an option for writing emails to files in your local filesystem. This is useful in test and for not spamming people in development. From the perspective of the architecture that you're learning, nothing will be affected, and when we get to configuring the mailer, you'll know what would need to change to actually send emails.

More importantly, though, you're going to learn how to orchestrate the work of more than one Component. identity doesn't and won't know how to send emails—that's the job of the send-email Component you'll write. You'll make identity get send-email to do something all while communicating over pub/sub and respecting our Component boundaries.

Discovering the Email Component Messages

The email Component will be the only part of the system that knows how to send emails, *and* sending emails is all it will know about. Sending email is a delightfully straightforward process that culminates in one of two possible events—Sent when it worked, and Failed when it didn't. We'll record having sent an email with the following:

```
{
  "id": "c5f672bd-cf5f-4e6b-91ad-60a17cd6bbab",
  "type": "Sent",
  "data": {
    "emailId": "e0c6e804-ae9e-4c9c-bd55-b0c049a03993",
    "to": "lucky-recipient@example.com",
    "subject": "Rare investment opportunity",
    "text": "12 million US pounds stirling",
    "html": "<blink>12 million US pounds stirling</blink>"
  }
}
```

to, from, and subject tell us whom the email is going to, who it's from, and what the subject line is, respectively. Each and every email will get a unique identifier, and we store that in emailId. text and html are the plain text and HTML versions of the email's body, respectively.

And again, when they fail, we get Failed:

```
{
  "id": "636401d3-6585-4887-8576-ec8003e6b380",
  "type": "Failed",
  "data": {
    "emailId": "e0c6e804-ae9e-4c9c-bd55-b0c049a03993",
    "reason": "Could not reach email provider",
    "to": "lucky-recipient@example.com",
    "from": "exiled-prince@example.com",
    "subject": "Rare investment opportunity",
```

```
    "text": "12 million US pounds stirling",
    "html": "<blink>12 million US pounds stirling</blink>"
  }
}
```

Same as Sent, with the addition of a reason property so that we can know why it failed.

Now that we have the events that make up the process, how does one kick it off? By writing a Send command, of course:

```
{
  "id": "636401d3-6585-4887-8576-ec8003e6b380",
  "type": "Send",
  "data": {
    "emailId": "e0c6e804-ae9e-4c9c-bd55-b0c049a03993",
    "to": "lucky-recipient@example.com",
    "subject": "Rare investment opportunity",
    "text": "12 million US pounds stirling",
    "html": "<blink>12 million US pounds stirling</blink>"
  }
}
```

Notice that emailId comes from the command. It's up to the portion of the system wanting to send the email to supply that ID. For idempotence to work, the client of an idempotent component must supply the ID.

As always, we record this message contract in a contract file. We'll name the Component we're building send-email, and put its message definitions in code/video-tutorials/src/components/send-email/contract.md. With the messages necessary for sending emails defined, our plan of attack will be to first implement this send-email Component, and second, we'll teach the identity Component to leverage send-email's capabilities.

Addressing Idempotence

Here's the deal. SMTP[1] is a wonderful protocol when it comes to getting emails from one machine to another. Most of the time it just works. But when it doesn't, well, we really won't be able to tell.

If we have our own SMTP server, we could guarantee that we sent the message, but it could fail to arrive because of the many hops it would have to go through across the internet. If we use a third-party email provider, we can send a request to that provider. That request could fail *after* the provider has already sent the email. So if we tried again, it might get sent twice. So what do we do?

---

1. https://en.wikipedia.org/wiki/Simple_Mail_Transfer_Protocol

This is why you work with your business team.

Which failure case is worse? Not sending an email, or sending it more than once? Is either of those cases correct for every kind of email we send? As developers, we can't make that call on our own. We know the technical details, and we need to communicate the trade-offs to the business team. They know the impact of each case better than we do, and we're unlikely to stumble on the best decisions on our own. And once the team has reached a decision, DOCUMENT IT! You'll notice that this Component's contract file explains the decision we made.

We'll "send" emails by writing their data to the local filesystem. We'll write the email file first and then record an event of sending it. An error might occur between writing that file and recording the RegistrationEmailSent event. If our Component restarts after the file is written but before the event is written, it will attempt to write the file a second time, which effectively sends the email a second time. Our other option is to make a new email protocol, but that is outside the scope of this book. Or left as an exercise to the reader. Take your pick as to why we won't do that here.

In any case, after consulting with our business team, we've concluded that sending our emails more than once is preferable to not sending them at all. Let's start sending some.

Adding the Component

The code for send-email will go in code/video-tutorials/src/components/send-email. Let's begin with the top-level function of send-email:

```
video-tutorials/src/components/send-email/index.js
const createSend = require('./send')
function build ({
  messageStore,
  systemSenderEmailAddress,
  transport
}) {
  const justSendIt = createSend({ transport })
  const handlers = createHandlers({
    messageStore,
    justSendIt,
    systemSenderEmailAddress
  })
  const subscription = messageStore.createSubscription({
    streamName: 'sendEmail:command',
    handlers,
    subscriberId: 'components:send-email'
  })
```

```
function start () {
  subscription.start()
}

return {
  handlers,
  start
}
}
```

Like all message handlers in autonomous components, this function's job is to set up handlers and a subscription to use those handlers. This function receives the following dependencies:

Dependency	Purpose
messageStore	A reference to the Message Store
systemSendEmailAddress	The "from" address the system uses for emails it sends
transport	An object that encapsulates a specific means of sending messages in nodemailer

Briefly Introducing nodemailer

We discussed earlier that we'd use a library called nodemailer,[a] but the truth is that it's more of a suite of libraries. If you use it, you'll always use the nodemailer core package which manages the process of sending emails. But you also create different "transports" which handle the particulars of sending emails with whatever provider you use.

Out of the box, nodemailer ships with transports that work with the sendmail unix command, AWS's SES service, and a transport that just puts the messages in memory. Beyond these transports there are plugins for almost every email-sending product under the sun, including SendGrid, Mailgun, and even a transport for using a Gmail account.

We're going to use nodemailer-pickup-transport.[b] This has nothing to do with small trucks. Rather, it has to do with writing emails to files in the filesystem. There are email-sending programs that could run independently and "pick up" these files to actually send messages over the wire. But we're going to use it so that when we send, we get an artifact in our filesystem that we can inspect for testing purposes.

---

a.   https://nodemailer.com/about/
b.   https://www.npmjs.com/package/nopl8;demailer-pickup-transport

In order to set up the handlers, we need one additional piece—the thing that will actually *send* emails for us. We instantiate it with the mystery createSend function that we'll write as soon as we're done with the top-level function here, but it does need to know what transport we're using. We pass its result, the enticingly named justSendIt, along with a reference to the messageStore and the systemSenderEmailAddress to make the handlers.

Those handlers then are used to make a subscription. Since the contract.md for this Component says that Send commands are written to the sendEmail:command category, that's the category we subscribe to.

The function finishes with a start function like we have in all our autonomous components.

We required createSend at the top of the file and used it in the top-level function. Let's write it now:

```
video-tutorials/src/components/send-email/send.js
const nodemailer = require('nodemailer')

const SendError = require('./send-error')

function createSend ({ transport }) {
  const sender = nodemailer.createTransport(transport)
  return function send (email) {
    const potentialError = new SendError()

    return sender.sendMail(email)
      .catch(err => {
        potentialError.message = err.message
        throw potentialError
      })
  }
}

module.exports = createSend
```

This file exports a single function at line 5. It receives the transport object we just talked about and uses it to build a nodemailer instance that we name sender. At line 7 it then returns a function called send that will send emails using this instance.

send takes an object named email that should have keys from, to, subject, text, and html. These correspond to the event properties you defined earlier in this chapter on page 134. send calls sender.sendMail, passing it that email at line 10 and doing any necessary error handling.

> **Joe asks:**
> ## What Is This potentialError Business?
>
> Why would any right-thinking person instantiate an error before we know that one has occurred? Due to the way Node.js works, if we do get an error when trying to send this email, when we get to the catch() handler, we won't have the actual stack trace of where the error occurred. By instantiating an error at line 8, we capture a stack trace that points to this function. Then if there is an error, we just copy over its message. Knowing what function led to the error being thrown will be very useful for debugging.

Sending the Email

With the infrastructure bits in place, we can move onto actually sending the email. Let's write the handler for the Send command:

```
video-tutorials/src/components/send-email/index.js
function createHandlers ({
  justSendIt,
  messageStore,
  systemSenderEmailAddress
}) {
  return {
    Send: command => {
      const context = {
        messageStore,
        justSendIt,
        systemSenderEmailAddress,
        sendCommand: command
      }

      return Bluebird.resolve(context)
        .then(loadEmail)
        .then(ensureEmailHasNotBeenSent)
        .then(sendEmail)
        .then(writeSentEvent)
        // If it's already sent, then we do a no-op
        .catch(AlreadySentError, () => {})
        .catch(
          SendError,
          err => writeFailedEvent(context, err)
        )
    }
  }
}
```

It uses a Promise chain to build a pipeline of functions that sends email. The first step is to build the context for the pipeline. That context contains:

messageStore

> The reference to the Message Store

justSendIt

> The function we wrote to wrap the actuation of nodemailer

systemSenderEmailAddress

> The "from" address for our system emails

sendCommand

> The Send command that we're handling

The first step is to project the email's stream to make sure we haven't already sent it:

```
video-tutorials/src/components/send-email/load-email.js
const emailProjection = {
  $init () { return { isSent: false } },
  Sent (email, sent) {
    email.isSent = true

    return email
  }
}
function loadEmail (context) {
  const messageStore = context.messageStore
  const sendCommand = context.sendCommand
  const streamName = `sendEmail-${sendCommand.data.emailId}`

  return messageStore
    .fetch(streamName, emailProjection)
    .then(email => {
      context.email = email

      return context
    })
}

module.exports = loadEmail
```

loadEmail starts by pulling the messageStore and the sendCommand it uses out of context, using that command to build the streamName where an existing email's state would be found if there is any. Then it fetches the email entity from the messageStore, using the projection defined at line 1. This entity has two states, sent and unsent, represented by isSent being true or false, respectively. If we haven't applied any messages, then it hasn't been sent, so $init sets isSent to false. If we see a Sent event, then we set isSent to true. We attach the entity to the context and return it.

The next step is where we check if we've already sent the email, defined here:

```
video-tutorials/src/components/send-email/ensure-email-has-not-been-sent.js
const AlreadySentError = require('./already-sent-error')
function ensureEmailHasNotBeenSent (context) {
  if (context.email.isSent) {
    throw new AlreadySentError()
  }

  return context
}

module.exports = ensureEmailHasNotBeenSent
```

It's just a quick check to see if the isSent property on the registrationEmail entity is true. If it is, we throw an AlreadySentError to signal that and break the Promise chain, otherwise we continue right along.

Now that we know we haven't already sent the email, we're just gonna send it:

```
video-tutorials/src/components/send-email/send-email.js
Line 1  function sendEmail (context) {
          const justSendIt = context.justSendIt
          const sendCommand = context.sendCommand
          const systemSenderEmailAddress = context.systemSenderEmailAddress

    5
          const email = {
            from: systemSenderEmailAddress,
            to: sendCommand.data.to,
            subject: sendCommand.data.subject,
   10       text: sendCommand.data.text,
            html: sendCommand.data.html
          }

          return justSendIt(email)
   15       .then(() => context)
        }

        module.exports = sendEmail
```

Remember the justSendIt function we set up in this Component's top-level function on page 136? We grab it out of context along with the sendCommand that we're handling and the systemSenderEmailAddress, which is the address all our emails will be sent from. At line 6 we assemble the email object that justSendIt expects. It's composed of the systemSenderEmailAddress and the data from sendCommand. We then invoke justSendIt with that email object, returning the context when we're done sending it. It's gonna be a good day.

The next step is to record that we've "sent" the registration email:

```
video-tutorials/src/components/send-email/write-sent-event.js
function writeSentEvent (context) {
  const sendCommand = context.sendCommand
  const streamName = `sendEmail-${sendCommand.data.emailId}`
  const event = {
    id: uuid(),
    type: 'Sent',
    metadata: {
      originStreamName: sendCommand.metadata.originStreamName,
      traceId: sendCommand.metadata.traceId,
      userId: sendCommand.metadata.userId
    },
    data: sendCommand.data
  }

  return context.messageStore.write(streamName, event)
    .then(() => context)
}

module.exports = writeSentEvent
```

This function builds a Sent event. We discovered the need for this event on page 134. We do some interesting metadata work here. We do the standard chaining of traceId and userId found in the message we're handling. But notice this originStreamName property. What is that all about?

Well, send-email is a general-purpose Component in our system. We'll modify the identity Component to use send-email to send registration emails when users register later in this chapter, but we could easily imagine other uses for sending email in a system like Video Tutorials. As you'll see on page 148, identity will subscribe to send-email's sendEmail streams, and it will need a way to know which events in those streams occurred because of registration. It doesn't care about emails sent for other reasons.

That's the purpose of originStreamName. Any component issuing a Send command adds a reference to one of its own streams in this property. For example, if identity were processing a registration for user 88513bc7-f472-4494-9764-c845cc62bea5, that user's registration events would live in identity-88513bc7-f472-4494-9764-c845cc62bea5. When identity writes the Send command to a sendEmail:command stream, it will set the originStreamName on that command's metadata to identity-88513bc7-f472-4494-9764-c845cc62bea5. Our job in send-email is to propagate that originStreamName property into the metadata of any events resulting from that command. Since we're coding that happy path right now, that means we put it into this Sent event.

With the event assembled, we then write it to the email's stream. In the future, if we ever reprocess the registration event, writing another Send command with the same emailId, this Sent event is what will tell us that the email is already out and that we shouldn't send it again.

That concludes the happy path. Let's revisit the Registered handler's Promise chain to deal with our errors:

video-tutorials/src/components/send-email/index.js
```
return Bluebird.resolve(context)
  .then(loadEmail)
  .then(ensureEmailHasNotBeenSent)
  .then(sendEmail)
  .then(writeSentEvent)
  // If it's already sent, then we do a no-op
➤  .catch(AlreadySentError, () => {})
➤  .catch(
    SendError,
    err => writeFailedEvent(context, err)
  )
```

The first thing we catch is the AlreadySentError. This handles the case where the registration email was already sent. This isn't an *error* per se, but we threw it to use the mechanics of Promises and JavaScript to break out of our pipeline, perform a no-op, and move on. However, if the actual act of sending the email caused an error, that will come to our pipeline as a SendError. In this case we want to record that sending the email failed, and we do so here:

video-tutorials/src/components/send-email/write-failed-event.js
```
function writeFailedEvent (context, err) {
  const sendCommand = context.sendCommand
  const streamName = `sendEmail-${sendCommand.data.emailId}`
  const event = {
    id: uuid(),
    type: 'Failed',
    metadata: {
      originStreamName: sendCommand.metadata.originStreamName,
      traceId: sendCommand.metadata.traceId,
      userId: sendCommand.metadata.userId
    },
    data: {
      ...sendCommand.data,
      reason: err.message
    }
  }

  return context.messageStore.write(streamName, event)
    .then(() => context)
}

module.exports = writeFailedEvent
```

This looks just like recording that it succeeded, except that we build a Failed event instead of a Sent event. Notice that we chain through the originStreamName. We also pass in the error's message property as the reason so that we have a record of what went wrong. Then we write the event to the email's stream. With failure events recorded, we could build admin tooling that would let us try to send it again. Or perhaps we could add a handler for this message type to implement an automatic retry (hint, hint).

Running the Component

Now that it's written, let's get this puppy actually running. Whenever we add a new component to the system, we head to config.js. We have a little bit more to do this time, since in addition to configuring the send-email Component, we also need to configure the node-mailer transport:

video-tutorials/src/config.js
```
Line 1   // ...
         const createPickupTransport = require('nodemailer-pickup-transport')
         const createSendEmailComponent = require('./components/send-email')
         function createConfig ({ env }) {
     5     // ...
           const transport = createPickupTransport({ directory: env.emailDirectory })
           const sendEmailComponent = createSendEmailComponent({
             messageStore,
             systemSenderEmailAddress: env.systemSenderEmailAddress,
    10       transport
           })
           const components = [
             // ...
             sendEmailComponent,
    15     ]
           return {
             // ...
             sendEmailComponent,
           }
    20   }

         module.exports = createConfig
```

Can't configure something if you don't first require it, so at line 2 we require the nodemailer-pickup-transport. Then at line 3 we require the Component.

Onto instantiation then, we first instantiate the transport at line 6. The pickup transport needs to know which directory to write the .eml files to. This directory is relative to the project root, and we pull it in through the environment. Line 7 then instantiates the Component, giving it the messageStore, systemSender EmailAddress, and the transport we just configured. Like the env.emailDirectory that the transport uses, env.systemSenderEmailAddress also comes from the environment. We'll add those to env.js right after we finish with the configuration.

This is a Component, so we need to add it to the components array at line 14. And then we add it to the return value at line 18.

Let's get those environment variables set up now:

```
video-tutorials/src/env.js
module.exports = {
  appName: requireFromEnv('APP_NAME'),
  cookieSecret: requireFromEnv('COOKIE_SECRET'),
  databaseUrl: requireFromEnv('DATABASE_URL'),
  env: requireFromEnv('NODE_ENV'),
  port: parseInt(requireFromEnv('PORT'), 10),
➤ emailDirectory: requireFromEnv('EMAIL_DIRECTORY'),
➤ systemSenderEmailAddress: requireFromEnv('SYSTEM_SENDER_EMAIL_ADDRESS'),
  version: packageJson.version,
  // ...
  messageStoreConnectionString:
    requireFromEnv('MESSAGE_STORE_CONNECTION_STRING')
}
```

Notice EMAIL_DIRECTORY and SYSTEM_SENDER_EMAIL_ADDRESS. These will end up on our environment object as emailDirectory and systemSenderEmailAddress, respectively. You'll want to add them to .env.development and .env.test as well.

Boom. If you happen to be holding a microphone right now, feel free to drop it.

Assuming you've pulled down the code and installed the dependencies with npm install, you can run the project with npm run start-dev-server. Navigate to localhost:3000 in a browser and click through to register. You'll then see a .eml file for that registration in video-tutorials/tmp/email/development, assuming you haven't changed the email directory location.

Adding Email to the Registration Process

Next, we'll teach the identity Component to send a welcome email when users register. Back on page 114 you wrote Registered events in the identity Component. We'll use those events as the trigger to send a registration email. Yes, when we're done, identity will respond to its own messages. There is absolutely nothing wrong with that.

We also need to introduce a new event owned by the identity Component. Since we're going to send emails in response to messages, we'll need a way to project an identity and know if the email has already been sent. To that end, we introduce the RegistrationEmailSent event:

```
{
  "id": "2ea97206-10a4-46ac-aa4a-ba48e0cdd450",
  "type": "RegistrationEmailSent",
  "data": {
    "userId": "e0c6e804-ae9e-4c9c-bd55-b0c049a03993",
    "emailId": "e31ecf6f-8eb2-4b75-aafb-dd715d4b2f3d"
  }
}
```

It records the userId of the identity and the emailId of the email that was sent. We don't need any additional information to know that the user's registration email has gone out.

The basic flow will be as follows:

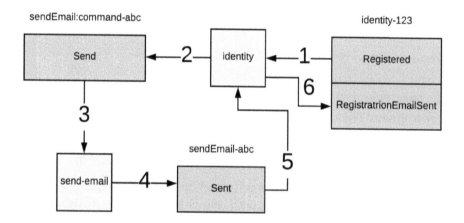

1. identity observes its own Registered event.

2. identity handles that Registered event by writing a Send command to a sendEmail:command command stream.

3. send-email observes the Send command.

4. send-email handles that Send command by sending the email and writing a Sent event a corresponding sendEmail event stream.

5. identity observes the Sent event.

6. identity handles the Sent event by writing a RegisteredEmailSent event to the original identity stream.

Let's make the changes that will get these emails sent. We'll start by writing a handler in identity to handle identity's own Registered events:

video-tutorials/src/components/identity/index.js

```
function createIdentityEventHandlers ({ messageStore }) {
  return {
    Registered: event => {
      const context = {
        messageStore: messageStore,
        event,
        identityId: event.data.userId
      }

      return Bluebird.resolve(context)
        .then(loadIdentity)
        .then(ensureRegistrationEmailNotSent)
        .then(renderRegistrationEmail)
        .then(writeSendCommand)
        .catch(AlreadySentRegistrationEmailError, () => {})
    }
  }
}
```

Standard fare. Build a context with the messageStore, event we're handling, and the identityId in question. That feeds into a Promise chain that starts with the loadIdentity function you wrote on page 112 and that will attach the identity in question to the context. Next, we do our idempotence check:

video-tutorials/src/components/identity/ensure-registration-email-not-sent.js

```
const AlreadySentRegistrationEmailError =
  require('./already-sent-registration-email-error')
function ensureRegistrationEmailNotSent (context) {
  if (context.identity.registrationEmailSent) {
    throw new AlreadySentRegistrationEmailError()
  }

  return context
}
```

We check the registrationEmailSent property on the loaded identity and throw an AlreadySentRegistrationError if it's truthy. Of course, for that property to ever be set, we have to add it to the projection in loadIdentity:

video-tutorials/src/components/identity/load-identity.js

```
const identityProjection = {
  $init () {
    return {
      id: null,
      email: null,
      isRegistered: false,
      registrationEmailSent: false
    }
  },
  // ...
```

```
➤    RegistrationEmailSent (identity) {
➤      identity.registrationEmailSent = true
➤
➤      return identity
➤    }
```

If we encounter a RegistrationEmailSent message, then we set registrationEmailSent to true.

If it wasn't sent though, then we'll write a Send command:

video-tutorials/src/components/identity/write-send-command.js
```
❶  const uuidv4 = require('uuid/v4')
   const uuidv5 = require('uuid/v5')

❷  const uuidv5Namespace = '0c46e0b7-dfaf-443a-b150-053b67905cc2'
❸  function writeSendCommand (context, err) {
     const event = context.event
     const identity = context.identity
     const email = context.email

     const emailId = uuidv5(identity.email, uuidv5Namespace)
❹    const sendEmailCommand = {
       id: uuidv4(),
       type: 'Send',
       metadata: {
         originStreamName: `identity-${identity.id}`,
         traceId: event.metadata.traceId,
         userId: event.metadata.userId
       },
       data: {
         emailId,
         to: identity.email,
         subject: email.subject,
         text: email.text,
         html: email.html
       }
     }
❺    const streamName = `sendEmail:command-${emailId}`

     return context.messageStore
       .write(streamName, sendEmailCommand)
       .then(() => context)
   }

   module.exports = writeSendCommand
```

❶ First off, we require functions to generate both v4 and v5 UUIDs. Version 5 UUIDs generate a UUID by hashing a piece of known data. This lets us get a predictable UUID given, say, an email address.

❷ UUID v5s also require a namespace string, which we hardcode into uuidv5Namespace.

❸ Next, we start writeSendCommand, pulling out of the context the bits that we need. We then generate an emailId by turning identity.email into a UUID.

❹ Next, we build a command like any other command we've built with the exception of the originStreamName. Earlier in this chapter on page 142 you chained that bit of metadata through the send-email Component's handlers. Here is where the originStreamName, um, originates.

In just a bit we're going to write handlers in the identity Component that subscribe to send-email's events. Because other components may also make use of send-email, any client component needs to be able to tell which emails it caused to be sent and which were caused by other components. The originStreamName is that mechanism. We set that value to the same stream that this identity's events go in.

❺ We then build a streamName for the Send command and finally write it to the Message Store.

This will of course require a subscription in the top-level function:

```
video-tutorials/src/components/identity/index.js
function build ({ messageStore }) {
  // ...
  const identityEventHandlers = createIdentityEventHandlers({ messageStore })
  const identityEventSubscription = messageStore.createSubscription({
    streamName: 'identity',
    handlers: identityEventHandlers,
    subscriberId: 'components:identity'
  })
  return {
    identityCommandHandlers,
    identityEventHandlers,
    start
  }
}
```

Instantiate the handlers and pass them to the subscription.

Recording Registration Emails

With the identityEventSubscription running, we're sending Send commands to send-email. It will send those emails and record events when it does so. We just need to observe those Sent events and make a record of it in the corresponding identity stream so that identity can know that the email was sent and that it doesn't have to worry about it anymore.

To that end, let's write handlers to handle those Sent events:

video-tutorials/src/components/identity/index.js

```
Line 1  function createSendEmailEventHandlers ({ messageStore }) {
          return {
            Sent: event => {
              const originStreamName = event.metadata.originStreamName
    5        const identityId = streamNameToId(originStreamName)

              const context = {
                messageStore,
                event,
    10          identityId
              }

              return Bluebird.resolve(context)
                .then(loadIdentity)
    15          .then(ensureRegistrationEmailNotSent)
                .then(writeRegistrationEmailSentEvent)
                .catch(AlreadySentRegistrationEmailError, () => {})
            }
          }
    20  }
```

First off, at line 4 we get the originStreamName out of the event's metadata, and use it to extract the identityId of the identity we're working on. With that, we build a context and start a Bluebird pipeline. The first two steps are loadIdentity and ensureRegistrationEmailNotSent, which we've used before, most recently on page 145, so no need to rehash those.

writeRegistrationEmailSentEvent continues the chain:

video-tutorials/src/components/identity/write-registration-email-sent-event.js

```
function writeRegistrationEmailSentEvent (context, err) {
  const event = context.event

  const registrationEmailSentEvent = {
    id: uuid(),
    type: 'RegistrationEmailSent',
    metadata: {
      traceId: event.metadata.traceId,
      userId: event.metadata.userId
    },
    data: {
      userId: context.identityId,
      emailId: event.data.emailId
    }
  }
```

```
    const identityStreamName = event.metadata.originStreamName

  return context.messageStore
    .write(identityStreamName, registrationEmailSentEvent)
    .then(() => context)
}

module.exports = writeRegistrationEmailSentEvent
```

It builds the corresponding event and writes it to the stream name contained in event.metadata.originStreamName.

At the very end of the pipeline we have a catch for AlreadySentRegistrationEmailErrors, so that we can no-op if the work has already been done.

Next, we just need to set up the subscription for this handler:

video-tutorials/src/components/identity/index.js
```
function build ({ messageStore }) {
  // ...
  const sendEmailEventHandlers = createSendEmailEventHandlers({ messageStore })
  const sendEmailEventSubscription = messageStore.createSubscription({
    streamName: 'sendEmail',
    handlers: sendEmailEventHandlers,
    originStreamName: 'identity',
    subscriberId: 'components:identity:sendEmailEvents'
  })
  return {
    identityCommandHandlers,
    identityEventHandlers,
    sendEmailEventHandlers,
    start
  }
}
```

This subscription adds a new parameter, namely originStreamName. This may be a shocker, but this parameter tells the subscription to only send messages to the supplied handlers if the category of the metadata.originStreamName on the messages matches the supplied originStreamName. Of course, this doesn't actually exist in our Message Store code yet, so we'll need to add it.

Making the Message Store Aware of Origin Streams

In code/video-tutorials/src/message-store/subscribe.js we wrote getNextBatchOfMessages which retrieves the batches of messages in the category we're subscribing to. For subscriptions that have an originStreamName, we'll further filter that query result based on whether or not the messages have that originStreamName in their metadata.

First the filtering function:

```
video-tutorials/src/message-store/subscribe.js
const category = require('./category')
function configureCreateSubscription ({ read, readLastMessage, write }) {
  // ...
    function filterOnOriginMatch (messages) {
      if (!originStreamName) {
        return messages
      }

      return messages.filter(message => {
        const originCategory =
          message.metadata && category(message.metadata.originStreamName)

        return originStreamName === originCategory
      })
    }
}
```

On line 4 we start the function filterOnOriginMatch. It sits inside the main closure in this file because it needs access to the originStreamName parameter used when setting up a subscription. It receives the list of messages to filter.

On line 5, if the subscription has no originStreamName, then there's no filtering to do, and we just return the array of messages as is. If there was an originStream-Name, then we call messages.filter[2]. filter receives a function that will get called for each message in messages, returning a new array containing only those messages that evaluate to truthy when passed through this second function.

How do we actually filter? Well, at this point in filterOnOriginMatch, we know that the subscriber is interested in a particular originStreamName, otherwise we would have already bailed. On line 10 we therefore get originCategory from each message.metadata by first checking to see if the message has metadata, and then running message.metadata.originStreamName through a function named category which extracts the category from a given stream name. We then return whether or not the supplied originStreamName matches the originCategory we got from the message on line 13. The category function is just a few lines:

```
video-tutorials/src/message-store/category.js
function category (streamName) {
  // Double equals to catch null and undefined
  if (streamName == null) {
    return ''
  }
```

---

2. https://developer.mozilla.org/en-US/docs/Web/JavaScript/Reference/Global_Objects/Array/filter

```
    return streamName.split('-')[0]
}
module.exports = category
```

First, if there is no streamName, then there is no category, so we just return the empty string. However, if there is a streamName, we split it on - and take the first segment. That is the definition of what a category is.

With this filtering in place, the Message Store tick function will now have only messages that match the originStreamName we care about, and our component handlers that so specify will be guaranteed to receive only messages they caused to happen. And that also concludes our work to get registration emails to our users.

Revisiting Idempotence

Hooray for sending emails! Before closing, let's call out our idempotence choice. This Component interacts with a third-party system that isn't under our control (the email provider), so now you can build Components that interact with other third-party systems. This is one of the trickier parts of microComponent architectures (indeed, any architecture) because it involves state outside of our control. There is no way to guarantee that our system will agree with an external system about the state of the world, but by recording each step of our interaction with these external systems, we have a better shot at debugging when things go wrong.

When recording those interactions, failure can occur at any point along the chain. With our registration emails, we could "send" the email and crash before recording that we sent it. Upon restart, we'd try to send it again. We consulted with our business team to decide that sending it more than once is better than not sending it at all.

In other cases, that would be a terrible plan. Imagine if we were charging customer credit cards, for example. In that case, we'd want to write that we're attempting to charge the card *before* charging it, so that we'd never attempt to charge it twice. Handling it not being charged at all we could handle with admin tooling or manual intervention. Is that ideal? No. It sure beats the heck out of double charges, though. We would be scoundrels to put our users through that, and our payment provider would likely also drop us. Lose, lose.

Orchestrating Components vs. Choreographing Components

Now, in this chapter you made changes to identity so that it could leverage the functionality of the send-email Component by explicitly writing a command. The explicit control of the process is called *orchestration*. You may have come across the terms *process manager* and *saga*. These are both flavors of orchestrating Components, and what you built here is an example of "process manager."

Orchestration is in contrast to a technique called *choreography*. Imagine that instead of identity writing an explicit command to send-email that send-email had observed the Registered event and just known to send the registration email. That is like a group of dancers who each know their part to play without any specific direction from a coordinating actor.

We'll favor orchestration because it makes processes more explicit. For example, we can look in one place and know that as part of registration an email is supposed to go out. Had we choreographed this interaction, we'd have to look into multiple Components to see the complete registration process.

What You've Done So Far

Whew! You just added a Component that, um, actually does something. This is great! In the process, you also got experience working with the business team when considering idempotence trade-offs.

You've also made it so a Component can take advantage of the capabilities offered by another Component. One of the main points of this architecture is to be able to compose functionality from a collection of components, something you did in making identity leverage send-email to get registration emails out to users. Check out Eventide's documentation for additional insight into how this worked.[3]

But why stop here? You saw how nodemailer works. Could you configure it with a transport that would actually send an email? SendGrid is a fine option for that, and they wrote documentation on how to use nodemailer with their product.[4] There's also a Mailgun transport,[5] if that's your style. And if you prefer something else, there's probably a transport for it. Keep in mind that other

---

3. http://docs.eventide-project.org/user-guide/messages-and-message-data/metadata.html
4. https://sendgrid.com/blog/sending-email-nodemailer-sendgrid/
5. https://github.com/orliesaurus/nodemailer-mailgun-transport

transports will need other configuration information, so you'll need to get those settings into the Component or to wherever you set up the transport.

Now, remember how if the registration email *fails* to send, we just yawn and move on? Could you build some retries into the system? As a hint, you might consider adding a handler for RegistrationEmailFailed events. You'd probably want to limit the number of send attempts, so you'd need to know how many attempts were made. Can you add the number of failures to the projection in code/video-tutorials/src/components/send-email/load-registration-email.js? I bet you can.

Next up, you may be familiar with the concept of background jobs in web apps. There are certain things you don't want to do during an HTTP request/response cycle because they take too long. So you receive the information about what needs to be done and pass it off to some worker queue. How do we do something similar now that we're dealing with Components? Stay tuned for the next chapter, where you'll tackle this exact problem in the context of transcoding your users' videos.

Wrong models cause massive accidental complexity.

> Greg Young

CHAPTER 10

Performing Background Jobs
with Microservices

Have you ever ordered food over the telephone? Maybe you called a pizza delivery place that didn't yet have online ordering? Did it go something like this?

You phoned the location, maybe asking what they had on special. You ended up making a selection and getting an idea of when it would be delivered. Then you stayed on the phone, tying up the line so that no one else could call in until your pizza was delivered and ready to go into your belly.

Oh wait, that doesn't sound familiar? Well, good. Just like with this pizza-delivery scenario, there are certain things web applications do that have no business being completed during a request/response cycle. They would make that cycle take too long and degrade user experience. You've seen one example of that so far with sending registration emails. That likely is going to connect to a third-party API to actually send the message, and there's about one thing you can safely rely on when it comes to networks—they *will* fail from time to time. They are subject to the physical world. If you haven't accounted for that in your system, these external failures will become internal failures.

In this chapter we're going to look at how long-running processes are modeled in an autonomous, microservices-based system. SPOILER ALERT: We already have all the tools we need. By the end of this chapter, we'll build a video publishing Component that does post-processing on videos that users upload. This post-processing will take time to complete and kick off status updates as it goes along. In the process, we'll see a rather interesting idempotence trade-off, on page 170, where sometimes it's okay to accept duplicate work.

Accidental Complexity

If you've moved operations out of the request/response cycle before, you're likely familiar with terms like "delayed jobs," "background jobs," or "queues." There are libraries in various programming languages to make working with these concepts fairly straightforward.

If you take anything from this book, I hope it is a curiosity to move beyond specific tools and implementations into the ideas behind them. That includes Video Tutorials. There's a world of autonomous microservices that's far bigger than this book. So let's pose a question: what exactly is a background job? Well, a background job simply does some computing work in an asynchronous manner. It probably reports status along the way. It may or may not require setting up a new piece of infrastructure. DelayedJob[1] in the Ruby world just uses your database to track jobs, whereas node-resque[2] requires Redis or Sidekiq.

Hmmm...asynchronous work that reports status along the way. Does that sound awfully familiar?

Greg Young once asked, "What is a queue but a degenerate form of a stream?" Said another way, what does a queue offer that a stream does not? Streams are already the fundamental building block of the work we're doing.

Let's pretend that the RantAboutQueuesDelivered event didn't get written, and so the projection that would have prevented it appearing a second time didn't prevent it because this point is worth making over and over. Doing so-called "background jobs" requires *no additional setup* because background jobs are just a degenerate form of managing asynchronous work. Because we've chosen the right model for microservices, we're not left with the accidental complexity Greg Young warns against.[3] We don't have to set up a one-off worker queue system. This type of work just uses the primitive constructs an asynchronous, message-based system already provides.

You're going to see this in the context of sending emails and publishing videos, which will involve transcoding those videos. We've already covered the use case for sending emails. As for publishing videos, a Video Tutorials site sans videos is, um, well, we're not marketing experts, but if we're to trust our business team, they're telling us this is a rather important feature of the site.

---

1. https://github.com/collectiveidea/delayed_job
2. https://github.com/taskrabbit/node-resque
3. https://www.youtube.com/watch?v=hv2dKtPq0ME&t=1064

We need to allow content creators to upload their content. Once they've uploaded videos, we need to transcode them into formats suitable for streaming. Depending on the size of these videos, a transcoding job might take seconds to minutes. While that is considerably less time than it takes to get a pizza delivered, our tolerance for leaving an HTTP connection open is also considerably less. Let's tuck in.

"I Heard I Need to Use Kafka or RabbitMQ to Do Background Jobs. Do I?"

No.

"Okay, Seriously, Don't I Need to Use Kafka or RabbitMQ to Do Background Jobs?"

Seriously, no. Yes, this is getting repeated ad nauseam, but you've already built every construct you need to perform long-running processes outside of the request/response cycle. If you're still in doubt, just roll with it for the rest of this chapter.

Use Case #1: Sending Emails

Okay, this is a petty move on your humble author's part, but you've already moved sending emails out of the request/response cycle in Chapter 9, Adding an Email Component, on page 133. There isn't anything to add. But if you are one of the doubters, go back and read through that chapter to see how the Message Store has already provided everything you needed.

Use Case #2: Transcoding Videos

As we said earlier, content creators will upload videos, and then we'll transcode them into various formats that play nicely with our users' devices and internet connections. As always, before starting to build features, let's discover the messages we need.

The publishing flow will be something like:

The Creators Portal will have UI to simulate uploading videos directly to Amazon's S3 offering. Once the "upload" is complete, the UI will instruct the server to publish the video. This suggests a PublishVideo command that communicates who owns the video and where to find its source file. We'll only allow authenticated users to do this so that we don't end up being the world's Dropbox substitute.

> ## Joe asks:
> # Why Are We Only Simulating Uploads?
>
> That's a fair question. It's to avoid getting lost dealing with a complicated JavaScript client and the intricacies of configuring an AWS account to handle uploads. We need to stay focused on microservices, and simulating the upload to S3 won't change anything about the microservices aspect of our project. You'll see exactly where you'd need to change things to properly interact with S3.
>
> We'll do something similar with the transcoding process itself, but the flow through the microservices won't be changed. You would be able to swap in a Component that actually does transcode videos without changing any of the rest of the flow.
>
> In fact, once you see the whole flow, wouldn't that be a great exercise...

Here is an example PublishVideo command:

```
{
  "id": "f72ee7ab-066f-403c-b4b6-5f233fd34c81",
  "type": "PublishVideo",
  "data": {
    "ownerId": "bb6a04b0-cb74-4981-b73d-24b844ca334f",
    "sourceUri": "https://sourceurl.com/",
    "videoId": "9bfb5f98-36f4-44a2-8251-ab06e0d6d919"
  }
}
```

This command makes the distinction between the user issuing it, userId, and the owner of the video, ownerId. We may have an admin screen where admins need to move a video along the publishing flow. sourceUri tracks where the uploaded video file lives, and id is the video's identifier.

You may have noticed that this command transmits no name or description of the video. We'll handle naming videos in the next chapter, Chapter 11, Building Async-Aware User Interfaces, on page 173.

Something will observe that command, and said something will publish the video by transcoding it and then writing a VideoPublished event. Again we see a command/event pair where the command's type is the imperative form of the event's past-tense type. Here is an example VideoPublished event:

```
{
  "id": "d260b63a-8195-4488-b5e4-8884ac792c61",
  "type": "VideoPublished",
  "data": {
    "ownerId": "bb6a04b0-cb74-4981-b73d-24b844ca334f",
    "sourceUri": "https://sourceurl.com/",
    "transcodedUri": "https://someswankyurl.com/"
    "videoId": "9bfb5f98-36f4-44a2-8251-ab06e0d6d919"
  }
}
```

It copies the id, ownerId, and sourceUri from the command. It also adds the transcodedUri, letting us know where the transcoded file was stored. Writing this event is when the video becomes officially "published."

The last event we need to consider is when publishing fails. Our system runs on hardware that exists in the physical world, and things can happen and frequently do there. This gives us the VideoPublishingFailed event, and here is an example:

```
{
  "id": "3ed7c799-7a74-4e98-9759-013ef031ac10",
  "type": "VideoPublishingFailed",
  "data": {
    "reason": "Invalid format",
    "ownerId": "bb6a04b0-cb74-4981-b73d-24b844ca334f",
    "sourceUri": "https://sourceurl.com/",
    "videoId": "9bfb5f98-36f4-44a2-8251-ab06e0d6d919"
  }
}
```

This event copies over the same data from the command as the success event, adding reason why publishing failed. It's unlikely that we'd surface that reason word-for-word to our users, but it does provide debugging information. If you started seeing the same reason over and over again, you'd know where to first direct work to make the publishing process more robust.

Now, there are rumors that the business team is going to require multiple transcoding formats, so we'll want to make sure that whatever we choose now doesn't make adapting to that requirement difficult.

To transcode into multiple formats we could instead choose to make our transcodedUri property an array or we could write one of these events for each target format. Our events are supposed to represent what happens in our domain, and from that perspective using separate events for each target format makes more sense. We don't have to worry about supporting multiple targets right now, but we've chosen an event structure that will adapt to it well when and if the requirement hits.

In any case, these messages all logically fit together, and we'll write a video-publishing Component to own them and perform the work of publishing our creators' videos. You can see the full write-up of the messages and process in video-tutorials/src/components/video-publishing/contract.md.

Describing the Creators Portal

The Creators Portal is an Application that writes commands to the Message Store. We're not going to build it here because, uh, let's say our development efforts are going so well and we're showing so much value to our company and investors that they've brought on another team to work on the solid foundation we've put down. This other team will build the Creators Portal, but they're going to have questions for you since you designed the message contract. You'll need to advise them.

You can do this. You've built a few applications already, so think through the contract we just developed. Would you have the Creators Portal directly receive the video uploads? Would it have users upload directly to something like Amazon's S3 and then just have the browser UI call in after that happened? You could even pretend to be the other team and take a crack at writing the Creators Portal on your own.

If you get stuck or flat out would rather twiddle your thumbs, the book's code does have a fully functioning solution in code/video-tutorials/src/app/creators-portal. Its job is to respond to user stimulus and issue commands to the video publishing Component:

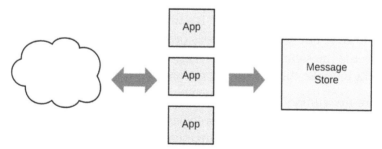

If you do want to give it a shot, see the screenshot on page 163 for some inspiration.

On the left is a list of videos the current user has uploaded, and on the right is the interface for uploading a new video. Don't forget to wire it up in code/video-tutorials/src/config.js and code/video-tutorials/src/app/express/mount-routes.js if you choose to give it a go.

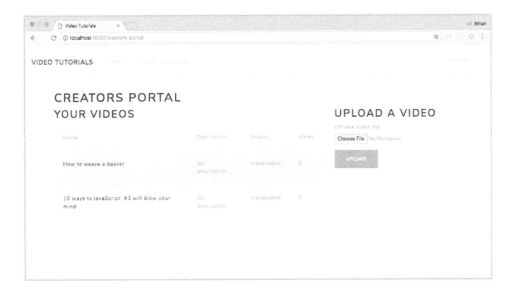

Aggregating Is Also for Other Teams

That other team is also going to build the Aggregator that populates the View Data the Creators Portal uses. Again, there is a working reference implementation in code/video-tutorials/src/aggregators/creators-videos.js with View Data defined in code/video-tutorials/migrations/20181013180427_create_creators-portal-videos.js, but you don't really need to know that because you have a message contract. You're about to write the Component backing the message contract from before, and we've all agreed to communicate through that contract rather than through each other's internals. Once the contract is in place, it really doesn't matter what order the individual pieces get developed in.

As it turns out, though, we're going to build the video publishing Component now.

Building the Video Publishing Component

Let's situate the video-publishing Component in the architecture as shown in the figure on page 164.

It's one of the system's lightning bolts, and it will read messages from and write messages to the Message Store. With this Component we get to the heart of "background jobs" in a microservices world. Remember that in a service-based architecture, communication with Components happens via asynchronous messages—nothing changes when you're doing a so-called background job. *Everything already is a "background" job.*

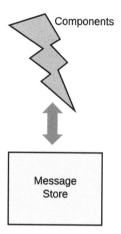

Start with the top-level function:

```
video-tutorials/src/components/video-publishing/index.js
function build ({ messageStore }) {
  const handlers = createHandlers({ messageStore })
  const subscription = messageStore.createSubscription({
    streamName: 'videoPublishing:command',
    handlers: handlers,
    subscriberId: `video-publishing`
  })

  function start () {
    subscription.start()
  }

  return {
    handlers,
    start
  }
}
```

Standard fare for an autonomous component. Note that we're subscribing to the videoPublishing:command category stream. With this set up, we'll first dive into the handlers.

Handling PublishVideo Commands

The Creators Portal application wrote a PublishVideo command to signal that a user wants to publish a video. It doesn't know precisely what will respond to it, or if anything will at all, nor does it care. Its job was to *issue* the command, and it is the job of the video-publishing Component to *handle* it:

```
video-tutorials/src/components/video-publishing/index.js
const Bluebird = require('bluebird')

const AlreadyPublishedError = require('./already-published-error')
const ensurePublishingNotAttempted =
  require('./ensure-publishing-not-attempted')
const loadVideo = require('./load-video')
const transcodeVideo = require('./transcode-video')
const writeVideoPublishedEvent = require('./write-video-published-event')
const writeVideoPublishingFailedEvent =
  require('./write-video-publishing-failed-event')
function createHandlers ({ messageStore }) {
  return {
    PublishVideo: command => {
      const context = {
        command: command,
        messageStore: messageStore
      }

      return (
        Bluebird.resolve(context)
          .then(loadVideo)
          .then(ensurePublishingNotAttempted)
          .then(transcodeVideo)
          .then(writeVideoPublishedEvent)
          .catch(AlreadyPublishedError, () => {})
          .catch(err => writeVideoPublishingFailedEvent(err, context))
      )
    }
  }
}
```

The first step is to set up a context at line 14 to flow through our processing pipeline which we start on line 20. The context just contains the command and the messageStore.

Now, the basic flow of any Component's handlers, whether we're transcoding videos or sending emails, is:

1. Load and project the current state of the entity we're modifying, on page 166 and on page 165.
2. Make the handler idempotent, on page 167.
3. Do the thing we're supposed to do, on page 168.
4. Write the events to show we've done the thing, also on page 168.

First, load the entity we're acting on:

```
video-tutorials/src/components/video-publishing/load-video.js
const videoPublishingProjection = require('./video-publishing-projection')
function loadVideo (context) {
```

```
    const messageStore = context.messageStore
    const command = context.command
    const videoStreamName = `videoPublishing-${command.data.videoId}`

    return messageStore
      .fetch(videoStreamName, videoPublishingProjection)
      .then(video => {
        context.video = video

        return context
      })
  }

module.exports = loadVideo
```

This function grabs the messageStore and command out of the context. It then builds the name of the stream the video entity is in and stuffs that into videoStreamName. With that stream name, it calls messageStore.fetch, passing videoStreamName and videoPublishingProjection to get the current state of the video. Once it gets the projected video, it stuffs it into context. We still have to write that projection:

video-tutorials/src/components/video-publishing/video-publishing-projection.js
```
Line 1  const videoPublishingProjection = {
          $init () {
            return {
              id: null,
    5         publishingAttempted: false,
              sourceUri: null,
              transcodedUri: null,
            }
          },
    10    VideoPublished (video, videoPublished) {
            video.id = videoPublished.data.videoId
            video.publishingAttempted = true
            video.ownerId = videoPublished.data.ownerId
            video.sourceUri = videoPublished.data.sourceUri
    15      video.transcodedUri = videoPublished.data.transcodedUri

            return video
          },

    20    VideoPublishingFailed (video, videoPublishingFailed) {
            video.id = videoPublishingFailed.data.videoId
            video.publishingAttempted = true
            video.ownerId = videoPublishingFailed.data.ownerId
            video.sourceUri = videoPublishingFailed.data.sourceUri
    25
            return video
          }
        }

    30  module.exports = videoPublishingProjection
```

The state of an entity is stored in a stream of events, and projections are how you turn a linear log of history into a shape you can work with right now. You built the core projection mechanism in Chapter 7, Implementing Your First Component, on page 105, but for a brief refresher, you implemented a projection as an object that takes an $init property whose value is a function returning the entity's state before you've applied any events to it. Then you reduce the list of events in the stream, checking the projection object to see if it has a key matching each event's type. If the projection has a corresponding handler, you call that function, passing it the entity's state up to that point and the event to apply. It returns the entity with that event applied, and you move on to the next event if there are more. If there are no more, then that return value is the state of the entity.

This projection, too, starts with an $init function at line 2. A video with no events has no id, publishingAttempted is false, and there is neither a sourceUri nor a trasncodedUri.

The publishing process so far has two state-changing events, VideoPublished and VideoPublishingFailed, which we handle at lines 10 and 20. For both types we extract the videoId, ownerId, and sourceUri from the event payload, and we set publishingAttempted to true. With VideoPublished events we also extract transcodedUri.

With the video projected and loaded into context, we head back to our pipeline on page 165, where the next step, ensurePublishingNotAttempted, makes this handler idempotent:

video-tutorials/src/components/video-publishing/ensure-publishing-not-attempted.js
```
const AlreadyPublishedError = require('./already-published-error')
function ensurePublishingNotAttempted (context) {
  const { video } = context

  if (video.publishingAttempted) {
    throw new AlreadyPublishedError()
  }

  return context
}

module.exports = ensurePublishingNotAttempted
```

You wrote a similar check earlier on page 141 when we were making sure sendemail hadn't already sent a given email. From the point of view of a microservices architecture, publishing a video isn't really any different from sending an email. It's all the same building blocks for both features of the system. When sending emails, when transcoding videos, when moving funds around, whenever modifying an entity, *our message consumers* make sure we're not processing the same messages twice.

So, if the video in context has a publishingAttempted of true, then we throw an AlreadyPublishedError. If not, just return context.

The next step in our pipeline on page 165 is to "transcode" the video:

video-tutorials/src/components/video-publishing/transcode-video.js
```
Line 1  const FAKE_TRANSCODING_DESTINATION =
          'https://www.youtube.com/watch?v=GI_P3UtZXAA'
        function transcodeVideo (context) {
          console.log('We totally have a video transcoder installed that we are')
     5    console.log('totally calling in this function. If we did not have such')
          console.log('an awesome one installed locally, we could call into a')
          console.log('3rd-party API here instead.')

          const { video } = context
    10    context.transcodedUri = FAKE_TRANSCODING_DESTINATION
          console.log(`Transcode ${video.sourceUri} to ${context.transcodedUri}`)

          return context
        }
    15
        module.exports = transcodeVideo
```

The current implementation of this function contains a fair amount of hand waving. Remember when Joe asked about all the simulating on page 160, and we said that we were going to simulate the actual transcoding to keep the focus on the microservices architecture? That's why this function currently just shows some text assuring us that this is where the transcoding would happen. It would be a great exercise to flesh this out to and actually transcode your videos here. A few options are ffmpeg[4] and Zencoder,[5] but diving into either is beyond the scope of this book. You could just replace the console.log statements with the actual implementation code.

The only real bit of work we do here is at line 10 where we attach the location where the "transcoded" video is "stored."

We're at the final step of the golden path we wrote on page 165. With all the actual work of publishing done, now it's time to record that we did the work in writeVideoPublishedEvent:

video-tutorials/src/components/video-publishing/write-video-published-event.js
```
function writeVideoPublishedEvent (context) {
  const command = context.command
  const messageStore = context.messageStore
```

---

4. https://www.ffmpeg.org/
5. https://zencoder.com

```
const event = {
  id: uuid(),
  type: 'VideoPublished',
  metadata: {
    traceId: command.metadata.traceId,
    userId: command.metadata.userId
  },
  data: {
    ownerId: command.data.ownerId,
    sourceUri: command.data.sourceUri,
    transcodedUri: context.transcodedUri,
    videoId: command.data.videoId
  }
}
const streamName = `videoPublishing-${command.data.videoId}`

return messageStore.write(streamName, event)
  .then(() => context)
}

module.exports = writeVideoPublishedEvent
```

This is a typical write-X-event function. In this case you build a VideoPublished event, copying the data from the command in context. We also get the transcodedUri that the transcodeVideo function attached and put all of these values into our event, honoring our contract in code/video-tutorials/src/components/video-publishing/contract.md. We build a streamName to write to, and then call messageStore.write to write the event.

Congrats—you've just published videos. You've successfully published videos without so-called background jobs, and learned how a microservices architecture makes this kind of work feel native. And these transcoding jobs will always work just like we have planned here.

Except when they don't. Because, sometimes, they won't. That's why at the end of the pipeline on page 165 we have these two lines:

video-tutorials/src/components/video-publishing/index.js
```
    .catch(AlreadyPublishedError, () => {})
    .catch(err => writeVideoPublishingFailedEvent(err, context))
)
```

The first catches the AlreadyPublishedErrors that ensureVideoIsNotPublished will throw if the video has already been published. With the next we catch any other type of error and call writeVideoPublishingFailedEvent:

video-tutorials/src/components/video-publishing/write-video-publishing-failed-event.js
```
function writeVideoPublishingFailedEvent (err, context) {
  const command = context.command
  const messageStore = context.messageStore
```

```
  const transcodingFailedEvent = {
    id: uuid(),
    type: 'VideoPublishingFailed',
    metadata: {
      traceId: command.metadata.traceId,
      userId: command.metadata.userId
    },
    data: {
      ownerId: command.data.ownerId,
      sourceUri: command.data.sourceUri,
      videoId: command.data.videoId,
      reason: err.message
    }
  }
  const streamName = `videoPublishing-${command.data.videoId}`

  return messageStore.write(streamName, transcodingFailedEvent)
    .then(() => context)
}

module.exports = writeVideoPublishingFailedEvent
```

Like the other writeX functions, this one grabs the data it cares about out of the context and builds its event. In this case that's a VideoTranscodingFailed event. In addition to the videoId, ownerId, and sourceUri, this event type takes a reason, and the reason we'll give for the failure is the message we got from err. Then we write the event to the video's streamName. If something goes wrong, we'll have some excellent debuggable state. These failure events could also be used to retry transcoding the video if that requirement came along. That would require modifying the video publishing projection which sets publishingAttempted to true even in the case of failure.

In any case, the video-publishing Component is wired into the rest of the system in the same way that everything else is wired in. You can inspect that in code/video-tutorials/src/config.js, but we won't go through it here.

But that's a wrap on publishing, so let's reason through our choice for how to make this handler idempotent.

Accepting Potential Duplication

If you had an uneasy feeling as you went through how we handled idempotence here, that's awesome that you're developing a sense for it. Before publishing the video, we checked to see if the video was already *done*. We only have a single video-publishing instance, so we don't have to worry about two or more instances competing with one another. However, we could very well transcode the video and get restarted due to deployment or crash before writing the

VideoPublished event. When it restarts, it'll see the PublishVideo command and do it all over again.

Transcoding videos is cheap, and we absolutely cannot accept failing to transcode the videos—they don't go out to our viewers if they don't get transcoded. Also, the destination of where we'll put the result of the duplicate work won't change, so we won't end up with orphaned files. After consulting with the business team (which we must do to answer questions like this!), we all agree that it's okay to just let the duplicate work happen.

To recap, when deciding how to make a handler that executes a long-running process like video transcoding idempotent, we have to ask whether it's worse to do the thing zero times or do them more than once. In the case of transcoding our videos prior to publishing, we discovered that it would be worse to not transcode the video at all than it would be to transcode it twice. So we chose an idempotence strategy that may duplicate work. We accept that.

What You've Done So Far

Wow! You just built a video publishing system. More importantly, this was the classic sort of "background job" you may have encountered in your days as a purveyor of monoliths, where making it happen probably required some sort of one-off solution and flow that was different from everything else your system did. You just wrote such a process without having to pull in any new concepts. Whenever you're faced with incorporating a long-running process in a services architecture, you now have the machinery and understanding to do so.

Isn't it remarkable that once we had our message contract, we were able to let the other team build the UI and Aggregator while we focused on the Component? They weren't waiting on us!

To take your learning further, try getting the Component to actually transcode the videos. If you're particularly ambitious, you could actually upload files to S3 and pull them down when transcoding, or you could modify the command to write a local path that you can work on. I can't wait to see what you come up with!

Now, if you were to fire up the project and upload a video, you'll notice a, uh, sub-optimal feature of the system right now. Every video is named "Untitled." This isn't ready for primetime yet, so in the next chapter you'll give our creators a way to name their videos. In doing so, you'll see an aspect that our architecture makes more difficult—how do you create a pleasant user experience when the result of what they're doing isn't immediately available?

CHAPTER 11

Building Async-Aware User Interfaces

Have you ever been on a very large boat? Maybe an aircraft carrier or a cruise ship? If you have, or if you've seen pictures of one, you may have noticed that there are watertight doors interspersed throughout. Doors like that surely increase the cost of building such a vessel, since it would require less metal without them. So why bother?

Well, preventing water from moving from one part of the ship to another is a winning strategy if one part of the ship springs a leak. It could make the difference between a nuisance of a repair bill and the entire thing sinking.

The Video Tutorials site you're building would likely take less overall code if you built it as a monolith. In fact, a microservices-based system in general is going to have more moving parts than an MVC monolith.

Suppose that it took ten complexity points to be build a given monolith. It might take fifteen to build an equivalent microservices-based system. But when you're building the microservices-based system, you only have to hold two points of complexity in your mind at any given time. For the monolith, you have to hold eight points of complexity in your mind at any given time because there are no hard, fast doors sealing one portion off from another. The message contract gives you that kind of separation, and that's what keeps you more productive in a services system in the long run.

In this chapter, we're going to examine an aspect of our system that is *more* complex because of having a microservices architecture—building a UI in an async world. How do you give the user a seamless experience when the results of the actions they take are not immediately available? We'll discuss a couple of patterns, and you'll code one of them in the context enabling your users to name their videos.

Defining Video Metadata Messages

We introduced the Creators Portal in Chapter 10, Performing Background Jobs with Microservices, on page 157. Our other team built the first version, and we'll augment it, allowing users to see their uploaded videos via an interface like the following:

Let's open the Creators Portal application and see how the other team set up the application:

```
video-tutorials/src/app/creators-portal/index.js
Line 1  function createCreatorsPortal ({ db, messageStore }) {
          const queries = createQueries({ db })
          const actions = createActions({ messageStore, queries })
          const handlers = createHandlers({ actions, queries })
     5
          const router = express.Router()
          router
            .route('/publish-video')
            .post(bodyParser.json(), handlers.handlePublishVideo)
    10    router.route('/videos/:id').get(handlers.handleShowVideo)
          router.route('/').get(handlers.handleDashboard)

          return { handlers, router }
        }
    15
        module.exports = createCreatorsPortal
```

The other team built this application following the pattern we've used for all our applications. It receives dependencies and sets up queries, actions, and handlers. It builds a router and adds routes for publishing a video (line 9), showing an individual video (line 10), and displaying the Creators Portal dashboard (line 11). There are handlers for each of those routes, and be sure to check them out when you can.

Our business team is saying that we'll get more engagement with the site if the videos have names other than "Untitled," and that seems reasonable. So we need to let our users name their videos. Maybe even rename them. That sounds like another state transition for videos, so we need to modify the video publishing Component to provide this state transition as well as add an Aggregator to reflect the change back into appropriate View Data. In the process, you'll even see on page 178 a use for building different View Data structures from the same events. Surely, such power isn't meant for mere mortals, but here we are, so let's get to it.

First of all, new state transitions means new messages. The piece of state we'll record is that a video got named. This suggests a VideoNamed event:

```
{
  "id": "c022a493-4784-4e54-84a1-df5e4e08553a",
  "type": "VideoNamed",
  "data": {
    "name": "Prod Bugs Hate This Guy: 42 Things You Didn't Know About JS"
  }
}
```

It holds the name the creator supplied.

Now, Components own their data, and the first rule of user input is to never trust user input. It's quite possible for users to give us names we don't want to allow. For example, a blank name isn't much more useful than just naming a video "Untitled." We discussed validating eventually consistent data on page 99, when we implemented user registration. In that chapter we had the Application layer catch malformed email addresses. We did that because what makes a string a valid email address is not a unique property of our system—as awesome as Video Tutorials is, it did not invent email. However, it *is* our system declaring that users can't name a video with a blank name.

In this chapter you'll use a Component to validate input on page 181. The Application layer will let everything through. The catch is that everything a Component does is asynchronous. If we wait for the Component to validate a video's name, we won't know during the request/response cycle if the naming attempt succeeded. This means the Component will need an event to signal naming failures. That leads us to the VideoNameRejected event:

```
{
  "id": "19f71d45-eb38-4fde-9ed9-d1565ef61a2f",
  "type": "VideoNameRejected",
  "data": {
    "name": "",
    "reason": "ValidationError**{ \"name\": [ \"Can't be blank\" ]}"
  }
}
```

It captures the reason why the video naming didn't go through.

Then we need a command to request that the Component name the video. Let's call it NameVideo:

```
{
  "id": "b8723a39-f75a-41cb-a618-c4634e08da56",
  "type": "NameVideo",
  "data": {
    "videoId": "f94ce176-4a31-47e3-9593-c4ed4ee6ac84",
    "name": "Prod Bugs Hate This Guy: 42 Things You Didn't Know About JS"
  }
}
```

This one needs to know which video is supposed to get a name as well as what that name is. We allow the owners of videos to submit this command. If we ever have admins in our system, they'll be able to as well.

Responding to Users When the Response Isn't Immediately Available

We head back to the Creators Portal application to put these messages to use. The individual video screen has two forms on it, one for naming the video and one for describing it. Why two forms? We don't want to present users with an HTTP form sitting on top of a database table. They're not here to edit a video—they're here to *name a video*. This is an example of a task-based UI,[1] a UI geared toward achieving specific ends rather than raw editing.

That said, we'll only cover naming the videos, since describing them is an exercise at the end of the chapter. The name appears in a text box that submits back to our server, ending up at the handleNameVideo handler:

---

1.   https://cqrs.wordpress.com/documents/task-based-ui/

```
video-tutorials/src/app/creators-portal/index.js
function createHandlers ({ actions, queries }) {
  function handleNameVideo (req, res, next) {
    const videoId = req.params.id
    const name = req.body.name

    actions
      .nameVideo(req.context, videoId, name)
      .then(() =>
        res.redirect(
          `/creators-portal/video-operations/${req.context.traceId}`
        )
      )
      .catch(next)
  }
  return {
    handleNameVideo,
  }
}
```

Like all good HTTP handlers, it grabs the data it needs out of the incoming request and passes it to the business logic. In this case we need the videoId, found at req.params.id, the name the user supplied, which is found at req.body.name, and the request context. It passes these pieces to actions.nameVideo:

```
video-tutorials/src/app/creators-portal/index.js
function createActions ({ messageStore, queries }) {
  // ...
  function nameVideo (context, videoId, name) {
    const nameVideoCommand = {
      id: uuid(),
      type: 'NameVideo',
      metadata: {
        traceId: context.traceId,
        userId: context.userId
      },
      data: {
        name,
        videoId
      }
    }
    const streamName = `videoPublishing:command-${videoId}`

    return messageStore.write(streamName, nameVideoCommand)
  }
  return {
    // ...
    nameVideo
  }
}
```

actions.nameVideo's job is to take user input and turn it into a NameVideo command that the video publishing Component will process. So it does just that, writing that command to the video's command stream.

Now, we've issued a command into the wild that we want this video to be renamed, and we're in the middle of an HTTP request. We don't know when that command is going to get processed. Truth be told, we don't even know *if* it's going to get processed. That isn't our concern here. Our concern is to issue the command. But what about our users? What do we show them?

Every model has its strengths and weaknesses, including evented, autonomous microComponents. This type of user interaction is where our architecture is *more* difficult to work with than a monolith. Why? *Everything* is asynchronous. We don't have the familiar world of issuing an update query to the database and waiting for the result. We have a much richer domain model and an architecture that will scale to larger systems available to us, but we have to handle the fact that so much work is done asynchronously.

We don't know when that command will be processed, but we know what events to look for when it does—we defined those on page 174. But do we have a way to link these events to the command that originated them? Take a moment and see if you can answer that.

We sure do! That's what traceIds are. They link messages that all originated from the same user activity. The NameVideo command has a traceId, and any events written in response to that command will have the same traceId.

Okay, so we know what event types to look for, and we know how to link event instances to the command. If we just aggregated those into some sort of View Data, we'd be able to query that View Data to know if the naming has succeeded or failed. This View Data would need to link a traceId to the ID of the video being acted on. It would also need to record if the command was successful, and if the command failed, the View Data would need to record why so that we could show that to users:

video-tutorials/migrations/20181224101632_create-video-operations.js
```javascript
exports.up = function up (knex) {
  return knex.schema.createTable('video_operations', table => {
    table.string('trace_id').primary()
    table.string('video_id').notNullable()
    table.bool('succeeded').notNullable()
    table.string('failure_reason')
  })
}

exports.down = knex => knex.schema.dropTable('video_operations')
```

It has the four columns we just mentioned. If the succeeded column is true, then the failure_reason column will be null.

Okay, so let's look back at the HTTP handler for naming videos:

```
video-tutorials/src/app/creators-portal/index.js
function createHandlers ({ actions, queries }) {
  function handleNameVideo (req, res, next) {
    const videoId = req.params.id
    const name = req.body.name

    actions
      .nameVideo(req.context, videoId, name)
      .then(() =>
        res.redirect(
          `/creators-portal/video-operations/${req.context.traceId}`
        )
      )
      .catch(next)
  }
  return {
    handleNameVideo,
  }
}
```

We already went through the action, and the catch is for unpredictable errors like "hard disk blew up." Let's finish the happy path. We redirect users to /creators-portal/video-operations/:traceId, where :traceId is the traceId of the current request—the same traceId we attached to the command the action wrote. Let's write the handler for this redirect path:

```
video-tutorials/src/app/creators-portal/index.js
function handleShowVideoOperation (req, res, next) {
  return queries.videoOperationByTraceId(req.params.traceId)
    .then(operation => {
      if (!operation || !operation.succeeded) {
        return res.render(
          'creators-portal/templates/video-operation',
          { operation }
        )
      }

      return res.redirect(
        `/creators-portal/videos/${operation.videoId}`
      )
    })
}
```

First we query for a video operation with the traceId we get from our request params. Note that this is not the traceId of the current request. It's the traceId of the request that wrote the command. Here's queries.videoOperationByTraceId:

```
video-tutorials/src/app/creators-portal/index.js
function videoOperationByTraceId (traceId) {
  return db.then(client =>
    client('video_operations')
      .where({ trace_id: traceId })
      .limit(1)
  )
    .then(camelCaseKeys)
    .then(rows => rows[0])
}
```

It just uses knex to query the video_operations table for a row whose trace_id matches the traceId received as an argument.

The handler then checks to see if the query found either no matching operation, or if there was one, if the operation failed. In either of those cases, we render a page in response to the request. The context for the response is the value we have for operation, which is either undefined or a row with false for its succeeded property.

Here is a screenshot of the interstitial:

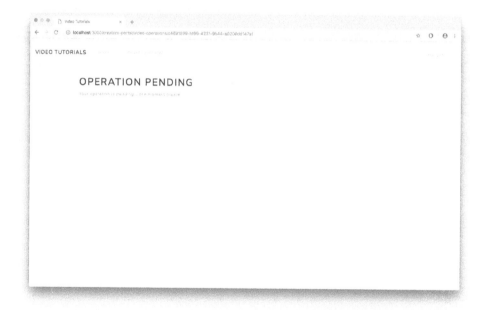

Let's write the Pug for this screen:

```
video-tutorials/src/app/creators-portal/templates/video-operation.pug
extends ../../common-templates/layout

block content
  - const pending = !operation
```

```
if pending
  .row
    .col-12
      h1 Operation pending

      p Your operation is pending... one moment please

  script.
    setTimeout(() => window.location.reload(), 1000)
else
  .row
    .col-12
      - videoUrl = `/creators-portal/videos/${operation.videoId}`

      h1 Operation failed

      p.alert.alert-danger= operation.failureReason

      p
        a(href=videoUrl) Back to the video
```

First off, we want this page to have the same basic look and feel as every page in our site, so we declare that it extends from ../../common-templates/layout, which resolves to the templates in code/video-tutorials/src/app/common-templates. Next, in block content, we declare a variable named pending, which will be true if queries.videoOper-ationBytraceId did not find a row. This means that the Aggregator has not yet picked up the result of the naming command. If that's the case, we tell users their operation is pending. We then add a small snippet of JavaScript that will reload the current page in 1 second. This will set up a polling loop so that when the operation completes, users will get the result.

However, if there was an operation row, the only reason we'd render this template is if said operation failed. If that's the case, we let users know why, and then we offer them a link to the video's page where they can enter a different name if they still want to rename the video.

Back to the HTTP handler then, if we found the operation, and it succeeded, we redirect them to the video's page. Boom! You just handled async UI. Is this always the right pattern? No. But it works for this use case.

Two steps remain. We need the video publishing Component to process the command, and we need an Aggregator to populate the video operations View Data. Let's tackle the Component.

Adding Validation to a Component

Let's handle that NameVideo command in the video-publishing Component:

```
video-tutorials/src/components/video-publishing/index.js
function createHandlers ({ messageStore }) {
  return {
    NameVideo: command => {
❶     const context = {
        command: command,
        messageStore: messageStore
      }

      return Bluebird.resolve(context)
❷        .then(loadVideo)
         .then(ensureCommandHasNotBeenProcessed)
         .then(ensureNameIsValid)
         .then(writeVideoNamedEvent)
❸        .catch(CommandAlreadyProcessedError, () => {})
❹        .catch(
           ValidationError,
           err => writeVideoNameRejectedEvent(context, err.message)
         )
    },
    // ...
  }
}
```

❶ First, build a context consisting of the command in question and the message-Store.

❷ Next, load the video's publishing history with loadVideo—you wrote that earlier on page 165. Then validate the command by ensuring it hasn't already been processed and that the name follows our rules for what makes a valid name. If that's successful, we write a VideoNamed event to show it worked. We'll look at these steps in just a moment, right after we look at our catches.

❸ If ensureCommandHasNotBeenProcessed detects that we've processed this command before, it throws a CommandAlreadyProcessedError, which we catch here and turn into a no-op.

❹ If ensureNameIsValid finds an invalid name for the video, it throws a Validation-Error, which we catch here. We use the message from the given error to call writeVideoNameRejectedEvent. That's our failure event, and err.message contains why it failed.

Let's break down the steps of that pipeline. You wrote load video on page 165, so we don't have anything more to say on it here.

Next, we make sure we haven't already processed this command:

video-tutorials/src/components/video-publishing/ensure-command-has-not-been-processed.js
```
const CommandAlreadyProcessedError =
  require('./command-already-processed-error')
function ensureCommandHasNotBeenProcessed (context) {
  const command = context.command
  const video = context.video

  if (video.sequence > command.globalPosition) {
    throw new CommandAlreadyProcessedError()
  }

  return context
}

module.exports = ensureCommandHasNotBeenProcessed
```

Imagine for just a moment that we have a property on our video entity named sequence which is the globalPosition of the last VideoNamed or VideoNameRejected event applied to this video. If we've already processed the command we're considering right now, either in the affirmative or in the negative, one of these two types of events would have been written. That event's globalPosition would necessarily be greater than this command's globalPosition, and thus sequence would be greater than the command's globalPosition. In that case, we throw a CommandAlreadyProcessedError.

Now, the only hitch is that the video's projection doesn't currently handle our naming events, so let's fix that:

video-tutorials/src/components/video-publishing/video-publishing-projection.js
```
const videoPublishingProjection = {
  $init () {
    return {
      id: null,
      publishingAttempted: false,
      sourceUri: null,
      transcodedUri: null,
➤     sequence: 0,
➤     name: ''
    }
  },
  VideoNamed (video, videoNamed) {
    video.sequence = videoNamed.globalPosition
    video.name = videoNamed.data.name

    return video
  },

  VideoNameRejected (video, videoNameRejected) {
    video.sequence = videoNameRejected.globalPosition

    return video
  },
```

First off, notice that we've added sequence and name to $init. Then we added two events to the projection, namely VideoNamed and VideoNameRejected. They assign the event.globalPosition into the sequence field on the projected value. The function for VideoNamed also assigns the video's name.

Now that you know this command has not already been processed, we can make sure the name is valid:

```
video-tutorials/src/components/video-publishing/ensure-name-is-valid.js
const validate = require('validate.js')

const ValidationError = require('./validation-error')

const constraints = {
  name: {
    presence: { allowEmpty: false }
  }
}
function ensureNameIsValid (context) {
  const command = context.command
  const validateMe = { name: command.data.name }
  const validationErrors = validate(validateMe, constraints)

  if (validationErrors) {
    throw new ValidationError(
      validationErrors,
      constraints,
      context.video
    )
  }

  return context
}

module.exports = ensureNameIsValid
```

This function validates the proposed name using the validate.js library. We used this same library when we were registering users on page 93. We define constraints at line 5, and in this case we're just checking to see if the user supplied a non-blank name for the video. If they didn't, we throw a ValidationError, which will contain the information we need to tell users how to correct their commands. This is some weak validation, to be sure. If we wanted to include other validation (for example, making sure that the name didn't contain profanity or other undesirable text), we'd add that here as well.

Assuming all our checks passed, we record this state transition in the video's history:

video-tutorials/src/components/video-publishing/write-video-named-event.js

```js
function writeVideoNamedEvent (context) {
  const command = context.command
  const messageStore = context.messageStore

  const videoNamedEvent = {
    id: uuid(),
    type: 'VideoNamed',
    metadata: {
      traceId: command.metadata.traceId,
      userId: command.metadata.userId
    },
    data: { name: command.data.name }
  }
  const streamName = `videoPublishing-${command.data.videoId}`

  return messageStore.write(streamName, videoNamedEvent).then(() => context)
}

module.exports = writeVideoNamedEvent
```

Construct a VideoNamedEvent using the values from the command stashed into context. Then build the streamName where we should write the event to, and write the event, concluding the happy path.

If one of our failure conditions was triggered, we need to record that:

video-tutorials/src/components/video-publishing/write-video-name-rejected-event.js

```js
function writeVideoNameRejectedEvent (context, reason) {
  const command = context.command
  const messageStore = context.messageStore

  const VideoNameRejectedEvent = {
    id: uuid(),
    type: 'VideoNameRejected',
    metadata: {
      traceId: command.metadata.traceId,
      userId: command.metadata.userId
    },
    data: {
      name: command.data.name,
      reason: reason
    }
  }
  const streamName = `videoPublishing-${command.data.videoId}`

  return messageStore.write(streamName, VideoNameRejectedEvent)
    .then(() => context)
}

module.exports = writeVideoNameRejectedEvent
```

Here again, construct an event, only this time it's a VideoNameRejected event. In addition to the same data the successful event needs, include the reason that comes from the error you caught. Then write this event to the video's history.

And that concludes doing the validation inside of a Component. Hopefully that wasn't too surprising. It really isn't ground-breaking tech to move a validation function from one file to another. However, we did reinforce the principle that Components are authoritative over their data, and that's a core principle.

Next we need to aggregate the results into the video operations View Data.

Aggregating Naming Results

You've built the application that allows users to manage their video metadata, and you've built the Component that powers that management. Now it's time to populate the View Data that feeds the application. It's a pretty straightforward Aggregator. First, its top-level function:

```
video-tutorials/src/aggregators/video-operations.js
function build ({ db, messageStore }) {
  const queries = createQueries({ db })
  const handlers = createHandlers({ queries })
  const subscription = messageStore.createSubscription({
    streamName: 'videoPublishing',
    handlers,
    subscriberId: componentId
  })

  function start (es) {
    subscription.start()
  }

  return {
    handlers,
    queries,
    start
  }
}

module.exports = build
```

It's all the usual suspects here. Receive the db and messageStore; set up the queries, handlers, and subscription. This Aggregator handles two events, namely VideoNamed and VideoNameRejected. Let's write the handler for VideoNamed events:

```
video-tutorials/src/aggregators/video-operations.js
function createHandlers ({ queries }) {
  return {
    VideoNamed: event => {
```

```
    const videoId = streamToEntityId(event.streamName)
    const wasSuccessful = true
    const failureReason = null

    return queries.writeResult(
      event.metadata.traceId,
      videoId,
      wasSuccessful,
      failureReason
    )
  },
}
```

This file also defines a streamToEntityId function, which we use to get the videoId from the event's stream. Remember that we write these events to streams of the form "videoPublishing-X", where X is the video's ID. Then we set a couple of convenience variables. This event means the naming operation succeeded, so wasSuccessful is true, and there is no failureReason.

We conclude by calling queries.writeResult, and if we're going to call it, we need to write it:

video-tutorials/src/aggregators/video-operations.js
```
function writeResult (traceId, videoId, wasSuccessful, failureReason) {
  const operation = {
    traceId,
    videoId,
    wasSuccessful,
    failureReason
  }

  const raw = `
    INSERT INTO
      video_operations (
        trace_id,
        video_id,
        succeeded,
        failure_reason
      )
    VALUES
      (:traceId, :videoId, :wasSuccessful, :failureReason)
    ON CONFLICT (trace_id) DO NOTHING
  `

  return db.then(client => client.raw(raw, operation))
}
```

This query assembles an operation object with the arguments we received. Then it runs an upsert query using PostgreSQL's ON CONFLICT feature. This also handles idempotence. The first time this is called, it will insert the result into the video_operations table. If subsequent calls occur, they'll have a conflict on trace_id, and when that occurs we DO NOTHING.

The handler for VideoNameRejected events is almost exactly the same thing:

```
video-tutorials/src/aggregators/video-operations.js
function createHandlers ({ queries }) {
    VideoNameRejected: event => {
      const videoId = streamToEntityId(event.streamName)
      const wasSuccessful = false
      const failureReason = event.data.reason

      return queries.writeResult(
        event.metadata.traceId,
        videoId,
        wasSuccessful,
        failureReason
      )
    }
  }
}
```

The differences here are that wasSuccessful is false, and since it didn't succeed, we also have a failureReason, which we get out of the event.data.reason. Then we make the same call to queries.writeResult.

And then wire it up in config.js:

```
video-tutorials/src/config.js
// ...
❶ const createVideoOperationsAggregator =
    require('./aggregators/video-operations')
function createConfig ({ env }) {
    // ...
❷  const videoOperationsAggregator = createVideoOperationsAggregator({
      db: knexClient,
      messageStore
    })
    const aggregators = [
      // ...
❸    videoOperationsAggregator,
    ]
    return {
      // ...
❹    videoOperationsAggregator,
    }
}
```

❶ First, require the Aggregator.

❷ Instantiate it, passing in a reference to the db and the messageStore.

❸ Add it to the aggregators array so that it gets picked up and started in src/index.js.

❹ Finally, include it in the config object so that it's available in test.

And that's it for the video operations Aggregator.

Applying Naming Events to the Creators Portal View Data

The Aggregator we just completed aggregates the status of the naming process. We use that View Data to tell if the NameVideo command has finished processing. At this point though, the new name will not be reflected in the Creators Portal dashboard or in the single video view. That's a different View Data, and it's a different Aggregator. We need to add a handler to the creators-videos Aggregator:

```
video-tutorials/src/aggregators/creators-videos.js
function createHandlers ({ messageStore, queries }) {
  return {
    VideoNamed: event =>
      queries.updateVideoName(
        streamToEntityId(event.streamName),
        event.position,
        event.data.name
      ),
  }
}
```

This handler uses streamToEntityId to get the video's ID and then passes that ID to queries.updateVideoName along with the event's version and the new name found in event.data.name. Let's write queries.updateVideoName:

```
video-tutorials/src/aggregators/creators-videos.js
function updateVideoName (id, position, name) {
  return db.then(client =>
    client('creators_portal_videos')
      .update({ name, position })
      .where({ id })
      .where('position', '<', position)
  )
}
```

This function updates the name column in the row whose id column matches the videoId argument. Two notes:

- Notice how we handle idempotence. This query will only run on a row whose position column is strictly less than the event's position.

- This function is another with the word "update" in its title. This is appropriate because this is a database function. The domain said "this video was named," and that domain event leads to a database record being updated.

Justifying Our UI Decision

Yes, the flow of communicating to users when their naming requests have been processed ain't pretty. Like we said in the beginning, every model we choose comes with its complexity, and autonomous components are no exception. Because the response to a user's request isn't immediately available, we need UI patterns to compensate. You just implemented one pattern—redirecting to a polling interstitial.

Here again is that screenshot of the video operations interstitial:

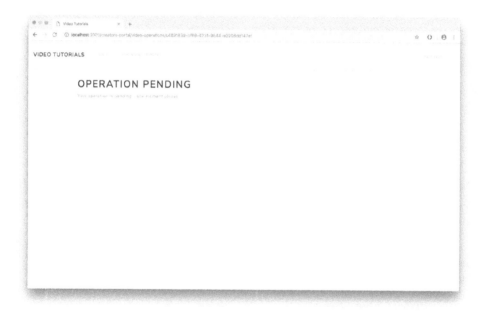

This page polls until the operation completes and then either shows users the failure reason or takes them back to the video's page. This works, but it isn't ideal. A big reason for the clunkiness here is that we're rendering our UI on the server. We didn't delay sending a response to the user until the command had finished processing, although that was an option. But keeping a request open while a potentially long-running process would tie up server resources.

We could mitigate a lot of this clunkiness by building a richer client application, using optimistic updates as our theatrics instead. A rich client-side application could do the polling in the background, and users wouldn't have to have it shoved in their faces. We didn't do that here because this isn't a book about, say, React.[2] If you have experience with browser app development, by all means, give it a shot!

The fact remains that making things asynchronous is something that will affect your user experience. If you try to use a service-based, asynchronous architecture but still use all the same UI idioms you've used before, you're going to have a bad time. We're still in our MVP stage right now, though, and once those sweet membership dollars begin flowing in, we can make a nicer UI.

What You've Done So Far

In this chapter you made it so that our creators can manage their videos. To make that happen, you came face to face with one of the things that is more difficult in a services architecture—rendering responses when they aren't immediately available.

While the content creators can name their videos, they still can't describe them. Can you add that? It wouldn't be much different than how the naming works.

As another exercise, think through and draw out how you might improve this experience with a richer browser client. Would part of how we did things still apply? Is there still going to be some polling? What would the flow of data look like?

One note before closing: when we decided on our message contract at the beginning of this chapter, we chose, for example, VideoNamed as an event. We could have chosen a name like VideoUpdated, but frankly, that's a very bland name. It doesn't even tell us what changed. Furthermore, it would betray an error in our thinking. A video isn't just some row in a database that a user updated a property on. It's a rich entity, with a history, and set of defined operations we can make on it. Naming it is one of those operations.

You've built a solid foundation so far in this book. Our users are registering, and we're spamming—err, sending useful emails to them. They're uploading videos, getting them transcoded, and editing their metadata. The time has come to get this puppy deployed, which just so happens to be the topic of the next chapter.

---

2. https://reactjs.org/

Part III

Tools of the Trade

Having built the functioning pieces of the system, we look at the tools we have to release what we built to the world. How do we deploy? What questions do we have to answer? And what if something goes wrong?

Covering everything to do with microservices is well beyond the scope of any book, so we conclude by calling out areas we didn't look at and show avenues for where you can continue the journey.

You can have a second computer once you've shown you know how to use the first one.

> ➤ *Paul Barham*

CHAPTER 12

Deploying Components

In 1889, France unveiled the Eiffel Tower as the entrance to that year's World's Fair.[1] If you were able to ask anyone who attended that moment whether they would trade it for what you're about to do in this chapter, well, you'd have a whole lot of spectators right now. It's the grand opening of Video Tutorials, and you're going to push it live on the internet.

The basic plan of attack is:

1. Sign up for Heroku,[2] if you haven't already.

2. Create a new "app"—Heroku has a different meaning for that word than we do in this project.

3. Configure that "app."

4. Deploy the code.

Once we're satisfied that the system is running properly, we'll then consider what it would take to run Video Tutorials as a distributed system and why we might choose to do so. Even though all of the code is in one codebase, we definitely still have a services-based system—the components are all autonomous. What we don't have so far is a distributed system. What you'll see is that having properly built the system, we can actually extract microservices—because unlike in a distributed monolith, we actually have some.

Finally, when we distribute the system, you might think it's a bit tedious, so we'll cover a different way of packaging the pieces of the system to make our deployment strategy more flexible.

---

1. https://en.wikipedia.org/wiki/Eiffel_Tower
2. https://www.heroku.com

Let's do call out one thing. Your humble author has no commercial interest in Heroku and is not receiving any compensation from them. It's just an easy-to-use platform that will help us get this system running. If you'd prefer to deploy it elsewhere, by all means use whatever you'd like.

Strap yourself in because here we go.

Creating the Heroku "App"

It's quite possible that you haven't heard of or have never used Heroku. It's a platform-as-a-service company, or PaaS for short. If you've ever used a cloud provider like Amazon Web Services, Google Cloud Platform, Digital Ocean, or Linode, then you've experienced deploying code to a cloud provider. Heroku is similar, only you exchange the high degree of control and responsibility you have over your instances for a very smooth deployment experience. You don't have to provision instances, do all the security hardening, etc. You just easily push code. Of course, sometimes you need that finer degree of control. We don't right now, so we won't bother with it.

Now, we won't walk through signing up for an account there. If you managed to get a copy of this book, you already know how to sign up for a website. In case you're concerned, unless you're already running a number of projects on Heroku, you won't have to pay any money to deploy Video Tutorials. So we're going to assume that you've registered and have made it to your Heroku dashboard.

Hopefully the UI there hasn't changed a lot by the time you're reading this, so assuming it hasn't, from the dashboard, choose the "New" button in the upper right and select "Create New App" in the menu that then appears:

From there choose a name for the app. Sadly, some, uh, unknown person already chose "video-tutorials" for deploying something else, so that name won't be available to you as shown in the screenshot on page 197.

After clicking "Create App" you'll be taken to that "app's" page. You'll need to get the project's code into a directory and make a Git repository out of it. Then follow Heroku's instructions for "Existing Git repository," and add the heroku remote.

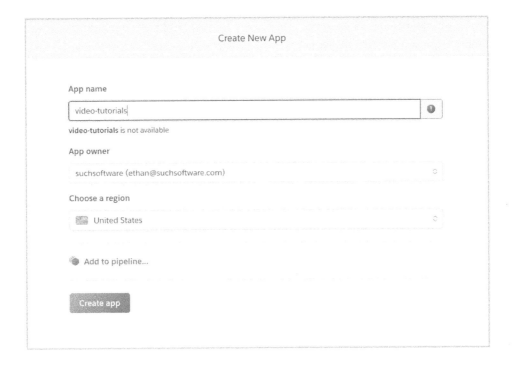

Next up, we need to add a database and configure the environment variables our system needs.

Configuring the "App"

From the main "app" page, click on "Resources:"

On the "Resources" page, type "postgres" and the option for "Heroku Postgres" should appear. Select that. It will then pop up a dialog asking you to select a "Plan." "Hobby Dev - Free" is good for now. IMPORTANT: Do this a second time. One will be for all View Data, and the other will be for Message DB. Having attached two databases, your "Resources" screen will resemble the following:

Yours will likely not say HEROKU_POSTGRESQL_COBALT, and guess what? Mine doesn't anymore either.

Next, click on the "Settings" tab. There will be a button in the "Config Vars" section that says "Reveal Config Vars." Click that button to reveal the environment variables:

On the Settings page, you'll type environment variable names into the box that says "KEY" and their corresponding values into the box that says "VAL-UE." You should already see the DATABASE_URL key–value pair. Click on the "Add" button and add the following pairs on page 199.

KEY	VALUE
APP_NAME	Video Tutorials
COOKIE_SECRET	*something of your choice*
EMAIL_DIRECTORY	tmp/email
MESSAGE_STORE_CONNECTION_STRING	*see below*
NODE_ENV	production
SYSTEM_SENDER_EMAIL_ADDRESS	no-reply@example.com

Notice that this list is very similar to the environment variables in .env. MES-SAGE_STORE_CONNECTION_STRING should get the same value as the second database URL. Using the screenshots above, Heroku named the second Heroku Postgres instance HEROKU_POSTGRESQL_COBALT. In the environment variables, Heroku pre-populated a HEROKU_POSTGRESQL_COBALT_URL. Duplicate the value of that key into a new key named MESSAGE_STORE_CONNECTION_STRING.

PORT is missing from this list, since Heroku will supply it at runtime.

For COOKIE_SECRET you'll want to put something good and random there, since that will be the key used to sign cookies in our system. There's a script at video-tutorials/src/bin/generate-cookie-secret.js. If you look at the project's package.json file, you'll see you can invoke it with npm run generate-cookie-secret. That will give you output resembling the following:

```
$ npm run generate-cookie-secret

> microservices-book@1.0.0 generate-cookie-secret
> node src/bin/generate-cookie-secret

eff41191a4c1f51742496bd07ec9ca5407a94e0e98fb995f920d8690828c7aa8
```

If you run that script, you can copy the resulting string and make that your COOKIE_SECRET value if you wish. Or you can put something else. Up to you. But, whatever you do, don't put the one that appeared in print in this book. No one else is supposed to know your secret. That's why it's called a secret.

Installing Message DB

Next we need to install Message DB into that second Heroku Postgres instance. There is a script in code/video-tutorials/script/install-message-store-in-heroku.js that will do the necessary installation. You'll need to have installed the psql client on your machine, so if you haven't, follow the directions at the PostgreSQL website[3] to get up and running.

---

3.   https://www.postgresql.org/download/

Assuming you have that client installed, you'll need your connection credentials. These are found in the value of the MESSAGE_STORE_CONNECTION_STRING value in Heroku. That string is of the form:

```
postgres://PGUSER:PGPASSWORD@PGHOST:PGPORT/PGDATABASE
```

Run the install-message-store-in-heroku.js script with a total of five environment variables. Windows and *nix-based systems differ in how they treat environment variables, but in Bash, you'd invoke the script as follows:

```
[video-tutorials]$ PGUSER=mqlztugqizopuz \
PGPASSWORD=fd2b16b923521a2312ee9a63a8fe7c37d869fdde860abdbf1c0e172de9a7820f \
PGHOST=ec2-174-129-253-175.compute-1.amazonaws.com \
PGPORT=5432 \
PGDATABASE=d2a0cj6ir00kc2 node script/install-message-store-in-heroku.js
```

which will produce output similar to the following:

```
psql://code/video-tutorials/node_modules/@eventide/message-db/database/types/
message.sql:15: NOTICE: type "message_store.message" does not exist, skipping
psql://code/video-tutorials/node_modules/@eventide/message-db/database/
indexes/messages-category.sql:1: NOTICE:  index "messages_category" does
not exist, skipping
psql://code/video-tutorials/node_modules/@eventide/message-db/database/
indexes/messages-id.sql:1: NOTICE:  index "messages_id" does not exist,
skipping
psql://code/video-tutorials/node_modules/@eventide/message-db/database/
indexes/messages-stream.sql:1: NOTICE:  index "messages_stream" does not
exist, skipping
```

You might see slightly different output, but don't be alarmed by the NOTICEs. You can use those same PGUSER etc. values to use a database connection tool and connect directly to the Heroku Postgres instance and verify the installation.

Deploying the System

Now that the "App" is configured, you should be able to deploy the system code. If you set things up the way that Heroku told you to, then you'll likely just need to run git push heroku master. If you named your Git remote something else, you'll want to push to that. You should see a wall of text telling you that the repo is being pushed and that the "App" is being built.

You should then be able to actually navigate a browser to the site. Since I can't know what you named your "App," it would be impossible to give an exact link. However, it'll be something of the form https://<your app name>.herokuapp.com. Navigate to there, and you should be treated to a page like the screenshot on page 201.

So while that is exactly the same page you loaded in development, this is special because it's actually deployed into the wild. Congrats! You just deployed a bona fide microservices-based system into the wild.

Distributing the System

To distribute or not to distribute; that is the question. Tyler Treat wrote, "The first rule of distributed systems is don't distribute your system until you have an observable reason to."[4] The following are not observable reasons to distribute:

- You want to use Kubernetes.[5]
- You read somewhere that microservices need to be distributed.
- You know how to put things in Docker containers.

Distributing a system is necessarily going to be more complicated than not distributing it. More things to deploy. More things to organize. More moving parts. But there are sometimes good reasons, and they revolve around *availability*.

Our system currently is deployed as a single unit. If you want to deploy a new version of the video-publishing Component, you end up taking the Creators Portal application down. If the user-credentials Aggregator crashes for some reason, it's taking the rest of the system down because it's running in the same process. Once we start scaling our development team, organizational structure may lead us to deploying pieces independently. By making all communication between pieces pub/sub-based and by respecting the message contract, we absolutely can have this kind of independent deployment without disturbing the rest of the system.

With the current size of Video Tutorials, we're okay leaving it as a single unit. We're not observing any problems requiring us to distribute our pieces. But let's pretend that we are, so that you can see how it's done.

---

4.   https://bravenewgeek.com/service-disoriented-architecture/
5.   https://kubernetes.io

Currently we have a codebase like the following—some of the pieces are omitted so that the chart fits.

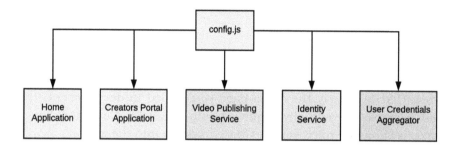

We have a single codebase, a single process tied together via a config.js file. The first obvious step in distributing this system and improving availability is to separate the Applications from the asynchronous components. Making this change will mean that if one of these components goes down, it won't bring down the website our users interact with. We'll put each side of this division into separate repositories, and connect those to new config.js files:

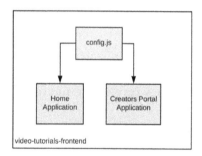
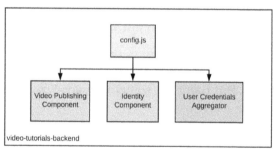

You can see how this is done in the distributed-video-tutorials folder. Because of the way the code for the book is distributed, you weren't able to download the code as two separate repositories. But, once you have the code downloaded, you can do the necessary filesystem manipulation. Make a Friday night out of it!

In any case, if you look in the distributed-video-tutorials folder, you'll see two folders under it, namely front-end and back-end. If you dig further into those folders, you'll find a familiar folder structure with a few changes. front-end doesn't have the aggregators or components folders, and back-end doesn't have the app folder. Furthermore, if you open the config.js files in each half, you'll see that the bits for the other half have been removed. Minor changes were made in src/index.js too; for example, in the front end's folder:

```
distributed-video-tutorials/front-end/src/index.js
const createExpressApp = require('./app/express')
const createConfig = require('./config')
const env = require('./env')

const config = createConfig({ env })
const app = createExpressApp({ config, env })

function start () {
  app.listen(env.port, signalAppStart)
}

function signalAppStart () {
  console.log(`${env.appName} started`)
  console.table([['Port', env.port], ['Environment', env.env]])
}
module.exports = {
  app,
  config,
  start
}
```

Notice that in the start function there are no longer references to aggregators and components. To reduce confusion, the Docker bit that starts the database isn't in both locations. We put it in the back-end because the Aggregators own the tables we write to, so they also own starting the database locally. So, locally, if you run the Docker image to get the database going and then run npm install followed by npm run start-dev-server in both folders, you'll be able to run the system just as you did before.

If you want to deploy the distributed version to Heroku, I recommend creating two new "apps." You can attach the Postgres Add-on to the back end. The code is set up so that front-end doesn't have any migrations. It certainly could, so that's why its config.js specifies a different table for storing its migrations, functionality you added back in on page 16:

```
distributed-video-tutorials/front-end/src/config.js
const knexClient = createKnexClient({
  connectionString: env.databaseUrl,
  migrationsTableName: 'front_end_migrations'
})
```

Note the new migrationsTableName. And one last note about deploying these together to Heroku. The back-end deployment won't start properly unless you run the following command from the back end's folder: heroku scale web=0 worker=1. By default, Heroku tries to run a web dyno.[6] However, no part of the

---

6. https://devcenter.heroku.com/articles/dynos

back-end deployment uses a web server, so we have to tell Heroku to not expect one (web=0) and to expect a worker (worker=1). And also, heads-up: the worker dyno will never sleep and will consume your free tier hours.

"Okay, that was a whole lot of work to just arrive at the same point," you might be thinking. It wasn't as pointless as that. First, notice that distributing the halves didn't actually require any code changes to the actual components themselves. You didn't have to open anything under app, aggregators, or components. There were no entanglements between any of those pieces. Second, the system is now distributed, and it's a distributed system of autonomous pieces. At the end of the chapter, you'll have an exercise where you intentionally bring down half of the system and see how the other half is not affected—and it won't take any code to make it work.

Deploying Databases

You've probably noticed that this entire project uses a single physical database, and that likely seems unsettling. If you analyze the code, you'll notice that a given instance of View Data is only ever written to by a single Aggregator. View Data are built with a single Application in mind as well.

Earlier we showed how we could take code out of our single codebase and begin to organize repositories around these separate pieces. It was mostly the config.js file that felt the impact of that change, but *all* of the change was felt at the outermost layer of the codebase. It was only the parts that connect the operating system to our code. Autonomy made it this easy. Autonomy made the deployment strategy independent of the actual system model.

Well, in a similar manner, we could move the tables in our single database to different databases. One very obvious division would be to put the Message Store in its own database, possibly its own server. But it's questions of availability that are going to determine that. As long as we honor the separation of concerns as Video Tutorials currently does, where to locate the tables is a very separate concern.

What You've Done So Far

You deployed Video Tutorials in this chapter! Hopefully it brings you joy thinking of all the people learning new things and all the content creators making a living using your creation. You've now operationalized a microservices-based system. This all started with an idea, and now you've taken that idea and are able to hit it in a web browser. Nice work!

To drive home the point of autonomy, consider the two halves in the distributed-video-tutorials folder. *These two halves can run completely independently.* Prove that to yourself. Start only the front end. Register a user. Click the "Record video viewing" button on the home page a few times. That view count won't increment, and your user won't be able to log in. Then stop the front end and start the back end. Maybe load the Message Store database in the database viewing tool of your choice. Notice that even though the front end is down, the back end continues chugging its way through the messages it needs to process. Then restart the front end and notice that all the operations you queued have completed.

Those chunks are autonomous. While it's unlikely you'd deliberately bring down such a large chunk of functionality for a long time on purpose, you probably will redeploy code from time to time. With autonomous components, a redeployment of one component doesn't make the whole system unavailable.

Now, of course this won't ever happen to us, but you may have friends that deploy systems that have bugs, and they'll ask you for help debugging their systems. What tools does this architecture provide for debugging? That's the topic of the very next chapter, so let's head over there to fix our sys—err, our friends' systems.

CHAPTER 13

Debugging Components

(2 weeks have passed...)

That go-live button was probably the most satisfying button anyone has ever pushed in the history of pushing buttons. Video Tutorials is live, people are learning, and our content creators are making a nice living.

The call just came in, though, that while we're getting a lot of signups, we've had a significant drop in the number of people who are actually logging into the site. We've got to figure this out and get things rolling again.

We're going to look at how we can use the event-based architecture to detect this problem in the first place and then how the architecture helps us debug it. All the information we need is already being kicked out in the form of events, so this chapter is going to be about interesting aggregations of that data.

Priming the Database with Example Data

First off, we're working out of the code/debugging-components folder in this chapter rather than our usual code/video-tutorials chapter, so make sure to switch there.

The story we're telling in this chapter will make a whole lot more sense if you prime your database with some good test data. It's worthwhile to completely destroy and rebuild your database before going any further. If you're using the Docker setup in this book, running docker-compose rm -sf followed by docker-compose up in code/debugging-components will do just that. If you're not using the Docker setup, well, then do whatever you do to rebuild it.

Once you've done that, also from within code/debugging-components, run npm run populate. That will inject 15 Register commands to prime the Message Store with data. When you start the server, the Components will get to work on those commands and produce corresponding events.

Now that we have data to work with, it's time to put on your sleuthing hat because the game is afoot!

Introducing the Admin Portal

What self-respecting system doesn't have an Admin Portal? Certainly not Video Tutorials!

Most of our work in this chapter is going to be working through building admin capabilities to explore the wealth of debugging information the Message Store provides for us. We don't have enough space to print every line of code that makes up this paragon of usefulness and good web design. Let's start, though, by exploring the first screen, which might help us debug what's going on:

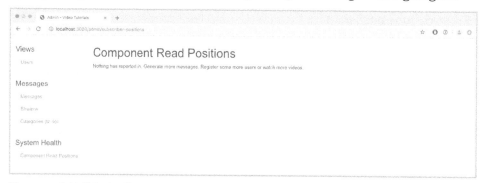

You can hit this in the running system by navigating to /admin/subscriber-positions. First, on the left, notice that the navigation is broken up into three main chunks. We have "Views," such as "User." Users are views, aggregations of data. Then we have the "Messages" section, which contains links for slicing and dicing the messages in interesting ways, such as a complete list of all the messages and a list of all the streams in the system. But for now, we're most interested in the third section, "System Health." Under this section we have "Component Read Positions." Remember those Read events we started writing in Chapter 5, Subscribing to the Message Store, on page 65? Well, we can aggregate those.

You can check out the code for that Aggregator in src/code/debugging-components/ aggregators/admin-subscriber-positions.js, but before you do, think through how you'd write this Aggregator. What would the columns be? What category would the subscription subscribe to? What message type(s) do you need to handle? How would this Aggregator handle idempotence?

Looking at that page, yeah, nothing has reported anything. Take a moment to think about why that is. How many messages did npm run populate write to the Message Store? Fifteen. How often do components write their progress?

Every 100 messages. There's not enough activity yet. This view has its uses, but it's pretty coarse. We need something finer.

Creating Users

Hopefully that header made you cringe. "*Creating* users? Didn't you start soapboxing on this in Beating a Dead Horse, on page 86?" Fair enough. Maybe "Assembling Users" or "Building Frankenstein's Monster" would be a more accurate title. While our users aren't monsters, we *are* going to take the various streams of data related to our users and assemble them into an aggregate view we'll call "users."

Specifically, we want a screen that shows users' email addresses, the number of times they've logged in, and whether or not we think we sent them their registration email. This will be our first step in tracking down why people aren't receiving their emails—*do we even think we've sent them?* If we think we have, then it might indicate that something is wrong with our email provider. But we need the data first.

The data we need is sitting in the identity and authentication category streams. But we don't want to look at lists of events, so that means we're going to write an Aggregator. Let's write the migration file for the view that we're going to populate with this Aggregator:

```
debugging-components/migrations/20190805180637_create-admin-users.js
exports.up = function up (knex) {
  return knex.schema.createTable('admin_users', table => {
    table.string('id').primary()
    table.string('email')
    table.boolean('registration_email_sent').defaultTo(false)
    table.integer('last_identity_event_global_position').defaultTo(0)
    table.integer('login_count').defaultTo(0)
    table.integer('last_authentication_event_global_position').defaultTo(0)

    table.index('email')
  })
}

exports.down = knex => knex.schema.dropTable('admin_users')
```

There is an id column for the user's ID, and then we two sets of columns. In each set there are the data points we're going to show in the admin screen and then an idempotence column. Because the data we're aggregating is in two separate stream categories, we're going to have two separate subscriptions. We have no guarantees of message order *across streams*. Even though registration events must necessarily be written before we encounter login events, we have no guarantee that the identity subscription will aggregate registration events before the authentication subscription aggregates login events. So, we need to track these last event IDs for each subscription.

Now we can get to the Aggregator itself:

```
debugging-components/src/aggregators/admin-users.js
function build ({ db, messageStore }) {
  const queries = createQueries({ db })
❶ const identityHandlers = createIdentityHandlers({ queries })
  const identitySubscription = messageStore.createSubscription({
    streamName: 'identity',
    handlers: identityHandlers,
    subscriberId: 'e482ed56-311c-486c-9bb8-8c2e2ca6f6f4'
  })

❷ const authenticationHandlers = createAuthenticationHandlers({ queries })
  const authenticationSubscription = messageStore.createSubscription({
    streamName: 'authentication',
    handlers: authenticationHandlers,
    subscriberId: '18b4c5d6-1f30-4a67-9b61-76a42884a9bb'
  })

❸ function start () {
    identitySubscription.start()
    authenticationSubscription.start()
  }

  return {
    authenticationHandlers,
    identityHandlers,
    queries,
    start
  }
}

module.exports = build
```

This is another multi-subscription Aggregator:

❶ First, we have the handlers/subscription pair for the identity category stream. This category gives us the user's email address, the result of our work in Chapter 7, Implementing Your First Component, on page 105, and whether or not we think we've sent the email, the result of our work in Chapter 9, Adding an Email Component, on page 133.

❷ Next up, we have the pair for the authentication category. In Chapter 8, Authenticating Users, on page 119, we set up this category to track user login activity.

❸ And then notice that each subscription is separately started in the start function.

Notice that each subscription has its own subscriberId. Remember from the discussion back in Chapter 5, Subscribing to the Message Store, on page 65, that the subscriberId becomes part of the name of the stream that periodically records the last message that a subscriber has processed? If we don't have unique subscriberIds, then subscribers will clobber each other's record of how far they've made it in the message history.

Let's add those two sets of handlers, starting with the Registered handler found in the identity handlers:

```
debugging-components/src/aggregators/admin-users.js
function createIdentityHandlers ({ queries }) {
  return {
    Registered: event =>
      queries
        .ensureUser(event.data.userId)
        .then(() =>
          queries.setEmail(
            event.data.userId,
            event.data.email,
            event.globalPosition
          )
        ),
  }
}
```

The identity subscription handles the Registered and RegistrationEmailSent events. And when it handles either one, it needs to make sure that the user in question exists, hence the call to queries.ensureUser passing in event.data.userId.

Here is queries.ensureUser:

```
debugging-components/src/aggregators/admin-users.js
function createQueries ({ db }) {
  function ensureUser (id) {
    const rawQuery = `
      INSERT INTO
        admin_users (id)
      VALUES
        (:id)
      ON CONFLICT DO NOTHING
    `

    return db.then(client => client.raw(rawQuery, { id }))
  }
  return {
    ensureUser,
  }
}
```

It's an idempotent query. We again use PostgreSQL's ON CONFLICT DO NOTHING capability to make it so that we can execute this query as many times as we care to without ill effect. All this query does is insert a row with the ID populated, ensuring that the row is in place before proceeding to handle either message.

One we've ensured we have the user's row, then we can go ahead and set the email address with queries.setEmail:

```
debugging-components/src/aggregators/admin-users.js
function createQueries ({ db }) {
  function setEmail (id, email, eventGlobalPosition) {
    return db.then(
      client =>
        client('admin_users')
          .update({
            email: email,
            last_identity_event_global_position: eventGlobalPosition
          })
          .where(
            'last_identity_event_global_position',
            '<',
            eventGlobalPosition
          )
          .where({ id: id })
    )
  }
  return {
    setEmail
  }
}
```

Again, because of the call to queries.ensureUser we get to assume that the user's row is in place. Making that assumption, this query then updates the email column of the corresponding row. It also updates the last_identity_event_global_position_id column, which we use for idempotence on identity events. But of course, to be idempotent, we only do this where last_email_event_global_position_id is less than the eventGlobalPosition that we are processing. Both of our query functions are idempotent, and thus this handler is idempotent, so we are good to go here.

Next up, RegistrationEmailSent events:

```
debugging-components/src/aggregators/admin-users.js
function createIdentityHandlers ({ queries }) {
  return {
    RegistrationEmailSent: event => queries
      .ensureUser(event.data.userId)
      .then(() =>
```

```
    queries.markRegistrationEmailSent(
      event.data.userId,
      event.globalPosition
    )
  )
  }
}
```

It's similar in shape to the Registered handler. Notice how this handler also starts with the call to queries.ensureUser. Our message flow doesn't allow an email to go out before a user registers, but we include this check as a safety measure against future changes because it doesn't cost much to keep it. But the site is currently on fire because users are reporting not getting their emails, so let's stop the idle chit chat and get back to making this view by writing queries.markRegistrationEmailSent, the query that this handler calls:

debugging-components/src/aggregators/admin-users.js
```
function createQueries ({ db }) {
  function markRegistrationEmailSent (id, eventGlobalPosition) {
    return db.then(
      client =>
        client('admin_users')
          .update({
            registration_email_sent: true,
            last_identity_event_global_position: eventGlobalPosition
          })
          .where(
            'last_identity_event_global_position',
            '<',
            eventGlobalPosition
          )
          .where({ id: id })
    )
  }
  return {
    markRegistrationEmailSent,
  }
}
```

This is the exact same shape as what we did for setEmail. Update the sent flag to true and the last message processed to the current event's ID, but only if the currently recorded last message global position is less than the current message's global position so that the call is idempotent.

We won't print the code for the authentication category handlers, which give us the login count, because you've already encountered a similar pattern in the code for queries.incrementVideosWatched on page 55. Do go read through it though in code/debugging-components/src/aggregators/admin-users.js.

Next we need to connect this Aggregator to the rest of the system so that it runs. This takes us to config.js:

```
debugging-components/src/config.js
// ...
const createAdminUsersAggregator = require('./aggregators/admin-users')
function createConfig ({ env }) {
  // ...
  const adminUsersAggregator = createAdminUsersAggregator({
    db: knexClient,
    messageStore
  })
  const aggregators = [
    // ...
    adminUsersAggregator,
  ]
  return {
    // ...
    adminUsersAggregator,
  }
}
```

This is the same pattern you used with, for example, the home page Aggregator on page 60 and the user credentials Aggregator on page 121:

1. Pull in the creator function.
2. Instantiate the Aggregator with a reference to the db and messageStore.
3. Add it to the aggregators array.
4. Add it to the config return object.

With the Aggregator connected, its View Data is getting populated. Now we need to display it.

Wiring the Users View into the Admin Portal

It's an application, so we start with our standard application preamble:

```
debugging-components/src/app/admin/index.js
function createAdminApplication ({ db, messageStoreDb }) {
  const queries = createQueries({ db, messageStoreDb })
  const handlers = createHandlers({ queries })

  const router = express.Router()

  router.route('/users').get(handlers.handleUsersIndex)
  router.route('/users/:id').get(handlers.handleShowUser)
```

```
    return {
      handlers,
      queries,
      router
    }
}

module.exports = createAdminApplication
```

Set up the queries, handlers, and router. We're going to start with two routes. The first is for the master list of users, and the second is for a particular user. Master list first:

```
debugging-components/src/app/admin/index.js
function createHandlers ({ queries }) {
  function handleUsersIndex (req, res) {
    return queries
      .usersIndex()
      .then(users =>
        res.render('admin/templates/users-index', { users: users })
      )
  }
  return {
    handleUsersIndex,
  }
}
```

Routes that just display data generally follow a "query for the data -> render it in a template" pattern, and this is no exception. That query is found in queries.usersIndex, so let's write that:

```
debugging-components/src/app/admin/index.js
function createQueries ({ db, messageStoreDb }) {
  function usersIndex () {
    return db
      .then(client => client('admin_users').orderBy('email', 'ASC'))
      .then(camelCaseKeys)
  }
  return {
    usersIndex,
  }
}
```

You just finished populating that admin_users table, and all we're doing here is querying it and ordering the results by email. NB: WE ARE NOT WORRYING ABOUT PAGINATION! Sorry to yell there. In future projects, you'll definitely want to paginate your results, but for Video Tutorials, we don't want to distract from the rest of the flow.

Once this query has completed, we render the template found at code/debugging-components/src/app/admin/templates/users-index.pug. It's a basic page with a table to display all the users and worth reprinting here. That finishes the Users view in the Admin Portal. Those user IDs are links that will show us a given user's activity, so let's hook that up too. In the top-level function on page 214 we wrote that the single-user endpoint is handled by handlers.handleShowUser, so let's handle that one:

```
debugging-components/src/app/admin/index.js
function createHandlers ({ queries }) {
  function handleShowUser (req, res) {
    const userPromise = queries.user(req.params.id)
    const loginEventsPromise = queries.userLoginEvents(req.params.id)
    const viewingEventsPromise = queries.userViewingEvents(req.params.id)

    return Promise.all([
      userPromise,
      loginEventsPromise,
      viewingEventsPromise
    ]).then(values => {
      const user = values[0]
      const loginEvents = values[1]
      const viewingEvents = values[2]

      return res.render('admin/templates/user', {
        user: user,
        loginEvents: loginEvents,
        viewingEvents: viewingEvents
      })
    })
  }
  return {
    handleShowUser,
  }
}
```

❶ This handler is a bit denser than others, and that's because the data we're going to put in this view is not stored all in one location. We're going to show the users' email addresses, their video viewing activity, and their login activity. So, we set up three Promises to query for that data. JavaScript Promises aren't just fancy new syntax to avoid callback hell. They're values that merely aren't available at the moment they're instantiated. Values can be given names, in this case userPromise, loginEventsPromise, and viewingEventsPromise.

❷ We then use the Promise.all[1] function to wait for these three Promises to resolve.

❸ Promise.all itself resolves to an array containing the result of each Promise passed to it and in the same order. So, we extract the actual values we were interested in. Notice the naming of the pairs. userPromise resolves to user and so forth.

❹ With all of these values extracted, we can then render the template at code/debugging-components/src/app/admin/templates/user.pug, passing in each of those results.

The queries.user function just queries the admin_users table where the id column is equal to the ID of the user in question—not very interesting at this point. The other two are worth diving into though, as they use the Message Store's messages table directly.

First, let's consider queries.userLoginEvents. In what stream would all the login events for a given user be located? Check out Chapter 8, Authenticating Users, on page 119 and the contract file at code/debugging-components/src/app/authenticate/contract.md for a refresher before we write the following code:

```
debugging-components/src/app/admin/index.js
function createQueries ({ db, messageStoreDb }) {
  function userLoginEvents (userId) {
    return messageStoreDb.query(
      `
      SELECT
        *
      FROM
        messages
      WHERE stream_name=$1
      ORDER BY global_position ASC
      `,
      [`authentication-${userId}`]
    )
      .then(res => res.rows)
      .then(camelCaseKeys)
  }
  return {
    userLoginEvents,
  }
}
```

First, notice that we're using the Message Store's db connection, so we're dealing with the lower-level pg interface rather than knex. Then, the events

---

1. https://developer.mozilla.org/en-US/docs/Web/JavaScript/Reference/Global_Objects/Promise/all

that we're after are in the authentication category, so for an individual user, we just want authentication-X where X is the user's ID. This is one of those rare instances where the way we wrote the data is also the way we wanted to read it, since we're effectively building an audit log here.

Next, let's write queries.userViewingEvents:

```
debugging-components/src/app/admin/index.js
function createQueries ({ db, messageStoreDb }) {
  function userViewingEvents (userId) {
    return messageStoreDb.query(
      `
      SELECT
        *
      FROM
        messages
      WHERE category(stream_name) = 'viewing' AND data->>'userId' = $1
      ORDER BY global_position ASC
      `,
      [userId]
    )
      .then(res => res.rows)
      .then(camelCaseKeys)
  }
  return {
    userViewingEvents,
  }
}
```

The trick here is that these streams are organized by the video that was viewed and not by the user doing the viewing. So we need to get messages in the viewing category, but that are also from our user. Message DB provides a category function that takes a stream_name and plucks out the category. The user that caused the event is of course stored in the messages's data, so we peek into that object as part of the query as well. This gets us a list of viewing events associated with the user in question.

Now, both of these views would be better accomplished with proper Aggregators. We wouldn't want to put unnecessary read burden on the Message Store, since that's not its job. In any case, we need to connect this admin application into the rest of the system, including our Express app.

Hooking the Admin Portal into the Rest of the System

We start with our standard config.js work, and then we'll deal with Express:

debugging-components/src/config.js
```
// ...
const createAdminApp = require('./app/admin')
function createConfig ({ env }) {
  // ...
  const adminApp = createAdminApp({
    db: knexClient,
    messageStoreDb: postgresClient
  })
  return {
    // ...
    adminApp,
  }
}
```

Require. Instantiate. Return. Sounds like the makings of a political candidate's slogan. Notice the Admin Portal takes a reference to the Message Store's database connection. We'll do some queries against the Message Store directly.

Let's mount it in Express:

debugging-components/src/app/express/mount-routes.js
```
function mountRoutes (app, config) {
  app.use('/', config.homeApp.router)
  app.use('/record-viewing', config.recordViewingsApp.router)
  app.use('/register', config.registerUsersApp.router)
  app.use('/auth', config.authenticateApp.router)
➤ app.route('/admin').get((req, res) => res.redirect('/admin/users'))
➤ app.use('/admin', config.adminApp.router)
}
```

We pull one bit of trickery here. We set up a route on /admin to redirect to /admin/users. That way, if we hit the root of the Admin Portal, we don't get a 404. And yes, you would want to secure your Admin Portal behind an authentication wall. Hiding it behind a predictable URL, even one that isn't linked to from anywhere on the site, is not a Security Best Practice™. And believe you me, nefarious actors will be gunning for this site.

Inspecting the Results So Far

All right, with the Admin Portal wired up, start your server with npm run start-dev-server and navigate to the /admin route. That'll land you at the master users list as shown in the screenshot on page 220.

Ouch! That's a whole lot of "no" on that screen. For every single user, the "registration email sent" column is telling us "no."

It's looking like we don't think we've sent the emails, but at this point, there are still two possibilities. Can you think of what they are? As a hint, you're looking at the output from an Aggregator.

It could be that the Aggregator isn't aggregating. It could also be that there are no RegistrationEmailSent events in the Message Store for our Aggregator to aggregate. Before we dive into that, let's confirm the symptom that no one is logging in by clicking through to one of those users:

Indeed, it seems this user hasn't logged in. We need to figure out what's going on.

Thinking Through the Expected Flow

We know what's supposed to happen when someone registers. The register-users application writes a Register command that the identity component picks up. It writes a Registered event in response to that command. It then handles its own Registered event by writing a Send command that send-email observes and handles by sending the email and writing a Sent event. identity is listening for that Sent event. How can we construct a view that tells us if these three things happened and in the proper sequence? Is there a piece of data we have that links these messages across time and component boundaries, also known as *distributed tracing*?

Sure is. Remember those traceIds we've been so careful to include? All three of those messages would have the same one. We can build a view off of that.

Correlators Gonna…Correlate?

Back to the Admin Portal application, let's set up another route:

```
debugging-components/src/app/admin/index.js
function createAdminApplication ({ db, messageStoreDb }) {
  // ...
  router
    .route('/correlated-messages/:traceId')
    .get(handlers.handleCorrelatedMessagesIndex)
  // ...
  return {
    handlers,
    queries,
    router
  }
}
```

Okay, here's the handlers.handleCorrelatedMessagesIndex handler:

```
debugging-components/src/app/admin/index.js
function createHandlers ({ queries }) {
  function handleCorrelatedMessagesIndex (req, res) {
    const traceId = req.params.traceId

    return queries
      .correlatedMessages(traceId)
      .then(messages =>
        res.render('admin/templates/messages-index', {
          messages,
          title: 'Correlated Messages'
        })
      )
  }
  return {
    handleCorrelatedMessagesIndex,
  }
}
```

Extract the traceId from req.params and then call queries.correlatedMessages with that traceId. When we get the results, we render the template at code/debugging-components/app/admin/templates/messages-index.pug. That template has a more generic name because it's used for displaying lists of messages beyond those just grouped by traceId, such as what you'll get if you navigate to /admin/messages.

Let's write that query:

```
debugging-components/src/app/admin/index.js
function createQueries ({ db, messageStoreDb }) {
  function correlatedMessages (traceId) {
    return messageStoreDb.query(
      `SELECT * FROM messages WHERE metadata->>'traceId' = $1`,
      [traceId]
    )
      .then(res => res.rows)
      .then(camelCaseKeys)
  }
  return {
    correlatedMessages,
  }
}
```

It SELECTs from messages looking for messages with the traceId we're after.

This Query Does Not Use an Index!

It is very worth calling out that this implementation does not use an index! With 45 messages in the Message Store—the count you'd have if you're running with a fresh database, ran the populate script, and started the server—that isn't going to be an issue. With millions of messages, well, that would be a different story.

If you were going to build an Aggregator, you *could* have a table with a trace_id column that stored one message per row. One message per row seems very similar to the Message Store, but you'd at least have an index on trace_id and pull these queries off of the operational Message Store.

You could also feed the messages into something like ElasticSearch or have a table with a JSONB column that stores an array of messages. You have the freedom to build what makes sense!

Back to the task at hand, let's go ahead and navigate our browser to the /admin/messages endpoint we mentioned a moment ago:

If you cleared your database and ran the populate script, then you'll have those fifteen commands at the top. Let's take the first one and click on its traceId. That takes us to the /admin/correlated-messages endpoint we just wrote before. Drum roll, please...

Uh-oh. There are only three messages. We expected five messages because our flow indicates five. We're missing the Sent event from send-email and the RegistrationEmailSent event from identity. Now, this could be because we sent the emails and then crashed before writing the Sent event, but the symptom our users are reporting is that they never got the emails. This suggests that send-email isn't running.

Imagining Our Way to Good System Monitoring

Okay, it's no secret that merely writing to STDOUT is not a great logging strategy. But let's imagine that we had some sort of logging system set up that consumed our STDOUT output—the same sort of thing you'd set up for any project. The microservices architecture doesn't change that.

We don't put domain state in this sort of thing because that goes in the Message Store. On the flip side, we don't put debug logging in the Message Store because debug logging isn't domain state.

Anyway, we looked at our system logging that we *totally* set up, and we didn't see any messages from our subscription indicating that the subscription tried to start and then crashed. It's almost like we never told it to start!

Starting from the Beginning

We know that our components get started in src/index.js where we call start on each of them. Since the other components are running, we know that line is getting called. Is it possible the Component isn't making it in there?

Let's head over to src/config.js to find out:

debugging-components/src/config.js

```
Line 1  const components = [
     2    // ...
     3    identityComponent,
     4    // sendEmailComponent, //
     5    videoPublishingComponent
     6  ]
```

What in tarnation is going on at line 4?! Amateur hour, that's what. We need to have a serious look at our internal development processes that allowed a stinker like this to make it onto actual servers. Someone commented out sendEmailComponent, so it never made it into the services array, which means it never got its start function called.

Go ahead and uncomment that line and start the server. send-email should start chewing through those UserRegistered events and start sending those emails. Mystery solved, sheesh. At least we have some nice debugging capabilities as a result of this hunt.

Let's add one more.

Viewing Messages by Stream

The Admin Portal also lets us explore all the streams that are in the Message Store:

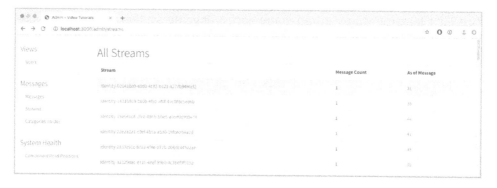

This view also gives us the number of messages in the stream and the global-Position of the last message that updated the stream's view. We could do this as a raw query on the Message Store, but that would be a hefty query to execute. We'll instead add another Aggregator to generate this view. Let's start with the migration that builds the database table we'll aggregate to:

```
debugging-components/migrations/20190830155603_create-admin-streams.js
exports.up = function up (knex) {
  return knex.schema.createTable('admin_streams', table => {
    table.string('stream_name').primary()
    table.integer('message_count').defaultsTo(0)
    table.string('last_message_id')
    table.integer('last_message_global_position').defaultsTo(0)
  })
}

exports.down = knex => knex.schema.dropTable('admin_streams')
```

Four columns. First, the stream_name becomes the primary key for this table.
Those are going to be unique. Then we're going to track a message_count so we
can know how many messages are in that stream. Then we have last_message_id,
which stores the ID of the last message written to this stream. Finally, all
handlers need to be idempotent, so we'll track last_message_global_position like
we've done for previous View Data so that we can use a message's global_position
as its idempotence key.

Let's populate this table by writing the admin streams Aggregator:

```
debugging-components/src/aggregators/admin-streams.js
function build ({ db, messageStore }) {
  const queries = createQueries({ db })
  const handlers = createHandlers({ queries })
  const subscription = messageStore.createSubscription({
    streamName: '$all',
    handlers: handlers,
    subscriberId: '6db9a0ab-7679-4b02-b5ad-2ebc8ae06b6a'
  })

  function start () {
    subscription.start()
  }

  return {
    handlers,
    queries,
    start
  }
}

module.exports = build
```

From the beginning, this is one part familiar, one part new. We have our
standard queries, handlers, and subscription trio. But look at that streamName the
subscription subscribes to. $all? What does that mean?

Well, it's a special stream name that we're coming up with that means "every message in the Message Store." We want to aggregate every stream in the Message Store. There isn't a single category we could subscribe to that gives us every message, and we don't want to have to whitelist every possible category we may ever come up with in the future. This is going to require augmenting the Message Store code, which we'll do right after working through the rest of this Aggregator.

Let's check out the handlers:

debugging-components/src/aggregators/admin-streams.js
```
function createHandlers ({ queries }) {
  return {
    $any: event => queries.upsertStream(
      event.streamName,
      event.id,
      event.globalPosition
    )
  }
}
```

"Handlers" with an "s" may have oversold this one. There's just one handler, and it is one of those very rare exceptions we talked about back on page 71 when we wrote the handleMessage function of the subscription mechanism in the Message Store. This handler uses an $any, which means that it wants to handle every type of message. This means we don't have to enumerate every message type in the system for this Aggregator. Yay!

It doesn't do much though, merely extracting the streamName, id, and globalPosition from the message—yes message, because this Aggregator is tracking all streams and not just entity streams—and passing them to queries.upsertStream:

debugging-components/src/aggregators/admin-streams.js
```
function createQueries ({ db }) {
  function upsertStream (streamName, id, globalPosition) {
    const rawQuery = `
      INSERT INTO
        admin_streams (
          stream_name,
          message_count,
          last_message_id,
          last_message_global_position
        )
      VALUES
        (:streamName, 1, :id, :globalPosition)
```

```
      ON CONFLICT (stream_name) DO UPDATE
        SET
          message_count = admin_streams.message_count + 1,
          last_message_id = :id,
          last_message_global_position = :globalPosition
        WHERE
          admin_streams.last_message_global_position < :globalPosition
    `

  return db.then(
    client => client.raw(rawQuery, { streamName, id, globalPosition })
  )
  }

  return { upsertStream }
}
```

This query has a few things going on. It's an upsert operation, which will insert a new row if the corresponding stream does not yet exist in the View Data or update said row if it already does. It helps to consider it in those two chunks.

First, it's a basic INSERT, setting the stream_name, last_message_id, and last_message_global_position to the values that were passed in. If we're actually doing the INSERT, then that means this is the first message we've encountered for this stream. So 1 is not only the loneliest number that you'll ever do,[2] it's also the correct number of messages for this stream at this point in time.

Now comes the upsert part. If we're handling this message a second time, by definition we're not taking the INSERT path. We again use PostgreSQL's ON CONFLICT functionality, using the stream_name column as the conflicting column. If that's the case we do a conditional UPDATE, incrementing message_count and setting last_message_id and last_message_global_position to the current message's values. That wouldn't be enough to make this idempotent, which is where the WHERE clause comes in. It restricts this UPDATE to cases where the current last_message_global_position is less than the incoming message's globalPosition.

That's a lot, so let's review the three cases we could encounter.

- Legitimately handling this stream for the first time—we take the INSERT path. All is well.

- Legitimately handling additional messages to the same stream—we take the ON CONFLICT branch. Because the incoming message's globalPosition is greater than the current last_message_global_position, we increment the count and update last_message_id and last_message_global_position. All is well.

---

2. https://www.youtube.com/watch?v=d5ab8BOu4LE

- Re-handling a message—we'll get a conflict on stream_name, but we won't UPDATE because the last_message_global_position will not be less than the incoming message's globalPosition. All is well.

And should the Aggregator die before the query is through? Well, it'll just restart later. All is well.

Augmenting the Message Store for $any and $all

Technically, we don't have to do anything to support $any, since we did that back on page 71 when we wrote the subscribe functionality's handleMessage function. That was too good of a header to pass up though.

Let's jump into the Message Store's read functionality to provide messages for $all:

```
debugging-components/src/message-store/read.js
const getAllMessagesSql = `
  SELECT
    id::varchar,
    stream_name::varchar,
    type::varchar,
    position::bigint,
    global_position::bigint,
    data::varchar,
    metadata::varchar,
    time::timestamp
  FROM
    messages
  WHERE
    global_position > $1
  LIMIT $2`
  function read (streamName, fromPosition = 0, maxMessages = 1000) {
    let query = null
    let values = []
    if (streamName === '$all') {
      query = getAllMessagesSql
      values = [fromPosition, maxMessages]
    } else
    if (streamName.includes('-')) {
      // Entity streams have a dash
      query = getStreamMessagesSql
      values = [streamName, fromPosition, maxMessages]
    } else {
      // Category streams do not have a dash
      query = getCategoryMessagesSql
      values = [streamName, fromPosition, maxMessages]
    }
```

```
return db.query(query, values)
    .then(res => res.rows.map(deserializeMessage))
}
```

First, we have the SQL we'll use to run the query, and then down in read we choose that SQL and the corresponding values based on streamName being $all.

With this additional functionality in place, the "Streams" view is now supplied with data. Explore it a little bit. The stream names are links to a view that shows all the messages in that particular stream, so click through to those to get a feel for how you slice and dice the messages in interesting ways.

What You've Done So Far

You can add "Code Sleuth" to your resume after this chapter. Sure, it was a contrived example, but in the process of exploring it, you built quite a few useful debugging capabilities. The tools you built in this chapter will save countless hours for your team members, so way to go.

This chapter was sprinkled with a lot of thought exercises, so let's add just one coding exercise here. The Admin Portal has a link to "Categories (to do)" under the "Messages" header. That portion of the Admin Portal is not at all done, so work through adding that. It will be very similar in spirit to the "Streams" view that closed this chapter, only instead of counting the individual stream, you'll need to map each stream to a category. So start with the database migration and then build the Aggregator and changes in to the Admin Portal that you need. And of course, remove "(to do)" from the link in the Admin Portal UI.

We're rapidly approaching the end of our journey, and up to this point, we have barely mentioned testing, let alone shown any examples of it. If you have been developing software for any length of time, surely you know how important it is to test your dang code. How else will you know you have a good system design? Rest assured that we do have tests for Video Tutorials, and it being a microservices-based system, there are some interesting things to say about testing that are particular to this architecture. Are you in for one more? Okay, let's go for it!

CHAPTER 14

Testing in a Microservices Architecture

In another life, your humble author studied economics instead of computer science and probably never would have started working with microservices architectures. That guy, of course, is missing out, and we wish him well. Hopefully, having made it this far in the book, you're not wishing reality had taken that other life's path though.

Among the many concepts in the field of economics, two that have had a profound impact on me are diminishing returns[1] and opportunity cost.[2] The former states that holding all else equal, increasing a factor of production begins to exhibit less benefit per unit added. You can intuit this. You have great use for roughly 64 ounces of water per day and probably less use for an additional 600 gallons. In fact, the only place where this concept doesn't hold true is in rock music where louder, faster, and more distortion will always make something better. We digress.

Opportunity cost is the idea that every choice you take comes at the expense of the best alternative choice you didn't take, and it goes hand in hand with diminishing returns. Each unit you add to a factor of production carries an opportunity cost. While diminishing returns doesn't necessarily mean that everything gets worse as you add more, it does means you get less and less bang for the buck. Since you're getting less and less increase in value, it might make sense to start deploying those units elsewhere.

It's really important to keep these ideas in mind in life in general, but for our purposes we're going to talk about testing in a microservices architecture. The fundamentals of testing software are sound, and if you don't test as part of your development process, well, start.

---

1. https://en.wikipedia.org/wiki/Diminishing_returns
2. https://en.wikipedia.org/wiki/Opportunity_cost

First and foremost, testing is an invaluable design tool. It forces you to *use* the code that you write! Your tests are a client of your code, and if your code is hard to test, chances are that it's also hard to use and maintain. If you find yourself resorting to unholy things like mocks and stubs, that's your code telling you, "Please design me better!" Of course, testing also helps you verify that your code produces your desired result.

But supposing that you do, things that are fundamental don't change from context to context, right? Gravity is a thing on Earth and on Jupiter. There is nothing about microservices that invalidates the fundamentals of testing and the laws of the universe. A full treatise on testing is well beyond the scope of this book, let alone this chapter. However, this chapter is going to give a flavor of how Video Tutorials has been tested and hopefully dispel some of the myths around testing in microservices architecture.

One of the biggest myths is that you need to be at FAANG scale to benefit from a microservices architecture, and an argument used in favor of that myth is that you need a complicated test framework when you build microservices. Bunkum and balderdash! Microservices make things simpler by making it so you don't have to hold as much in your head at any one time, and testing is no exception.

We're going to do three things in this chapter. We'll (a) revisit the fundamentals of our architecture so that we can (b) understand what needs automated testing, and then (c) discuss why complicated end-to-end automated testing falls squarely into the realm of diminishing returns.

Revisiting the Fundamentals

In Unmasking the Monolith, on page 25, we made the claim that the defining characteristic of a service-based architecture is autonomy. Autonomous components handle all of their communication through the Message Store. They receive commands, and sometimes events, and write new events in response. *They have only this one execution mode.* This is a subtle point with a profound implication.

How can an autonomous component tell the difference between running in a production environment and running in a test harness? Give up? It's a trick question. It can't. It has absolutely no idea if a message is coming from a live system or if it's coming from a test. It's kind of like the classic philosophical question of how we can't *really* be sure if our brains are sensing reality or if we're in a computer simulation. In the case of autonomous components, *they really can't tell.* They operate in the exact same manner.

Also, not microservices-specific, but not all testing needs to be automated. So, with these basic principles in mind, let's look at what it takes to test an autonomous component.

Writing Tests for Autonomous Components

Basically every test, microservices or not, is a three-step dance:

1. Set up the data for the test.
2. Exercise the (sub)system under test.
3. Make assertions about the results.

How does that work with autonomous components? Well, let's consider one of the very first autonomous components you wrote back in Writing Your First Aggregator, on page 53, the home page Aggregator. Its job was and still is to turn video view events into an aggregated global view count. Side by side with every bit of code in this book are test files. They're the ones that end in .test.js. The test for the home page Aggregator is no exception. Let's break down the basic skeleton of a test file:

```
video-tutorials/src/aggregators/home-page.test.js
const test = require('blue-tape')
const uuid = require('uuid/v4')

const { config, reset } = require('../test-helper')

test('It aggregates a VideoViewed event', t => {
})
```

First of all, we're using a library called blue-tape, which is a portemanteau of bluebird and tape. tape is a fantastic testing library,[3] and is your author's preferred testing library. Primarily, it keeps tests decoupled from one another, which is 100 percent in harmony with the goal of our overall system architecture. Let's not make this a chapter focused on tape though, so check out the fantastic article that Eric Elliot wrote about testing with tape for more information.[4] blue-tape makes tape Promise-aware.

The test-helper.js sets up some helper functions for running our tests. Check it out when you can, but for now config is the return value from config.js, and reset deletes the contents of the View Data tables.

Finally, a tape test takes a string describing the test and then a function that receives a single argument that we use to make test assertions.

---

3. https://www.npmjs.com/package/tape
4. https://medium.com/javascript-scene/why-i-use-tape-instead-of-mocha-so-should-you-6aa105d8eaf4.

Now for the three-step dance:

```
video-tutorials/src/aggregators/home-page.test.js
test('It aggregates a VideoViewed event', t => {
①  const userId = uuid()
   const videoId = uuid()
   const videoViewedEvent = {
     id: uuid(),
     type: 'VideoViewed',
     metdata: {
       traceId: uuid(),
       userId: uuid()
     },
     data: {
       userId,
       videoId
     },
     globalPosition: 1
   }

②  return (
     reset()
       .then(() => config.homePageAggregator.init())
③      .then(() =>
         config.homePageAggregator.handlers.VideoViewed(videoViewedEvent)
       )
       // Call it a second time to verify idempotence
       .then(() =>
         config.homePageAggregator.handlers.VideoViewed(videoViewedEvent)
       )
       .then(() =>
④        config.db.then(client =>
           client('pages')
             .where({ page_name: 'home' })
             .then(homePageData => {
               t.ok(homePageData, 'Got the home page data')

               t.equal(
                 homePageData[0].page_data.videosWatched,
                 1,
                 'Even though we see the event twice, there is still only 1'
               )
             })
         )
       )
   )
})
```

❶ Autonomous components function by responding to messages, so we set up this message by constructing a VideoViewed event.

❷ Then we reset the database so that we have a known starting point for the global count, followed by a call to the Aggregator's init function. Normal handling of events requires the row that the init function puts in place.

❸ Next we exercise the Aggregator's handler by just calling it with the event we built earlier. Handlers need to be idempotent, and if idempotence is important enough to warrant the number of exclamation points we've used throughout this book, then it's important enough to explicitly test it. So we immediately call the handler a second time.

❹ This Aggregator operates on the home page row in the pages table, so we finally assert correct operation by querying for that row and then seeing that the videosWatched count is 1, even though we handled the event twice. We're getting the right count, and it's idempotent.

And that's the basic pattern. It's no different for the Components, even ones that seem complicated, like video publishing:

```
video-tutorials/src/components/video-publishing/publish-videos.test.js
test('Writes a VideoPublishingFailed event when publishing fails', t => {
❶   function lousyFetch () {
      throw new Error('No can haz fetch')
    }
    const lousyMessageStore = {
      ...config.messageStore,
      fetch: lousyFetch
    }
❷   const videoPublishingComponent = createVideoPublishingComponent({
      messageStore: lousyMessageStore
    })
❸   const traceId = uuid()
    const ownerId = uuid()
    const userId = uuid()
    const sourceUri = 'https://www.youtube.com/watch?v=dQw4w9WgXcQ'
    const videoId = uuid()

    const command = {
      id: uuid(),
      type: 'PublishVideo',
      metadata: {
        traceId,
        userId
      },
      data: {
        ownerId,
        sourceUri,
        videoId
      }
    }
```

```
    return videoPublishingComponent.handlers.PublishVideo(command)
      .then(() =>
        config.messageStore.read(`videoPublishing-${videoId}`)
          .then(messages => {
            t.equal(messages.length, 1, '1 event written')

            t.equal(messages[0].type, 'VideoPublishingFailed', 'It failed')
            t.equal(messages[0].data.reason, 'No can haz fetch')
          })
      )
})
```

We're just looking at one test in this file, the one that makes sure we capture failures when publishing videos. For this test, we employ the dependency injection we've set up in the project to make a Message Store substitute that fails when attempting to fetch a stream.

❶ We first construct that substitute by making an aptly named lousyFetch function. Then we build a lousyMessageStore by swapping in lousyFetch in place of fetch.

❷ Then we make an instance of the video-publishing Component that uses this lousyMessageStore.

❸ Then we have the normal kind of setup. This Component responds to PublishVideo commands, so we build one of those.

❹ Then we exercise the Component's handler.

❺ The results this time are in the stream associated with this video, so we read the stream and assert that we got a VideoPublishingFailed event.

Notice that when a test doesn't involve View Data, there's no need to reset the database. By using UUIDs for all the test IDs, we won't have test collisions.

Writing Tests for Message-Writing Applications

Application tests are simpler as well. Generally, they just write a message and then respond. Here's a test used as part of registering users:

video-tutorials/src/app/register-users/register-users.test.js
```
test('Issues the registration command when user submits good data ', t => {
  const userId = uuid()
  const attributes = {
    id: userId,
    email: 'finally@example.com',
    password: 'adsfasdf'
  }
```

```
②   return supertest(app)
      .post('/register')
      .type('form')
      .send(attributes)
      .expect(301)
      .then(res => {
        t.assert(res.headers.location.includes('registration-complete'))
      })
③   .then(() =>
        config.messageStore
          .read(`identity:command-${userId}`)
          .then(retrievedMessages => {
            t.equal(retrievedMessages.length, 1, 'There is 1 message')
            // Various assertions to make sure the command was filled out right
      )
  })
```

The same phases:

❶ Setup in this case is assembling a POST body to submit to the HTTP handler.

❷ Then we make the HTTP POST to exercise the application.

❸ Then we retrieve the messages in the stream where the application is supposed to write the command and do various assertions on the command.

None of this is any different from what you've likely done before, only you're writing a message instead of updating various tables or NoSQL equivalents.

Keeping It Simple

So why does any of that matter? Well, you just saw what it takes to test autonomous components. Notice how there's no complicated orchestration of every piece of the system simultaneously. Even in the case of registering users, which has a three-message flow to it, we don't set up a difficult-to-maintain replica of the whole system.

Each component can act in only one way—responding to messages. There's no need to replicate live, direct communication between components because (a) our components don't communicate directly with each other, and (b) we weren't *mocking* their interaction in test. *In test we exercised them in exactly the same way they get exercised in production.*

Dropping Testing?

Does that mean we don't have to test how the pieces work together? It depends on how finely you want to split hairs.

Ed Keyes gave a wonderful presentation titled "Sufficiently Advanced Monitoring Is Indistinguishable from Testing."[5] In it he brings up how things fail in production in ways we can't predict. So we can't write tests to capture those in advance. So what do we do? We rely on good monitoring.

You actually took this path in the previous chapter when you were debugging why users weren't getting their emails. You wrote a few screens that showed you exactly where to look to fix the problem, such as the list of users starting in Creating Users, on page 209, and then the view that puts correlated messages together starting in Correlators Gonna...Correlate?, on page 221.

We could have instead spent several chapters setting up an elaborate pipeline that would deploy a new full environment for each test that also could have caught this, but *at what cost*? This is where diminishing returns and opportunity cost come in.

If we had infinite time at our disposal, there would be great value in automating all the things. Our time is not infinite, however, and we have to deal with trade-offs. Not all testing has to be automated, and in an architecture like ours, it's quite all right to monitor production rather than try to predict every test case and attempt to run the whole system in test. Why?

In addition to what Ed Keyes said, remember that we're storing our state as a complete log of every state transition. We can sample message workflows in production and verify that they're correct after the fact. Because we have a complete state history, fixing things that go wrong is possible. Banks do this sort of thing, and few domains can have as much impact on people's lives as the financial sector.

We could even automate some of the monitoring. We could have observers that notice a Register command was written but that no RegistrationEmailSent was written within an acceptable window of time. Monitoring like that is far easier to set up than replicating the whole system. It's cheaper too. And it could make a record of what it has verified, providing even more useful data.

---

5.   https://www.youtube.com/watch?v=uSo8i1N18oc

What You've Done So Far

In this chapter you wrote some tests for the pieces of Video Tutorials that we've done as part of this book. You've learned that this architecture makes testing simpler because it doesn't introduce disparity between how things run in test and how they run in production. You also learned that not all testing has to be automated and that with proper tools, you can bring human eyes to your testing efforts.

You also got exposed to the idea that monitoring in production can be a more cost-effective way of verifying system integrity, and we mentioned how we could have something observing registrations and timing out if it does not see the process complete in a reasonable amount of time. Can you work through how you might write that, and maybe even give it a shot? This component would probably observe UserRegistered events because until those are written, no email is supposed to go out. It would likely record those events into a table that it would check on periodic heartbeat and then make some kind of noise if too much time has passed between users registering and their emails going out.

(slow exhalation) This is it. We've come to the end of our time on this project. Thank you for sharing this journey. The next chapter is the last one, and in it we're going to list a bunch of topics we weren't able to cover in this book and where you can go to keep learning.

Once you start down the [path of services-based architecture],
forever will it dominate your destiny. Consume you it will.

> Software Architect Yoda

CHAPTER 15

Continuing the Journey

Well, here we are, the final chapter. You started this journey tasked with building the web's new e-learning sensation, and you dove in, applying your craft as we knew it. You quickly hit roadblocks and pivoted, starting down the path of services-based architecture. You defined monoliths on page 25, discovered event-based modeling on page 30, and built a Message Store (starting in Chapter 2, Writing Messages, on page 25).

You modeled common use cases using events, use cases like registering and authenticating users (Chapter 6, Registering Users, on page 83 and Chapter 8, Authenticating Users, on page 119, respectively), and you performed long-running tasks with this architecture Chapter 10, Performing Background Jobs with Microservices, on page 157. You scratched the surface of building async-aware UIs in Chapter 11, Building Async-Aware User Interfaces, on page 173 and began learning how to reason through the challenges this architecture presents.

After all that, you considered deployment options and actually shipping code to production in Chapter 12, Deploying Components, on page 195 right before you hunted down and dealt with a major bug in Chapter 13, Debugging Components, on page 207. And you wrapped it up with learning about testing in an autonomous, microservices-based system in Chapter 14, Testing in a Microservices Architecture, on page 231.

That's a lot of words to simply say you've done a lot. You've worked through the fundamentals of what microservices actually are and how they work, and that's something to be proud of. Video Tutorials is a success because of your efforts.

Our time here is rapidly drawing to a close, and we weren't able to cover everything relating to service-based architecture. This chapter will highlight some of the bigger issues we weren't able to cover and give you resources to help you continue your learning.

Handling Concurrency

A frequently asked question is "How do you scale microservices?" We have these single-threaded, stateful Components—what happens if they don't keep up? Are there other reasons to run concurrent instances? We have completely ignored dealing with concurrency in this project.

You're right to think it isn't as simple as just running more instances. That works very well for applications because they are inherently stateless. Autonomous components, on the other hand, are very much stateful.

And it isn't just intentional scaling that would lead us to multiple instances. We might accidentally cause two instances to be running at the same time through our own error with our deployment system. Or perhaps we want to have two going for redundancy's sake. In either of these two cases, we have two instances trying to do the same work. Let's tackle this case first.

What happens when we have two instances of the identity component running trying to do the same work? Here's the Register handler again:

```
video-tutorials/src/components/identity/index.js
function createIdentityCommandHandlers ({ messageStore }) {
  return {
    Register: command => {
      const context = {
        messageStore: messageStore,
        command,
        identityId: command.data.userId
      }

      return Bluebird.resolve(context)
        .then(loadIdentity)
        .then(ensureNotRegistered)
        .then(writeRegisteredEvent)
        .catch(AlreadyRegsiteredError, () => {})
    }
  }
}
```

Both instances of the component will start at the beginning, loading an identity that has not yet been registered as shown in the first figure on page 243.

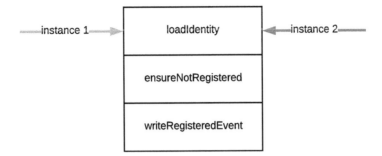

Then they'll both make their idempotence check:

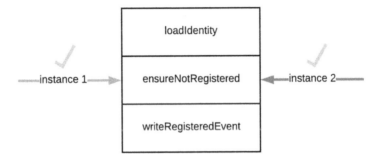

Since nothing has written a Registered event, they both pass the idempotence check and proceed to writing a Registered event:

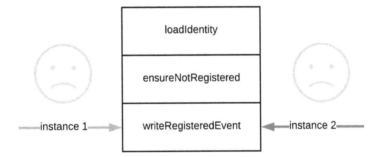

And we get two Registered events in the stream, which isn't correct. Imagine if instead of user registration that was a $1 million wire transfer. Bad news for our employment prospects.

This isn't an *idempotence* issue. This handler is 100 percent idempotent in that a single subscriber handling this message a second time will not register a user a second time. This is a *concurrency* issue, and we do need to design our systems to handle concurrency.

Let's dive into that writeRegisteredEvent function. Here again is its code:

video-tutorials/src/components/identity/write-registered-event.js
```
function writeRegisteredEvent (context, err) {
  const command = context.command

  const registeredEvent = {
    // ...
  }
  const identityStreamName = `identity-${command.data.userId}`

  return context.messageStore
    .write(identityStreamName, registeredEvent)
    .then(() => context)
}
```

There isn't a way to prevent both of the concurrent instances from reaching the call to messageStore.write function. Is there a way for this double write call to not actually write two events? What tools do we have to work with?

Well, registration should be the first event in an identity's stream. The first event in our streams is always at position 0. Is there a way we can tell the Message Store that we're expecting an event we write to be the first event in a stream?

There sure is. It's that third optional parameter, expectedVersion, that we handled back under Adding Optimistic Concurrency Control to Our Writes, on page 47, when we were writing the write function. If you change that call to write to .write(identityStream, userRegisteredEvent, -1), you're telling the Message Store that you expect there to be no messages in the stream when writing the UserRegistered event. The first instance to pass through here would successfully write the event, but the second one would fail, getting a VersionConflictError. The second instance could then crash, and because we have good system monitoring in place, it would get started again. When it does, the first instance's event will be sitting in the stream, so when the second handles the Register command a second time, it'll load and project an identity that has been registered, and the idempotence check will kick in.

The expectedVersion parameter is your friend. Though we haven't used it in our writes throughout the project because we were explicitly disallowing concurrency, it's a good idea to use it on all your writes. Your projections would need the store the position from the events they handle, and then you would use that value as the expectedVersion when you go to write.

Now, in the case of scaling, we want the multiple instances to be working on different work items. In this case, we need to make sure that different instances won't try to handle the same messages.

The basic idea is to divvy up the streams between each instance. If, say, we had three instances of the same component running, we would assign each instance a number from 0 to 2 inclusive. Then we'd make a numeric hash of the stream name and take the modulo of that number by 3, yielding a number 0 through 2 inclusive. If that result matches the instance's number, then that instance would handle the message. Here is a short potential snippet for doing just that:

```
const crypto = require('crypto')

const consumerIdentifier = 1
const numberOfConsumers = 3

const hash = crypto.createHash('sha256')

hash.update('streamCategory-20c27c90-ca76-4dc9-b3b8-afea34137103')

const number = hash.digest().readUInt32BE()
const owningConsumerIdentifer = number % numberOfConsumers
const owningConsumer = owningConsumerIdentifier === consumerIdentifier

if (owningConsumer) {
  console.log('I will process the message')
} else {
  console.log('I will not process the message (not event for $20)')
}
```

Our Message Store code can't currently support this, so if you were going to keep using this book's code—not recommended in real-life systems—you'd probably end up putting this filtering code in the message handlers of the component you're scaling. A more robust implementation would provide this as part of its toolkit.

There certainly is more to concurrency than what we've covered here, but this gives you a starting point for your research.

Snapshotting

If you've read about event sourcing, you've likely read about snapshotting. You might also have heartburn from reading that our projections work by reloading all the events in a stream every time we need to project them. Snapshotting is a performance enhancement that makes it so that we don't need to keep projecting entire streams when we need an entity.

Since streams are append-only logs of immutable events, their underlying data can't change. When you implemented projections back in Chapter 7, *Implementing Your First Component*, on page 105, you loaded a stream's events and ran them through a call to Array.prototype.reduce, passing in the result of calling a projection's $init property as the starting point. Let's consider this in the context of our video publishing projection. Suppose we have a video that has been published and named twice times. When we project it, we end up with a video named "Rework":

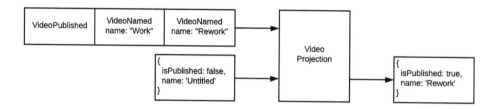

Now suppose that a third VideoNamed event makes it into this video's stream. If we reprojected the whole stream, starting from the $init value, we'd end up a video named "Snapshot!" We expect that:

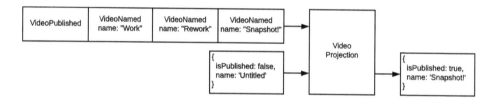

However, suppose we had saved the result from projecting this stream when there were only three events. When we went to project the stream, what if rather than reprocessing every event starting with $init, we instead started with that saved projection and only reduced the fourth event into it?

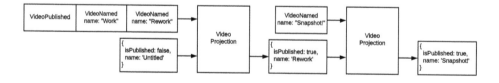

Well, we'd end up with the same result while having processed fewer events. This only works because we have immutable data. If events could change, then we'd always have to project everything every time.

Now, two important points. Computers are fast, and snapshots won't make a huge difference until you start having a lot of events in the same stream. So, this isn't as critical of a feature as you may think.

Second, *we don't snapshot streams!* We snapshot entities, and we get entities by projecting streams. We snapshot the result of projecting a stream through a projection. Snapshots are meaningless without projections, so a single stream could have multiple snapshots associated with it because a stream can be projected in different ways.

Snapshotting is again something our Message Store code doesn't handle. If you were to implement it, code that is fetching entities from the Message Store shouldn't know about the particulars of snapshotting. That ought to be hidden behind the fetch function.

Changing the Message Contract

First of all, don't. Message contracts are supposed to be immutable, and things that are immutable require more thought, consideration, and design than things that aren't. Do not just sit down and start writing code. To do so is to elect the way of pain with this architecture, and if you do that, well, don't blame the architecture.

That said, it *may* so happen that you need to evolve an existing contract. In that case, your humble author will proudly punt to Greg Young, who has a book on the subject.[1]

But seriously, spending more than 15 minutes designing something doesn't mean you've abandoned Agile for Big Up-Front Design. It's not only okay to think things through sufficiently before you start coding, but that's our job as software developers.

Using Different Programming Languages

While you may not *want* to use multiple programming languages because of increased operational costs and training overhead, if something can speak PostgreSQL, it will work in this system. You'd have to reimplement the Message Store code in each language, of course, or if you use Ruby, you can directly use the Eventide Project's libraries.[2]

Making Use of Monoliths

I have certainly been a critic of monolithic architectures in this book, but that doesn't mean that they are without value. That kind of architecture is a

---

1. https://leanpub.com/esversioning
2. https://eventide-project.org

special-purpose tool. I can't imagine a faster tool for prototyping than an MVC ORM web framework.

But if you follow American football, you may be aware of a play called the fake punt. A team lines up as if it were going to punt the ball to the other team, but instead attempts an actual play to score a touchdown or some such (go sports!). Whenever I play video game football, I attempt this on every play, and you can imagine how good the results are. Or poker. I don't always play poker, but when I do, I bluff on every hand. A special-purpose tool is one that gets used in rare circumstances, dare we say *special* circumstances.

Now, if you find yourself in one of these special circumstances, then your knowledge of service-based architecture will help you write a monolith that is more easily transitioned to long-term foundation. In Chapter 2, Writing Messages, on page 25, we demonstrated how the essence of a monolith is having things like "the users table," a table that aggregates data from diverse concerns and pretends it's all a single concept. There's no reason you can't break apart that users table into its constituent pieces, joining them together when you need to display a user's page.

If you did break it up, you're arguably not building a monolith anymore, but your MVC tools could make building an application like this go quickly. And then, when you've figured out what you need to build, your application already has its concerns separated giving you a much easier time converting to a pub/sub architecture with autonomous components.

But remember—special-purpose.

What You've Done So Far

Sadly, books are finite, as is your time. In this chapter, you went over a number of topics that are important to a service-based architecture but that we couldn't cover in detail in this one volume. You now have some jumping-off points to continue your learning.

Why not close our journey together by picking one of the topics we briefly covered in this chapter and seeing if you can implement it?

Whether you do or don't, though, you have my sincerest gratitude for sharing this journey. Let's connect online and continue the discussion! Architecture like this is a blast, and I can't wait to see what you create.

Until then, happy coding.

ES6 Syntax

For better or for worse, we used JavaScript to build Video Tutorials. It's a fine language, but like all human creations, it isn't without its warts. Since its first release in 1995, it has undergone some changes, some of which we use in this book.

Two years after JavaScript's release, Ecma International made a formal specification for the language. This formal specification is named ECMAScript, and JavaScript is still the best-known implementation of ECMAScript.[1] This specification is in its sixth version, commonly referred to as ES6. This appendix is not meant as a full-on primer for the changes introduced with ES6. Rather, it explains some of the syntax we use that may be unfamiliar if you haven't been writing JavaScript day in and day out. Readability is of course extremely subjective, but it is your humble author's sincere opinion that use of these syntactic conventions removes a lot of the noise that you'd otherwise be subjected to when writing JavaScript.

const and let

JavaScript variables used to always be declared with var. You may have noticed we never once used var.

ES6 brought us const and let. const is somewhat misnamed. It doesn't mean that the thing it points to can't be modified. For example, the following is perfectly valid:

```
const obj = {}
obj.key = 42
```

---

1. https://en.wikipedia.org/wiki/ECMAScript

However, once a name has been assigned in a scope with const, that name can't be reassigned to anything else in the same scope. It's the name that is constant and not the thing the name refers to. So you can't do the following:

```
const obj = {}
const obj = 'SyntaxError: Identifier 'obj' has already been declared'
```

let, however, lets the name be assigned to something else.

Both const and let brought something else, namely block-level scoping. var is scoped to its function, regardless of where in the function it is defined. If you have:

```
function iterate () {
  for (var i=0; i < 42; ++i) {
    console.log(i)
  }
  console.log(i) // `i` is still in scope, and its value is 42
}
```

We only need i as an iteration variable, but it remains in scope even after the for loop concludes. If we had instead used let to define i, the console.log call at the end would give an error, since i is no longer in scope.

For the most part, we always use const unless we have some reason to reuse the name.

Arrow Functions

Arrow functions give us a shorthand for defining functions that we use mostly when defining inline functions. Here is an example of one from the book, taken from the identity component's handlers:

```
video-tutorials/src/components/identity/index.js
return {
  Register: command => {
    const context = {
      messageStore: messageStore,
      command,
      identityId: command.data.userId
    }

    return Bluebird.resolve(context)
      .then(loadIdentity)
      .then(ensureNotRegistered)
      .then(writeRegisteredEvent)
      .catch(AlreadyRegsiteredError, () => {})
  }
}
```

We're defining an object literal with key Register whose value is a function. This function takes one parameter, namely command. Previously we would have had to write this function as follows:

```
return {
  Register: function (command) {
    // body omitted
  }
}
```

We still do define some functions that way (for example, our top-level, dependency-receiving functions are defined this way), but for inline functions, the arrow syntax has less noise.

Arrow functions are not quite semantically equivalent to the longer version. They differ in what the this keyword means in their body. We have not once used the this keyword in this entire project to avoid the confusion it introduces, but in short, inside an arrow function, this refers to whatever it referred to at the time the arrow function was defined. In a traditional function definition what this refers to is determined by how that function was invoked.

Object Destructuring

Speaking of top-level, dependency-receiving functions, their syntax might be new to you. Continuing with the identity component, consider its top-level function:

```
function build ({ messageStore }) {
  // body omitted
}
```

The parameter list on this function has curly braces, and those smell like object literals. But you're probably used to having to write object literals with key–value pairs separated by colons, such as: { key: 'value' }.

ES6 introduced shorthand for extracting values out of objects and binding them to names in local scope. For example, let's examine the identity component's loadIdentity function:

video-tutorials/src/components/identity/load-identity.js
```
function loadIdentity (context) {
  const { identityId, messageStore } = context
  const identityStreamName = `identity-${identityId}`

  return messageStore
    .fetch(identityStreamName, identityProjection)
    .then(identity => {
      context.identity = identity
```

```
    return context
  })
}
```

We receive the context object, which has two keys we're interested in. The first line of the function is aware that this object is supposed to have a command key and a messageStore key. We use the values of those keys in the rest of the function, and so we need a way to refer to them.

const { command, messageStore } = context introduces the two key names into the local scope and sets their values to the corresponding values in the object. We could have written that function as follows:

```
function loadIdentity(context) {
  const command = context.command
  const messageStore = context.messageStore
  // ...rest of body
}
```

It can get multilevel too. We could have gone bonkers and done something like:

```
function loadIdentity(context) {
  const { command: { data: { userId } }, messageStore: { fetch } } = command
  // ...rest of body
}
```

That would have introduced userId and fetch into the scope with the values found at context.command.data.userId and context.messageStore.fetch, respectively. The intermediate keys don't become names in the local scope. However, one can imagine this getting out of hand. We've kept our destructuring to a single level.

Getting back to function definitions, you can also destructure parameter lists. Getting back to the identity component's top-level function, we wrote:

```
function build ({ messageStore }) {
  // body omitted
}
```

That is equivalent to:

```
function build (dependencies) {
  const { messageStore } = dependencies
  // body omitted

}
```

or the old-school version:

```
function build (dependencies) {
  const messageStore = dependencies.messageStore
  // body omitted
}
```

Object Literal Property Value Shorthand

Sometimes you put into an object a value contained in a variable. Suppose that you want to put a userId into a message's metadata and you want to put it at the key userId. In days of yore, you would have to write { metadata: { userId: userId } }. That double userId is a wee bit redundant. It's also repetitive.

The committee that maintains the JavaScript language spec thought so too, and so now, if you have a variable whose name is the same as the key you want in an object, you can use the shorthand of just putting they key name directly in the curly braces like so: { metadata: { userId } }.

And it doesn't have to be all shorthand or no shorthand. The following is also valid:

```
const userId = uuid()
const event = {
  metadata: {
    userId,
    traceId: uuid()
  }
}
```

Index

Thank you!

How did you enjoy this book? Please let us know. Take a moment and email us at support@pragprog.com with your feedback. Tell us your story and you could win free ebooks. Please use the subject line "Book Feedback."

Ready for your next great Pragmatic Bookshelf book? Come on over to https://pragprog.com and use the coupon code BUYANOTHER2020 to save 30% on your next ebook.

Void where prohibited, restricted, or otherwise unwelcome. Do not use ebooks near water. If rash persists, see a doctor. Doesn't apply to *The Pragmatic Programmer* ebook because it's older than the Pragmatic Bookshelf itself. Side effects may include increased knowledge and skill, increased marketability, and deep satisfaction. Increase dosage regularly.

And thank you for your continued support,

Andy Hunt, Publisher

Node.js 8 the Right Way

Node.js is the platform of choice for creating modern web services. This fast-paced book gets you up to speed on server-side programming with Node.js 8, as you develop real programs that are small, fast, low-profile, and useful. Take JavaScript beyond the browser, explore dynamic language features, and embrace evented programming. Harness the power of the event loop and non-blocking I/O to create highly parallel microservices and applications. This expanded and updated second edition showcases the latest ECMAScript features, current best practices, and modern development techniques.

Jim R. Wilson
(334 pages) ISBN: 9781680501957. $33.95
https://pragprog.com/book/jwnode2

Small, Sharp Software Tools

The command-line interface is making a comeback. That's because developers know that all the best features of your operating system are hidden behind a user interface designed to help average people use the computer. But you're not the average user, and the CLI is the most efficient way to get work done fast. Turn tedious chores into quick tasks: read and write files, manage complex directory hierarchies, perform network diagnostics, download files, work with APIs, and combine individual programs to create your own workflows. Put down that mouse, open the CLI, and take control of your software development environment.

Brian P. Hogan
(326 pages) ISBN: 9781680502961. $38.95
https://pragprog.com/book/bhcldev

Docker for Rails Developers

Docker does for DevOps what Rails did for web development—it gives you a new set of superpowers. Gone are "works on my machine" woes and lengthy setup tasks, replaced instead by a simple, consistent, Docker-based development environment that will have your team up and running in seconds. Gain hands-on, real-world experience with a tool that's rapidly becoming fundamental to software development. Go from zero all the way to production as Docker transforms the massive leap of deploying your app in the cloud into a baby step.

Rob Isenberg
(238 pages) ISBN: 9781680502732. $35.95
https://pragprog.com/book/ridocker

Modern Vim

Turn Vim into a full-blown development environment using Vim 8's new features and this sequel to the beloved bestseller *Practical Vim*. Integrate your editor with tools for building, testing, linting, indexing, and searching your codebase. Discover the future of Vim with Neovim: a fork of Vim that includes a built-in terminal emulator that will transform your workflow. Whether you choose to switch to Neovim or stick with Vim 8, you'll be a better developer.

Drew Neil
(166 pages) ISBN: 9781680502626. $39.95
https://pragprog.com/book/modvim

Designing Elixir Systems with OTP

You know how to code in Elixir; now learn to think in it. Learn to design libraries with intelligent layers that shape the right data structures, flow from one function into the next, and present the right APIs. Embrace the same OTP that's kept our telephone systems reliable and fast for over 30 years. Move beyond understanding the OTP functions to knowing what's happening under the hood, and why that matters. Using that knowledge, instinctively know how to design systems that deliver fast and resilient services to your users, all with an Elixir focus.

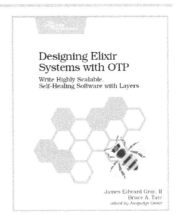

James Edward Gray, II and Bruce A. Tate
(246 pages) ISBN: 9781680506617. $41.95
https://pragprog.com/book/jgotp

Programming Phoenix 1.4

Don't accept the compromise between fast and beautiful: you can have it all. Phoenix creator Chris McCord, Elixir creator José Valim, and award-winning author Bruce Tate walk you through building an application that's fast and reliable. At every step, you'll learn from the Phoenix creators not just what to do, but why. Packed with insider insights and completely updated for Phoenix 1.4, this definitive guide will be your constant companion in your journey from Phoenix novice to expert as you build the next generation of web applications.

Chris McCord, Bruce Tate and José Valim
(356 pages) ISBN: 9781680502268. $45.95
https://pragprog.com/book/phoenix14

The Pragmatic Bookshelf

The Pragmatic Bookshelf features books written by professional developers for professional developers. The titles continue the well-known Pragmatic Programmer style and continue to garner awards and rave reviews. As development gets more and more difficult, the Pragmatic Programmers will be there with more titles and products to help you stay on top of your game.

Visit Us Online

This Book's Home Page
https://pragprog.com/book/egmicro
Source code from this book, errata, and other resources. Come give us feedback, too!

Keep Up to Date
https://pragprog.com
Join our announcement mailing list (low volume) or follow us on twitter @pragprog for new titles, sales, coupons, hot tips, and more.

New and Noteworthy
https://pragprog.com/news
Check out the latest pragmatic developments, new titles and other offerings.

Save on the ebook

Save on the ebook versions of this title. Owning the paper version of this book entitles you to purchase the electronic versions at a terrific discount.

PDFs are great for carrying around on your laptop—they are hyperlinked, have color, and are fully searchable. Most titles are also available for the iPhone and iPod touch, Amazon Kindle, and other popular e-book readers.

Buy now at *https://pragprog.com/coupon*

Contact Us

Online Orders:	*https://pragprog.com/catalog*
Customer Service:	*support@pragprog.com*
International Rights:	*translations@pragprog.com*
Academic Use:	*academic@pragprog.com*
Write for Us:	*http://write-for-us.pragprog.com*
Or Call:	+1 800-699-7764

Milton Keynes UK
Ingram Content Group UK Ltd.
UKHW030759190724
445759UK00003B/7